MATTHEW HALL

Body Language Psychology

Your Definitive Guide On How To Analyze Body Language And Learn All About The World Of Dark Psychology Secrets And Persuasion

Copyright © 2020 Matthew Hall
All rights reserved.

© **Copyright 2020 - All rights reserved.**

The content contained within this book may not be reproduced, duplicated or transmitted without direct written permission from the author or the publisher.

Under no circumstances will any blame or legal responsibility be held against the publisher, or author, for any damages, reparation, or monetary loss due to the information contained within this book. Either directly or indirectly.

Legal Notice:

This book is copyright protected. This book is only for personal use. You cannot amend, distribute, sell, use, quote or paraphrase any part, or the content within this book, without the consent of the author or publisher.

Disclaimer Notice:

Please note the information contained within this document is for educational and entertainment purposes only. All effort has been executed to present accurate, up to date, and reliable, complete information. No warranties of any kind are declared or implied. Readers acknowledge that the author is not engaging in the rendering of legal, financial, medical or professional advice. The content within this book has been derived from various sources. Please consult a licensed professional before attempting any techniques outlined in this book.

By reading this document, the reader agrees that under no circumstances is the author responsible for any losses, direct or indirect, which are incurred as a result of the use of information contained within this document, including, but not limited to, — errors, omissions, or inaccuracies.

Introduction *7*

Chapter 1. How Non-Verbal Communication Works *14*

Chapter 2. How to Understand People Through Body Language *23*

Chapter 3. Manipulation Through Body Language *31*

Chapter 4. Uses of Body Language *36*

Chapter 5. Guide to an Effective Body Language *42*

Chapter 6. How to Persuade People *48*

Chapter 7. How to Analyze People *54*

Chapter 8. Dark Psychology Secrets *60*

Chapter 9. How to Defend Ourselves of Dark Psychology *66*

Chapter 10. The Power of Hands *73*

Chapter 11. Body Language of a Child *78*

Chapter 12. Reading People Through Their Mind *83*

Chapter 13. Myths About Body Language *90*

Chapter 14. Who Is a Manipulator? *96*

Chapter 15. Dark Psychology and Women *101*

Chapter 16. Techniques of Dark Psychology *107*

Chapter 17. Practical Exercises For Mind Control Prevention *113*

Chapter 18. Touch As a Form of Body Language *118*

Chapter 19. Facial Expression As a Form of Body *123*

Chapter 20. Manipulation In a Relationship *130*

Chapter 21. How to Know if Someone Is Lying Through Body Language *136*

Chapter 22. How Body Language Improves Your Mindset *142*

Chapter 23. Proxemics *149*

Chapter 24. Muscular Core, Posture, and Breathing *152*

Chapter 25. Hand Gestures and Arm Signals 157

Chapter 26. Different Types of People and How They Fit In the Social Circle 162

Chapter 27: Conclusion of Body Language 168

Chapter 28: Dark Psychology 170

Chapter 29. What Is Dark Psychology? 173

Chapter 30. Explication of Dark Psychology 178

Chapter 31. How To Use Dark Psychology 182

Chapter 32. Delving Into Dark Psychology 187

Chapter 33. The History of Dark Psychology 192

Chapter 34. Advanced Techniques to Manipulate Human Psychology 198

Chapter 35. Mind Control 203

Chapter 36. Mind Control Techniques 209

Chapter 37. Influence People With Mind Control 214

Chapter 38. Dark Persuasion 219

Chapter 39. Dark Persuasion To Lookout For 224

Chapter 40. Subliminal Persuasion 230

Chapter 41. Psychological Manipulation 234

Chapter 42. Psychological Manipulation Technique 238

Chapter 43. Covert Emotional Manipulation 244

Chapter 44. Covert Emotional Manipulation Tactics 250

Chapter 45. Brainwashing 253

Chapter 46. Brainwashing Technique 257

Chapter 47. Hypnosis 261

Chapter 48. Hypnosis Techniques 267

Chapter 49. Mind Controls Hypnotism 273

Chapter 50. Dark NLP *279*

Chapter 51. The Positive and Negative Aspects of Neuro Linguistic Programming *285*

Chapter 52. Understanding Body Language *289*

Chapter 53. Deception *296*

Chapter 54. Dark Cognitive Behavioral Therapy *302*

Chapter 55. The Art Of Using Your Mind to Succeed *307*

Chapter 56. Dark Personalities *312*

Chapter 57. The Dark Triad *319*

Conclusion *325*

BODY LANGUAGE PSYHOLOGY

Introduction

Body language involves using our physical behavior, expressions, and manners to reveal nonverbal information about ourselves, which is usually done unconsciously. Many people are not mindful of it, but you are continually giving out body cues and wordless signals that reinforce the interaction or contradict what you are trying to say in all your interactions.

Your entire nonverbal behavior transmits a loud and strong message that continues even after you stop talking. There are instances when what someone says might differ from what their body language is communicating. Hence, in this case, it will be easy for the person you are interacting with to pass you off as a liar. If someone asked for a favor and you gave a smile after giving a no, you have ended up confusing the person. With this kind of mixed-signal, the person might be confused about what to believe. However, if the person understands the concept of body language, they would probably just walk away since the body language is unconscious and gives someone away by revealing their real intention.

The Essence of Nonverbal Communication

The cues you are unconsciously giving out from your body are pretty essential and, as said earlier, give meaning to the interaction you are in. From your body cues, the person you are with will know whether you are interested in the relationship or not, whether you are hiding information or being explicit, and whether you are paying attention.

With nonverbal communication signals that complement what you say, you can build trust, rapport, and clarity. I am pretty sure you know what happens when your words and body language cues contrast!

In reading body language signals, you have to notice the body language people are giving out. It does not stop at that, and you have to be sensitive to yours as well. In understanding nonverbal communication, pay attention to the following roles it plays:

Repetition

In other words, it enforces the message you are trying to pass. You made a marriage proposal to your girlfriend, for instance. After popping the question and she accepted, you would generally expect her to smile, jump up and be excited. However, if she said yes with a straight face, I am pretty sure you know something is not right.

Contradiction

It can also refute the message you pass across, thus giving the signal that you might be lying. You came home from a two-week journey. Your wife greeted you and said she was excited to see you, but without a hug, a smile, or any facial expression to corroborate the statement. Something was off.

Substitution

Body cues often stand in place of verbal communication. In African culture, for instance, let us assume a guest visited a family. As this person was leaving, he offered the child some money. The mother gave the child "that kind of look," and the child took it as a cue to reject the offer.

Complementing

Body language cues might add more weight to the meaning of the message you are passing across verbally. Consider a man who tells his wife, "I love you" and drives off. Another man plants a kiss on the wife's forehead and says, "I love you" while looking into her eyes. Of these two, it is clear which one meant what he was saying.

Accenting

Your nonverbal cues can also emphasize the point you are trying to make. Saying no, alongside a shaking of the head, emphasizes the weight of the negation.

Without beating around the bush any more, let us examine how you can read various clues from body parts.

Reading Various Parts of the Body

Head Movement

Head movement is one of the meekest body languages to decode. However, for someone who has no clue what this nonverbal communication signal means, hardly will they make sense of it. To explain the head movement, I have here two scenarios:

As part of the exercise to get a job, a candidate must decide why he is the best candidate for the job. During the presentation, his audience, the hiring manager, nods quickly while the candidate desperately keeps trying to sell himself. He is unaware of the hiring manager's message, which clearly shows he is wasting his time.

Consider another candidate giving the same presentation. As he goes off trying to sell himself, the hiring manager leans back with his head tilted. Oblivious to the meaning of this body language, the candidate does not try to shed light on the point that triggered the manager's body reaction. He is ignorant of the body language; hence, he keeps on blabbing.

Reading the Face

There are many expressions we can reveal with our faces. Even babies and toddlers are smart enough to decode this body language cue. That a smile reveals happiness or satisfaction or a frown shows dissatisfaction or sadness. There are times when the facial expression could give insight into what is going on with a person. A person who says they're fine with a slight frown, for instance, could be lying.

It is a universal expression that conveys a wide range of emotions, such as sadness, fear, panic, anxiety, worry, disgust, distrust, happiness, and many others. The best part is that this expression does not change or vary with people.

Many people, in a bid to hide their real intention, desperately try to control the face. However, a careful study of the face can give you a clear glimpse into the message someone is trying to pass across. There are times when someone might hide primary body language, such as raised eyebrows, smiles, frowns, etc. Be sure to look out for the subsequent:

A warm and genuine smile does light up the whole face. It indicates happiness. It is also an unmistakable symbol that the other party is enjoying your company.

On the other hand, a phony smile is a polite way of showing approval, even if they do not enjoy the conversation or interaction. For you to detect a phony smile, take a look at the side of the eyes. The lack of crinkles is all you need to pass a smile off as fake.

The Eye Window

The eyes disclose a lot regarding a person. It explains why the eyes are referred to as the window to the soul. Besides, it is an essential and natural communication process for you to note all interactions' eyes.

In communicating with people, it is customary to note eye contact, whether someone is averting your gaze or not, the rate of blinking, and their pupils' size.

The following explains some nonverbal clues from the eyes:

Eye gaze

A person interested and paying attention to a conversation will look directly into your eyes while having a conversation. However, they might break eye contact once in a while because prolonged eye contact is rather uncomfortable. A distracted and uninterested person, on the other hand, will often break eye contact and look away. This person might be awkward or is trying to hide their true feelings.

Blinking

While blinking is an entirely natural process, the frequency matters. A person uncomfortable or in distress will blink more often. On the other hand, infrequent blinking means that a person is intentionally trying to control their eye movements.

Pupil Size

Pay attention to pupil size as it is very subtle and affected by the room's light level. However, emotions also affect pupil dilation, causing small changes in the pupil's size. It explains why someone with highly dilated eyes is either aroused or interested in a person.

Hand Movements

Some cues can easily be found from the hand's position and pattern of movement. We explain this in detail:

When someone has their hands in their pockets, they could be lacking confidence, hiding information, or just being defensive.

When a person unconsciously points to another person in a group or meeting while making a speech, there might be some common ground they share.

In communicating with someone, there is the presence of an obstacle. It is in the form of an object between you, and the person translates to the person trying to block you out. In this circumstance, your goal should be to build rapport and gain such a person's trust.

A person talking with the palms facing up is likely, to be honest. Such a person is not hiding the palm since they most likely have nothing to hide.

The Mouth

The expressions and movement of the mouth are pretty vital in decoding body language as well. It is why a worried, anxious, or insecure person will likely chew their lower lip. Some forms of nonverbal communication cues from the mouth will be examined below. A person, to be polite, might cover the mouth if the other party is yawning. Be watchful, as it can be done to cover up a frown as well.

Pursed lips

When a person tightens up their lip, it could signal objection, disapproval, or distaste.

Lip biting

It is common when a person is anxious, worried, or stressed.

Covering the Mouth

It could be done to hide emotional reactions like smiles or smirks.

A Slight Change in Direction

A person's feelings can be seen through the direction of the mouth. As a result, someone happy or in a good mood might have their mouth slightly turned up. A slightly turned-down mouth, on the other hand, could signal sadness or displeasure.

The Importance of Reading People

The world is made of people. Life is better enjoyed when you have people to relate with. However, your survival in the world also depends on your ability to decide when not cooperating with some people. So, your ability to read people is essential.

There are times you are unconsciously cooperating with others. The fact that you walk gently to your place of work without causing a scene or doing anything to warrant unnecessary attention is an act of cooperation with the rest of the society on some level. You don't just awaken up one day and choose to go on a killing spree. You are connected to the Internet and the rest of the world alike. All these things require some form of human cooperation.

For this to occur, people unconsciously have to come to an appropriate form of agreement and acceptable behavior on some level. All in all, cooperating with people is pretty important, and your decision whether to cooperate or not comes down to your ability to read people.

The best salesman knows how to coax you because they are good at analyzing people. They can get you into buying what they have to offer, even if you do not need what they are offering. The better you are at reading other people's motives, the better you can deal with such a person.

Chapter 1. How Non-Verbal Communication Works

Being able to connect well is extremely important when wanting to succeed in the personal and professional world, but it isn't the words you say that scream. It is your body language that does the screaming. Your gestures, posture, eye contact, facial expressions, and tone of voice are your best communication tools. These can confuse, undermine, offend, build trust, draw others in, or put someone at ease.

There are many times where what someone says and what their body language says is different. Non-verbal communication could do five things:

- Substitute—It could be used in place of a verbal message.

- Accent—It could underline or accent your verbal message.

- Complement—It could complement or add to what you are saying verbally.

- Repeat—It could strengthen and repeat your verbal message.

- Contradict—It could go against what you are trying to say verbally to make your listener think you are lying.

Many different forms of Non-verbal communication will be looked at, and we are going to cover:

- Gestures—These have been woven into our lives. You might speak animatedly; argue with your hands, point, wave, or beckon. Gestures do change according to cultures.

- Facial expressions—You will learn that the face is expressive and shows several emotions without speaking one word. Unlike what you say and other types of body language, facial expressions are usually universal.

- Eye contact—Because sight tends to be our strongest sense for most people, it is an essential part of Non-verbal communication. The way someone looks at you could tell you whether they are attracted to you, affectionate, hostile, or interested. It might also help the conversation flow.

- Body movement and posture—Take a moment to think about how you view people based on how they hold their heads, stand, walk around, and sit. The way a person carries gives you much information.

Lower Body

The arms share much information. The hands share a lot more, but legs give us the exclamation point and tell us precisely what someone is thinking. The legs could say to you if a person is open and comfortable. They could also imply dominance or where they want to go.

Upper Body

Upper body language can show signs of defensiveness since the arms could easily be used as a shield. Upper body language could involve the chest. Let's look at some upper body language.

Leaning

If someone leans forward, it will move them closer to another person. There are two possible meanings to this. First, it will tell you that they are interested in something, which could just be what you are talking about. But this movement could also show romantic interest. Second, leaning forward could invade a person's personal space; hence, leading to a threat. It is often an aggressive display. It is done unconsciously by influential people.

The Superman

Bodybuilders, models commonly use this, and it was made famous by Superman. It could have various meanings depending on how a person uses it. Within the animal world, animals will try to make themselves look bigger when they feel threatened. If you look at a house cat when they get spooked, they will stretch their legs, and their fur stands on end. Humans also have this, even if it isn't as noticeable. It is why we get goosebumps. Because we can't make ourselves look bigger, we have to develop arm gestures like putting our hands on our waist. It shows us that a person is getting ready to act assertively.

The Chest in Profile

If a person stands sideways or at a 45-degree angle, they are trying to accentuate their chest. They might also thrust out their chest, more on this in a minute. Women do this posture to show off their breasts, and men will show off their profile.

Outward Thrust Chest

If someone pushes their chest out, they try to draw attention to this part of their body. It could also be used as a dreamy display. Women understand that men have been programmed to be aroused by breasts. If you see a woman pushing her chest out, she might be inviting intimate relations. Men will thrust out their chests to show off their chest and possibly trying to hide their gut. The difference is that men will do this to women and other men.

Hands

Human hands have 27 bones, and they are a very expressive part of the body. It gives us much capability to handle our environment.

Reading palms isn't about just looking at the lines on the hands. After a person's face, the hands are the best source for body language. Hand gestures are different across cultures, and one hand gesture might be innocent in one country but very offensive in another.

Hand signals may be small, but they show what our subconscious is thinking. A gesture might be exaggerated and done using both hands to illustrate a point

Face

People's facial expressions could help us figure out if we trust or believe what they are saying. The most trustworthy expression will have a slight smile and a raised eyebrow. This expression will sow friendliness and confidence.

We make judgments about how intelligent somebody is by their facial expressions. People who have narrow faces with a prominent nose were thought to be extremely intelligent. People who smile and have joyous expressions could be thought of as being smart rather than someone who looks angry.

Mouth

Mouth movements and expressions are needed when trying to read body language. Chewing on their lower lip might indicate a person who is feeling fearful, insecure, or worrying.

If they cover their mouth, this might show that they are trying to be polite if they are yawning or coughing. It might be an effort to cover up disapproval. Smiling is the best signal, but smiles can be interpreted in many ways. Smiles can be genuine, or they might be used to show cynicism, sarcasm, or false happiness.

Negative Emotions

The silent signals that you show might harm your business without you even knowing it. We have over 250,000 facial signals and 700,000 body signals. Having poor body language could damage your relationships by sending other signs that you can't be trusted. They might turn off, alienate, or offend other people.

You have to keep your body language in check, and this takes much effort. Most of the time, you may not know that you are doing it, and you might be hurting your business and yourself.

Here are some emotions and how to spot them:

Fear, Anxiety, or Nervousness

Fear could happen when our basic needs get threatened. There are many different levels of fear. Suppose might be mild anxiety or full-blown blind terror. The various bodily changes that get created by fear can make this one easy to spot.

- Voice trembling.
- Errors in speech.
- Pulse rate extremely high.
- Vocal tone variations.
- Sweating.
- Lips trembling.
- Muscle tensions like their legs wrapped around something, clenched hands or arms, elbows are drawn in, jerky movements.
- Damp eyes.
- Holding their breath or gasping for breath.
- Not looking at one another.
- Fidgeting.

- Dry mouth indicated by licking their lips, rubbing their throat, or drinking water.
- Defensive body language.
- Face is pale.
- Fight or flight body language.
- Breaking out in a cold sweat.
- Any symptoms of stress.

Sadness

- Lips trembling.
- The flat tone of voice.
- Body drooping.
- Tears.

Anger

- Clenched fists.
- Invading body space.
- Leaning forward.
- Baring their teeth or snaring.
- Using aggressive body language.
- Neck or face is red and flushed.

- Displaying power body language.

Embarrassment

- Not making eye contact.

- Looking down and away.

- Neck or face is red and flushed.

- Changing the subject or trying to hide their embarrassment.

- Grimacing.

- Fake smiles.

Positive Emotions

When you have positive body language, it means that you are engaging, approachable, and open. It isn't saying that you need to use this kind of body language all the time or that it is the best signs that will show a person is friendly. It's just a good beginning point for reading positivity in others as well as yourself.

Non-verbal Signals Used Universally

Non-verbal communication is different for everybody and in different cultures. A person's cultural background will define their non-verbal communication since some communication types, like signs and signals, need to be learned.

Since there are different meanings in non-verbal communication, there could be miscommunication when people from different cultures try to communicate. People might offend others without really meaning to due to cultural differences. Facial expressions are very similar around the world.

Seven micro expressions are universal, and we will go more in-depth about these, but they are hate/contempt, anger, disgust, surprise, fear, happiness, and sadness. It might be different in the extent of how people show these feelings since, in specific cultures, people might readily show them where others won't.

Nods might also have different meanings, and this can cause problems, too. In some cultures, their people might not say "yes," but people from different cultures will interpret as "no." If you nod in Japan, they will solve it as you are listening to them.

Here are other non-verbal communications and how they differ in various cultures:

Eye Contact

Many Western cultures consider eye contact as a good gesture. It shows confidence, attentiveness, and honesty. Cultures such as Hispanic, Asian, Native American, and Middle Eastern don't think eye contact is a good gesture. They believe it is rude and offensive.

Unlike Western cultures that think it's respectful, others don't think this way. In Eastern countries, women absolutely can't make eye contact with men since it shows the power or sexual interest. Many cultures accept gazes as only showing an expression, but staring is thought of as rude in most.

Gestures

You need to be careful doing a "thumbs up" because it is very different in many cultures. Some view it as meaning "okay," but in Latin America, it is vulgar. Japan views it as meaning money.

Snapping your finger may be acceptable in some cultures, but it is disrespectful and offensive in others. In some Middle Eastern countries, showing your feet can be offensive. Pointing your finger is an insult in some cultures. People in Polynesia will stick their tongue out when they greet someone, but other cultures see it as a sign of mockery.

Touch

Touch is thought of as rude in most cultures. Some cultures look at shaking hands to be acceptable. Kissing and hugs, along with other touches, are looked at differently in different cultures. Asians are too conservative with these types of communications.

Patting someone's head or shoulder has different meanings in different cultures. Patting a child's head in Asia is extremely bad since their head is the sacred part of their body. Middle Eastern countries think people of opposite genders touching to be horrible character traits.

How and where a person gets touched could change the meaning of that touch. You need to be careful if you travel to various places.

Appearance

It is an acceptable form of non-verbal communication. Their appearance has always judged people. Differences in clothing and racial differences could tell a lot about anyone.

Making yourself look good is an important personality trait in many cultures. What is thought to be a good appearance will vary from country to country. How modest you get is measured by your appearance.

Chapter 2. How to Understand People Through Body Language

The Capital Importance of Body Language

Our bodies cannot show anything but what is in us. Our emotions use the sounding board. Therefore, we understand that our body's non-verbal part of communication always reflects our mental state, whatever the situation. Indeed, where does it come from, if not our psyche?

Body language is subject to physical law: energy does not vanish; it transforms. As electricity becomes light, heat, or movement, our psyche becomes body language.

Beware, the same gesture may have different meanings. For example, a person with arms crossed, a gesture generally interpreted as a negative signal. Indeed, arms crossed the pass to outsource refusal, withdrawal, skepticism, antipathy, etc. Sometimes this interpretation is accurate, but not always. What about a man struck, waiting for the bus? Is it expressly rejected? If so, to whom? Facing the bus? To other people like him at the bus stop? What if nobody exists? In this situation, arms crossed indicate nothing but being able to do nothing but wait. No reason to move, our man folds his arms.

To correctly decipher body language, you must first consider the action context. Also, as with verbal language, an "expression" that does not fit into a situation will have a high potential for misunderstanding.

Incorrect posture can reveal insecurity, fear, distrust, etc. On the other hand, the right posture gives the impression of strength, power, and confidence.

Understand more about using body signals to convey the desired impression.

Negative Body Language

Often, during a conversation, you can pass negative body language without realizing it.

Facial expressions and gestures end up showing several details.

Some negative postures that you should avoid in your client meetings:

- Hands-on-hips or pockets;
- Knees pointing to the exit door;
- Legs wide open;
- Crossed arms.

These attitudes are perceived, even if unconsciously, by the other person and can ruin a sale's progress.

Know other signs you should avoid avoiding transmitting the wrong body language.

Hand to Mouth

Experts analyze that when a person is not telling the truth, they usually cover their mouths.

Disparities of this posture habit are:

- Rub your lips;
- Dash the chin;
- Put stuff in front of the mouth.

Compressed Lips

Another negative body language is to compress your lips.

This act shows that the person is trying to avoid saying what he thinks.

That is, hiding your lips reveals that you don't want to answer any questions.

Defocused Look

Body language says a lot by looking.

A look without focus, or looking up and to the right, indicates confusion.

It is because, when looking away, the person is looking for a mental image.

Therefore, he shows a lack of clarity in his speech, as well as insecurity.

Forehead Contracted

In conversation, if the other person wrinkles his forehead, that's not a good sign.

These horizontal lines show a certain level of tension, doubt, or nervousness, which is a bad sign of body language.

Restricted Hand and Arm Movements

Keeping your hands behind your back or clinging to your body conveys the message of little confidence.

Another gesture to be avoided is to put your hands back or feet crossed behind the chair.

These are signs of discomfort.

Reading Body Language

Reading body language may help to assess the feeling behind or instead of the words spoken. The adult can quickly and instinctively understand that a child is frightened by thunder when they see the child screaming and covering their ears. However, there are misconceptions about body language, causing miscommunication unless the whole-body language is read.

The eyes have long been named the windows to the soul, and it may be this concept that created the greatest myth in reading bodies. It is widely assumed that if a person avoids eye contact or does not hold it, that person does not say the facts. It is a mistaken assumption though popularly known. Pathological liars may maintain sustained contact with the eyes because they realize most people assume that looking away from the eyes shows an untruth. People who say the truth do not keep eye contact because they clearly state evidence and feel no need to convince anyone of this.

When a person is depressed or uncomfortable, and avoidance of eye contact occurs. For example, a child being chastised by a parent would always look down on the ground instead of him looking in the parent's eyes. Painfully shy or nervous people, too, are having a tough time meeting another person's eyes in conversation. Someone with little actual knowledge of reading body language would find the people lying by the standard error in each of these instances. Instead, the child shows authority, the adult, contrite, and the shy person shows typical distress or uncomforted sign.

In addition to the eye movement, the overall body language used needs to be looked at. Fidgeting, drumming fingers, or playing with hair matched to a lack of eye contact shows that a person is dissatisfied with the situation or discussion topic. Still, eyes fixed on a distant point by a person with arms crossed, attentive to the conversation, shows, instead, serious attention and intense thinking on the topic of discussion.

The precise interpretation of body language may provide an insight into another person's thoughts, feelings, and emotions. However, to read correctly, it is essential to remember to look at the entire body's movements, or words, rather than treating part of the body as separate from the other parts.

Keys to Reading Body Language

Body language is the type of communication a person uses to respond to circumstances, including facial expressions. More than 54% of the way we communicate with each other consists of body language, 39% consists of how the voice is used, and just 7% consists of the words spoken. Developing one's ability to interpret and understand gestures and signs of body language would greatly benefit because it will help better understand and interact with other human beings.

Body language involves body expressions, gestures, eye contact, muscle tension, skin coloring, breathing rate, etc. Of course, you should remember that body language is different from people to people and various nationalities and cultures. Consequently, it is at all times good to check what is seen in a person. It can be achieved by answering similar questions and endeavoring to better-known individuals.

There is also a lot of myths about interpreting body language. Most deceptive books and internet guides don't teach people the right thing. There's the truth you need to learn about this, while popular reasoning can trick you into believing a person's ability to read body language is the real secret to finding lies. Some important body language secrets are:

Posture

In most situations, if you take the correct pose, you should build the right impression on people. Leaning a little towards a person can create an image of friendliness. It could also be that you have an interest in others. At the same time, seeing a level head establishes a sense of self-assurance and trust.

Legs

When a person is anxious, the legs are always moving around. It happens when the person tells lies and is bored too. It is safer to keep those legs crossed or even to give the opposite impression, to appear confident and polite to others.

Eye contact

If you keep healthy eye contact, you show concern and respect for others. And you still need to find a balance. When you hold too much eye contact, the other person would feel self-conscious. Sometimes, if you don't have enough eye contact, you can make the other person believe you're not involved in what's being addressed.

Arms

If you have primary arms crossed, you can make yourself look nervous or defensive. On the other hand, if you hold open arms, you will make yourself comfortable and embrace others.

Distance

If you hold a person close, you can make yourself look pushy or put yourself in his face. At the same time, keep a distance away may mean that you don't care about what's being addressed or don't care about it at all.

You can study a lot regarding other people through body language. Many people show all sorts of thoughts in the way they push the body. Here are examples of how to discover other people's opinions:

Confidence

A comfortable person will always stand tall, holding eye contact sold while smiling at you simultaneously. The person can go even further with the hands when making gestures.

Tips for Reading Body Language

Eye movement, gestures, posture, and facial expressions are characteristics of human body language. American human behavior expert Eric Barker explains that it is best to look at "unconscious behaviors that are not easily controlled and may contain a message." Can anyone decipher this language? Barker reveals eight tips.

Use Common Sense

For the expert, analyzing the context is essential. Crossing your arms can mean adopting a defensive posture or even trying to deceive you. However, if it is cold or if the person concerned is sitting in an armless chair, the meaning can be different (much more straightforward and harmless).

Observe the Mime

Imitating a gesture or verbal expression may mean that the person is in tune with you. The act of agreeing with someone or something is difficult to fake, so the expert believes that the best thing is to think in these cases.

Nerve Energy

The other's level of activity can reveal your interest and enthusiasm for what you are saying. Research from the University of Manchester in England states that women shake their feet when they are interested in a man. Men, on the other hand, are tending to do so when they are nervous.

Consistency

Someone who reveals a fluid and consistent speech, emphasizing certain words, demonstrates control and concentration. Showing determination as they speak, these people are difficult to influence (and seduce).

Don't Care About Individual Signs

It is not possible to distinguish what a person means by body language through a single action. It is best to look at the actions as a whole, as two or three signals can help identify what goes in the other person's head.

Create A Reference

Uneasiness and the habit of always talking do not necessarily reveal any problem. However, something may be wrong when these people suddenly become calm.

Consider Your Previous Considerations

A judgment about another person will be affected if you have an initial impression, whether positive or negative. The inclination is to give the benefit of the doubt to someone you think is similar to you.

The Most Significant Thing Is to Focus on The Whole Context

Eric Barker argues that the ability to understand body language will increase when "understanding that body language is part of a larger context. Then you will begin to pay attention to other facets of interaction: voice, appearance, clothing, etc."

Chapter 3. Manipulation Through Body Language

After leaving the University heading to the golden paved streets of London, a man saw a woman who was also a model for the entire newspaper–at this point in his life. He hadn't met anyone attractive in the real world. Every day he walked and tried to be friendly, even cool, and afterward, he knew that he had just made himself a fool!

Why did trump react to her in that way? How was it that she was so successful? Have you ever addressed people with a lack of trust? And what about those other people in his class- his friend knew almost nothing about them as adults, he had never really been told, but he wasn't shocked by their performance.

They all had a certain aura about them that all these people could have a hypnotic effect on the people around them without opening their mouths. He wants to talk about this hypnotic body language today because it can help you achieve more and perfection without really having to do so much other than subtly alter your non-verbal communication.

3 Non-verbal keys for Hypnotic communication:

True Smile and Real Laughter

He can remember when his parents invited friends for supper when he was a child when his mother always told him to make sure that he was smiling and to show his teeth when the guests were arriving (I was never cheeky enough to grow, although the man was tempted). His mother knew that smiles produced positive reactions from people on an intuitive level.

This man speaks here of a real, genuine smile—a smile from the center of your body, which reflects joy. A natural smile makes the eyes and face wrinkle; insincere people smile with their mouths alone. Genuine smiles are often from the subconscious mind; individuals can sense, see, and feel real. A genuine smile implies you smile all over your face-your muscles move, your cheeks rise, your eyes shrink, and your eyebrows slightly go down.

Smile more, then. However, smile happily, fun, and joyfully. Smile in the future.

The explanation of why a photographer uses 'cheese' is because it's a term that helps you relax your face muscles. It often gives a crooked smile. How many pictures did you see that the smiles are cheese-powered and not authentic?

Professor Ruth Campbell, University College London, says that in the brain there is a "mirror neuron" which triggers the neurology responsible for the acknowledgment of face expressions and causes an immediate, unconscious mirroring response. The world smiles at you once you smile. In other words, know it or not, very often the facial expressions we see are unintentionally expressed.

So, if you smile more often than not-people around you smile more sincerely-it means, they feel better about you. You build for yourself and others around you a better immediate environment. How would you feel if you walk down the street and seeing someone with such an unhappy or cross face? Science has exposed that the more you smile, the more positive reactions people give you.

Would you smile more if you watch a funny movie with friends? Robert Provine found that Laughter in people in social situations was more than 30 times more likely than alone. He discovered that Laughter has less to do with jokes and funny storytelling and more to do with relationship building. Laughter creates a connection.

If you smile (a real smile) at another man, they almost always return the smile with a genuine smile that gives both of you and you genuinely positive feelings because of cause and effect. It creates a cycle of comfort: you smile, and you feel the perfect smile, and feel good, etc.

Studies show that most meetings run smoother, last longer, have better results, and improve relationships dramatically if you make a point of regularly smiling and laughing until it becomes a custom. He guesses you already knew all this-yet you smile a lot. Does recent research show that we smile 400% more-how as a kid often? Do you smile at the world today?

Confidence

The person was missing when he was younger, embarrassingly answering the receptionist.

I remember watching a documentary about a schoolgirl murdered in Great Britain. The girl's parents gave a press conference calling for help in the apprehension of the killer. It was the fall of the murderers. The way the father behaved at this press conference prompted the police to suspect him and to show him that he killed his daughter at last.

Many criminals are caught not because they have clues but because they are responsible, conscious of themselves, and lack trust. These feelings are sufficiently communicated to create suspicions.

When we are emotionally congruent and trustworthy, our body language is positive and expresses it to the world.

Psychologists advise us that by modifying our physical actions, we can alter our attitudes. Thus, adopting the physiology of trust can help you appear and become more trustworthy. When you are confident and hold your body that way more often, cause and effect mean having your body feel secure.

I recall reading a book a little while ago, and it taught you three great ways to build confidence with your body alone: first, he suggested that you be a' front seater.' Wherever you go to movies, classrooms, meetings, and presentations, the back lines appear to fill up fastest, aren't they? Many people go back so that they aren't too visible. It often shows a lack of confidence in him. Start sitting up today, relaxed with other people's eyes, and build confidence.

Furthermore, making direct contact with the eyes tells you a lot about confidence. If someone avoids contact with the look, we might start wondering what's wrong with them or what they must hide. Lack of eye contact may indicate that you feel weak or that you are, in some way, afraid. Conquer this and let the person in the eye look–you don't have to stare hard! Just look in your eyes to tell them that you believe you are honest, open, confident, and comfortable.

Suppose you seem confident and think of yourself. In that case, the other person tends unconsciously to agree that there is something worth knowing about you-why should anybody else be if you aren't confident or feel good about yourself? It is implicitly conveyed beyond conscious minds, often with these sages' good feelings. David Schwartz gave the other great tip to walk 25% faster. This man knows that his father always told him to slow down when he was taken to football to see his beloved Nottingham Forest as a boy because he was enthused and enthusiastic about their destination.

Psychologists link Slovenian stances and slowness to disagreeable attitudes towards oneself, work, and the people around us. But psychologists also tell us that by changing your posture and movement speed, you can change your attitudes. Body action is the result of mental action-and vice versa-as this man already said; cause and effect! The person with low morality is shuffling with little confidence and stumbles through life. Likewise, ordinary people are on average. You can see it, and you can hear it.

Confident people travel purposefully, they have to go somewhere important, and they will succeed when they get there. Open your chest, throw your shoulders back, lift your head, be proud of yourself, move a little faster, feel that your trust will grow. It doesn't have to be dramatic; just keep your body safe.

The Right-Hand Side of the Brain

Most people are right-handed, and as such, their thoughts and lives are processed on the right-hand side of their brain, and motor reactions and functional brain use reside on their brain's left-hand side.

Evolutionary psychologists debate it; most of them think we all have six raw emotions. All else is derived from these. Those six emotions are central: happiness. Surprise. Disgust. Fear. Rage. Anger. Sadness.

It's worth noting here that only two of them are good. If we are real, only one is guaranteed to be great to ourselves, isn't that? Following April's foolish day, he is reminded how much he enjoys' his surprise!

The vast majority of our thoughts in our minds are somehow negative. It is accurate, and bad things tend to stand out much more than our minds' good things.

So, if you respond to anybody's right brain, you may unconsciously associate yourself in the right mind with all those emotions. You don't want to do it.

If you first meet someone to use this knowledge in life instead, put yourself, so they have to look slightly right to look at you. See your right eye when you shake your hands. He believes that this picture is so much on his website's right-hand side. That in his rooms, the man places his chair so that his customers need to look correct when we communicate.

There are three powerful things to remember when improving your success and performance without opening your mouth.

Note that if you smile and smile with enthusiasm, if you behave with faith and connect with the right brain pieces, you start resonating far more gradually with the whole world.

Chapter 4. Uses of Body Language

Body language and self-esteem go hand in hand. It allows for a beautiful mechanism to observe and monitor how people behave and feel. Awareness of our body language is essential for becoming effective and persuasive communicators. Hence, there are several applications for using, reading, and changing body language.

Therapeutic Applications

Body language plays a significant role in counseling, NLP, and hypnotherapy. For psychologists, body language allows them to read their clients' emotional state and gives them a way to build rapport. Observing the client's body language can help the psychologist read how the client responds to a specific discussion or questioning line.

Body language speaks when we can't. Health care professionals have known this for some time. Many studies have been conducted in it and psychology academic studies for professionals, including modalities on body language.

Common issues which can be examined and treated through the use of body language include:

Bipolarity

Individuals with this condition suffer a chemical imbalance that leads to severe depression and the inability to make decisions. They often have low self-esteem that accompanies this disorder, and it is incredibly challenging to understand effectively or treat correctly. The person with bipolarity can be taught to manage their daily situations. Considering the link between body language and emotion, they can also enjoy relief by being trained to use positive body language. It is a means for them to use their body language to persuade their emotions to stabilize and improve. For their families, body language reading is also an effective way to monitor their loved one's state and intervene before incidents happen. Depression can often go unnoticed, and people will rarely speak out about it. They are not likely to say: "I'm feeling depressed."

Low Self-Esteem

Many of us have suffered the disturbing effects of low self-esteem in one way or another. The first victim is our ability to progress in life. A positive belief in yourself is needed to convince the rest of the world to believe in you. People can be trained in positive body language such as open positions, eye contact, and lifting the head. It's a case of falsifying it until you feel it. With enough repetitive use of persuasive body language, you can even convince yourself that you are stronger than you believe.

Trauma

Survivors of trauma suffer from a loss of power, feelings of inadequacy, and loss of confidence. They also have the burden of guilt, where they hold themselves responsible for what happened to them. Whether the trauma is due to a violent act, these individuals' emotional state is reflected in their body language. Body language may have been positive and inviting before the incident. The person may display negative body languages, such as crossed arms, slumping, excessive facial touching, and nervous ticks such as repetitive movement. With effective counseling, their progress to recovery can be tracked through counseling and monitoring their body language.

Abuse

Abuse can be physical, emotional, and sexual, but whichever of these it is, there is bound to be an overwhelming sense of a loss of power. The victim may need to be convinced that they can regain their strength and that it is okay to trust people. Body language is extremely efficient in this regard. Helping these survivors of abuse establish strong body language will increase their sense of their strength. Suffering abuse is also linked to a loss of trust in people and the world around them.

By helping the abuse victim understand others' body language, they can be aided in evaluating the world and those around them regarding what they see, not what they fear. It is already great empowerment to the abuse victim, as they can become a participant in life again and feel like they can make informed decisions.

Self-Development

Being an effective communicator is one of life's excellent skills that will open doors and lead to the self's emboldening. Self-development programs often include body language modalities where the participants are trained in positive body language and assertiveness.

Group Dynamics

People can be classed into two groups: introverts and extroverts. Introverts, as we know, are those people who tend to thrive in one-on-one communications and prefer to spend more time alone, while extroverts are the life of the party and go through life with a the-more-the-merrier attitude. Introverts often suffer a form of depression based on social settings. They do not do well in groups. As a result, their communication within a group dynamic tends to fizzle. Yet, communication is a learned skill. As we learn the words, sentence structures, and grammar of a new language, we can also learn how body language works.

Depression

People suffering from depression tend to convince themselves that they are not worthy, that they are to blame for some usually imaginary flaw, and that everyone around them judges them.

People with depression sometimes think that everyone else has it right, while they alone are suffering. In creating awareness of body language, they can see the world in a more realistic sense and realize that people everywhere go through trying times and are not alone.

By learning to focus on using positive body language, they can also begin to manage their condition, encouraging well-being.

OCD

This condition is known for the repetitive behavior that someone engages in to make themselves feel in control of their lives. At the root of this tragic condition lies the fear of losing power and a profound distrust in themselves and others. In extreme cases, this can even encompass excessive washing of hands to remove imaginary germs and avoid people because people have germs.

People with OCD tend to have a very negative view of the world, and their only safety comes from their repetitive behaviors. Using body language, they can be trained to notice positive feelings in others and incorporate them into themselves. As they learn to project a positive self-image, they will feel their stress levels diminish, which will lead to a reduction of their anxiety-driven obsessions. When they feel more balanced, they will begin to develop trust in themselves and those around them.

Destructive Body Imagery (Bulimia and Obesity)

Low body image is a tragic and very destructive condition to suffer from. It goes with low self-esteem, lack of trust, feelings of abandonment, and severe depression. Bulimia leads the sufferer to obsessively lose weight, while obesity is a condition where the sufferer wants to fill themselves due to their emotional disabilities.

Both these conditions are associated with a loss of reality. These people begin to see the world not as it is, but as they believe it to be, and their world view is almost always negative. They eat or refuse to eat, to hide from the world and themselves.

Body language is a way to find a connection back to the real world. In reading the body language being projected by those around us, we can see that many individuals are just like us. We are not alone. Using positive body language is a therapeutic way to recover a sense of self that is realistic and beneficial.

The Biological Feedback Mechanism of Body Language

Due to our loss of trust in other humans, we often turn to animals for comfort and assurance. We read into what people do, what they say, how they say it, and how they react. A salesperson will do this on a second-by-second basis to monitor the client's body language and adjust their body language to match. Techniques such as mirroring, open position, advancing or retreating, and touching can be used to have an effect on the other person and monitor how persuasive we are on them. If they have begun to trust us enough, they will start to do something we want; in which case, we will trust them since they've done something for us. This endless, nonverbal loop is known as a biological feedback mechanism.

Training and Exercises

Some numerous academies and colleges strive to train people in body language detection and application. They mention facts and case-studies, what to do and what not to do; however, not many of them detail precisely how to improve your body language in a step-by-step way. When considering the activities and desired results, we suggest the following steps be followed:

Observe

Look at the world around you. Notice the people in it and how they interact with each other. Identify people in similar situations to those that challenge you. It could be someone applying for a promotion at work, asking a girl on a date, and even haggling for a discount. Each situation will use the same skills but in different ways. It all boils down to body language.

Practice

It will require some bravery, which is perhaps why people do crazy things in foreign lands where no one knows them. Find some friends, set up a hidden camera if you have to, or undergo obedience training with your dog. The goal is to place yourself in a situation where you can practice some of the skills and how they can be used.

If you feel overwhelmed, you can practice at home with a mirror. You might even find some online help with an online counselor who can perhaps observe you over Skype.

Evaluate

Look at the recording you made of yourself, or talk to friends who are helping you. Don't look at your awkwardness; instead, focus on each body language technique, how you applied it, and what the response to it was.

You may even give yourself a score or write down what you need to focus on. Recall rejoicing the successes, no matter how small. Then it's time to repeat step two, practice.

It may seem like an incredibly arduous task to learn body language, but it certainly is worth it. These skills of using space, posture, facial expressions, eye contact, gesture, and touch are vital to leading a fulfilling life that has less conflict and misunderstanding in it.

Chapter 5. Guide to an Effective Body Language

Research has shown that, when you are aware of your own body's happenings, you can manipulate it by training yourself to have control and even mold it to have effective communication. Further research recommends that you take some breathing exercises before going into a meeting or presentation. It will help you calm and have the ability to take note of your posture and gestures while on presentation. As you have noted by now, mirroring is a good technique. Always try to be keen on what the next person is doing non-verbally and copy that. It will help you turn out to be more effective in your communication with them. They will understand you better because this tunes your mind to communicate more truthfully at a place of relaxation.

However, you should be careful while shaping your body language. It is to ensure that the body language that you portray matches with what you are trying to present. A mismatch may bring confusion and may not be relevant at the moment. The person you are in conversation with my mistake you for meaning something else contrary to what you intended. The secret to having control of your body language is taking your time to learn it and being aware of your non-verbal cues as you apply what you know.

The Body Language That Will Help You Take Charge of Your Space

Effective management involves individuals being able to encourage and have a positive influence. In planning for a necessary appointment, maybe with your employees, management team, or partners, you focus on what to say, memorizing critical points, and rehearsing your presentation to make you feel believable and persuasive. It is something you should be conscious of, of course.

Here is what you should know if you want to control your position, at work, in presentation, or as a leader.

Seven Seconds is What You Have to Make an Impression

First impressions are essential in market relationships. When somebody psychologically marks you as trustworthy, or skeptical, strong, or submissive, you will be seen through such a filter in any other dealings that you do or say. Your partners will look for the finest in you if they like you. They will suspect all of your deeds if they distrust you. While you can't stop people from having quick decisions, as a defense mechanism, the human mind is programmed in this way. You can learn how to make these choices useful to you. In much less than seven seconds, the initial perceptions are developed and strongly influenced by body language. Studies have found that nonverbal signals have more than four times the effect on the first impression you create than you speak. It is what you should know regarding making positive and lasting first impressions. Bear in mind several suggestions here:

- Start by changing your attitude. People immediately pick up your mood. Have you noticed that you immediately get turned off after finding a customer service representative with a negative attitude? You feel like leaving or request to be served by a different person. That will happen to you, too, if you have a bad mood, which is highly noticeable. Think of the situation and make a deliberate decision about the mindset you want to represent before you meet a client, or join the meeting room for a company meeting, or step on the scene to make an analysis.

- Smile. Smiling is a good sign that leaders are under using. A smile is a message, a gesture of recognition, and acceptance. "I'm friendly and accessible," it says. Having a smile on your face will change the mood of your audience. If they had another perception of you, a smile can change that and make them relax.

- Make contact with your eyes Looking at somebody's eyes conveys vitality and expresses interest and transparency. An excellent way to help you make eye contact is to practice observing the eye color of everybody you encounter to enhance your eye contact. Overcome being shy and practice this excellent body language.

- Lean in gently the body language that has you leaning forward, expresses that you are actively participating and interested in the discussion. But be careful about the space of the other individual. It means staying about two feet away in most professional situations.

- Shaking hands. This will be the best way to develop a relationship. It's the most successful as well. Research indicates that maintaining the very same degree of partnership you can get with a simple handshake takes a minimum of three hours of intense communication. You should ensure that you have palm-to-palm touch and also that your hold is firm but not bone-crushing.

- Look at your position. Studies have found that uniqueness of posture, presenting yourself in a way that exposes your openness and takes up space, generates a sense of control that creates changes in behavior in a subject independent of its specific rank or function in an organization. In fact, in three studies, it was repeatedly found that body position was more important than the hierarchical structure in making a person think, act, and be viewed more strongly.

Building your credibility is dependent on how you align your non-verbal communication

Trust is developed by a perfect agreement between what is being said and the accompanying expressions. If your actions do not entirely adhere to your spoken statement, people may consciously or unconsciously interpret dishonesty, confusion, or internal turmoil.

By the use of an electroencephalograph (EEG) device to calculate "event-related potentials"–brain waves that shape peaks and valleys to examine gesture effects prove that one of these valleys happens when movements that dispute what is spoken are shown to subjects. It is the same dip in the brainwave that occurs when people listen to a language that does not make sense. In a somewhat reasonable way, they simply do not make sense if leaders say one thing and their behaviors point to something else. Each time your facial expressions do not suit your words. For instance, losing eye contact or looking all over the room when trying to express sincerity, swaying back on the heels while thinking about the company's bright future, or locking arms around the chest when announcing transparency. All this causes the verbal message to disappear.

What Your Hands Mean When You Use Them

Have you at any point seen that when individuals are energetic about what they're stating, their signals naturally turned out to be increasingly energized? Their hands and arms continuously move, accentuating focus, and passing on eagerness.

You might not have known about this association before. However, you intuitively felt it. Research shows that an audience will, in general, view individuals who utilize a more prominent assortment of hand motions in a progressively ideal light. Studies likewise find that individuals who convey through dynamic motioning will, in general, be assessed as warm, pleasant, and vivacious. In contrast, the individuals who stay still or whose motions appear to be mechanical or "wooden" are viewed as legitimate, cold, and systematic.

That is one motivation behind why signals are so essential to a pioneer's viability and why getting them directly in an introduction associates so effectively with a group of people. You may have seen senior administrators commit little avoidable errors. When pioneers don't utilize motions accurately on the off chance, they let their hands hang flaccidly to the side or fasten their hands before their bodies in the exemplary "fig leaf" position. It recommends they have no passionate interest in the issues or are not persuaded about the fact of the matter they're attempting to make.

To utilize signals adequately, pioneers should know how those developments will be seen in all probability. Here are four basic hand motions and the messages behind them:

- Concealed hands—Shrouded hands to make you look less reliable. It is one of the nonverbal signs that is profoundly imbued in our subliminal. Our precursors settled on endurance choices dependent on bits of visual data they grabbed from each other. In ancient times, when somebody drew nearer with hands out of view, it was a sign of potential peril. Albeit today the risk of shrouded hands is more representative than genuine, our instilled mental inconvenience remains.

- Blame game—I've frequently observed officials utilize this signal in gatherings, arrangements, or meetings for accentuation or to show strength. The issue is that forceful blame dispensing can recommend that the pioneer lose control of the circumstance, and the signal bears a resemblance to parental reprimanding or play area harassing.

- Eager gestures—There is an intriguing condition of the hand and arm development with vitality. If you need to extend more excitement and drive, you can do such by expanded motioning. Over-motioning (mainly when hands are raised over the shoulders) can cause you to seem whimsical, less trustworthy, and less incredible.

- Laidback gestures—Arms held at midsection tallness, and motions inside that level plane, help you—and the group of spectators—feel focused and formed. Arms at the midsection and bowed to a 45-degree point (joined by a position about shoulder-width wide) will likewise assist you with keeping grounded, empowered, and centered.

In this quick-paced, techno-charged time of email, writings, video chats, and video visits, one generally accepted fact remain: Face-to-confront is the most liked, gainful, and impressive correspondence medium. The more business pioneers convey electronically, all the more squeezing turns into the requirement for individual communication.

Here's the reason:

BODY LANGUAGE PSYHOLOGY

In face to face gatherings, our brain processes the nonstop course of nonverbal signs that we use as the reason for building trust and expert closeness. Eye to eye collaboration is data-rich. We translate what individuals state to us just halfway from the words they use. We get a large portion of the message (and most passionate subtlety behind the words) from vocal tone, pacing, outward appearances, and other nonverbal signs. What's more, we depend on prompt input on others' quick reactions to assist us with checking how well our thoughts are being acknowledged.

Strong is the nonverbal connection between people. When we are in a certified affinity with somebody, we subliminally coordinate our body positions, developments, and even breathing rhythms with theirs. Most intriguing, in up close and personal experiences, the mind's "reflect neurons" impersonate practices, yet sensations and sentiments too. When we are denied these relational prompts and are compelled to depend on the printed or verbally expressed word alone, the cerebrum battles and genuine correspondence endures.

Innovation can be a great facilitator of factual data, but meeting in an individual is the key to positive relationships between employees and clients. Whatever industry you work in, we're always in the business of individuals. However, tech-savvy you could be, face-to-face gatherings are by far the most successful way of capturing attendees' interest, engaging them in a discussion, and fostering fruitful teamwork. It is said that if it doesn't matter that much, send an email. If it is crucial for the task but not significant, make a phone call. If it is extremely important for the project's success, it is advised to see someone.

Chapter 6. How to Persuade People

Persuasion is a deliberate effort to change or alter a person's opinions, beliefs, or attitudes toward an issue, situation, object, or person. It is usually achieved by transmission of a message which could be verbal or symbolic.

While persuasion could be used in a manipulative sense, it is, in an actual purpose, different from manipulation. It is because, when persuading a person, he/she is usually aware of your efforts at changing their point of view and willingly or reluctantly allows you to try. In this instance, the person listens and concentrates on what you are saying and then tries to rationalize your ideas with reality before then putting whatever conclusions they come to comparison with what they believed.

Your role in the entire dynamic is to state your reasons for the change you are prescribing, give illustrations and evidence supporting your views and try to convince the target of your advances that your line of action or advice is their best bet. The main goal of this is getting them to switch to a state of reasoning. In this, persuasion resembles manipulation because your goal is still to push the target towards an outcome that they might ordinarily not have considered right.

The success attained in persuasion usually depends on the target's preconceptions and their strength, their perception of the person sharing the new message or idea, their perception of the message or idea, and finally, their perception of the conclusion on offer. Upon outlining these reasons, it should be clear to you that the subject of your effort would probably possess ideas that are at least dissimilar. If not contradictory to yours and as such, the entire process would either hinge on your persuasion being very convincing or the target's ability to meet a compromise between the conflicting ideas that would majorly mirror the changes you want.

Below are six major theories that explain how the human mind absorbs and reacts to information. Knowledge of these would greatly increase the odds of persuasion if you could pinpoint it in your target.

The Attribution Theory

It concludes that people would either attribute actions and characters to people and objects, respectively, either relative to the context they are being considered in or according to their emotional disposition.

When they attribute using context as a guide, they are likely to come to decisions that consider the environment of origin and situational factors. Such is seen when a person refrains from calling a product inferior or calling a person insensitive. Instead of arguing that the product has been made from the best possible items available to the manufacturer. The person is merely reacting as he has learned from his childhood environment.

However, when considering their emotional disposition, they tend to believe that whatever is convenient for them is the only right decision or approach for every other person. Consider this situation:

You meet a person at an event or gather and try to start a conversation with them, but instead of giving you a polite audience, the person appears preoccupied with their thoughts or acts aloof. Angered or annoyed, you walk away, and when asked for an opinion on the person, you characterize them as proud, arrogant, or self-important.

In this case, the characterization you have concluded is based solely on your emotional disposition and does not consider the situation or possible problems the other person might have. The idea is not to determine whether you are wrong or right but rather to analyze how you are likely to process information about people and things. You might be right about the person.

Another situation is when you have been accused of doing something wrong, and you claim that your accusers have failed to see things from your perspective and are only interested in their point of view.

It is a perfect example of considering things as regards context. In this case, probably because the things said are negative, you'd notice the emphasis placed on contextual understanding of actions. There is also a minor hint of the dispositional thinking coinciding.

The Conditioning Theory

In this case, the person is likely to do things. It is if they are conditioned to look like their own decisions instead of coercion. It is mostly utilized in the advertising industry where commercials, advertisements, and billboards convey information that would provoke positive feelings in the population of interest. They then connect such sentiments to their products, making you feel that the work would bring such a feeling into your life since you are more likely to purchase their product, thinking that your decision was an independent one.

It is usually possible because we generally perceive things based on our emotions and are more likely to buy things because they make us feel good.

The Cognitive Dissonance Theory

Based on this theory, it is assumed that people tend to aim for consistency in their thoughts, attitudes, and decisions. It is the cause why most individuals create principles that they strive to follow. Most people also seem intent on reconciling the contradictions as much as they can until they feel comfortable. I would give two examples of this.

Example 1

You have an extreme and deep-rooted need for canned food, either due to the laziness of having to cook meals or the frustrations at having to wait in queues for food. Then you are told that such canned meals could lead to cancer, and you don't want to have cancer. But you also don't want to stop eating canned food. So, instead of stopping with the habit, you comfort yourself that millions of people like you have the same habit and never have cancer.

The cancer theory might be untrue, but your eagerness to dispute the fact or at least make the consequences seem less severe is your own way of changing your mind or making the facts you have just learned seem less important or true. It is one of the ways of dealing with cognitive dissonance theory.

Example 2

Imagine a criminal with a conscience. It is probably hard to envision, but they do exist. Their criminal tendencies are clashing with their tender hearts and causing a bit of discomfort in such a situation. Such a person is very likely dealing with his/ her problems by giving in to the rationale that a criminal and wealthy life far outweighs the benefits of having a clean conscience or right heart.

Again, I am refraining from judging whether such a rationale is sound but am more focused on the fact that the person seems to give in to a motivation that overlaps with most people's general aim to deal with his discomfort.

The Judgment Theory

This one is straightforward to grasp. It merely proposes that when faced with a new piece of information or idea, a person's reaction is dependent on the way he/she currently feels on the topic. What this means is that we're likely to accept something that resonates with our current belief, reject something that doesn't fit in with our beliefs, or stay indifferent to something never considered before.

Therefore, when attempting to persuade a person, it is better first to determine their views on the topic to gauge whether you'd be successful and if your effort would eventually be worth it.

The Inoculation Theory

The inoculation theory supports the view that even if uninterested before in two points of view, once argued for, you are likely to pick the dominant point of view and stick with it. Here is an example:

You have never viewed a soccer game in your life, but one day you are relaxing on the beach and happen to find yourself stuck between two diehard soccer fans who support rival teams. An argument begins about whose team is better and more dominant, and they both turn to you, presenting their points like you are a seasoned fan and, after some time, ask you to judge who's better. You obviously would pick the person with the better argument to not betray your lack of knowledge on the subject. If another individual were to pose a question to you in the future, inquiring about which of those two teams is better, you'd probably find yourself arguing in favor of the choice you made then, maybe even with some of the same points that were used then.

It is the power of inoculations; the most powerful initial idea always takes root first.

Narrative Persuasion Theory

From experience, I think we would all accept that stories have a more enhanced effect on perception and opinions than abstract advice. People's attitudes and views towards objects and others tend to change when they are told compelling stories of such subjects.

The theory simply attempts to explain the heightened effect that can have on people if appropriately utilized. In this, the listener feels transported, which significantly affects their perception of events, making them more pronounced and vivid than they might have been if they had been expressed ordinarily and abstractly.

The Psychological Perspective

Ordinarily, persuading people would be difficult without the ability to organize and present an argument properly. But if inexperience in any or both of this is coupled with an inability to understand moods and stances. Your task would be made many times more likely to fail.

The ability to instantly sense and recognize a person's stance on an issue is difficult, not to talk of performing the same trick on an audience. Because of this difficulty, most speakers who are attempting to introduce people to a new point of view always tend to ask questions that would enable them to gauge the audience's stance before moving on with their presentation.

After asking such questions immediately, they usually watch out for visible reactions from the audience members, maybe a smile to indicate a knowledge of the topic, sitting up to indicate interest, turning away, or sighing to indicate disagreement, boredom, or even a person willing to answer. These simple markers give you an idea of how your message may be received and help you map out a strategy of approach. It is also a useful tool as people express themselves more sincerely when they do not feel particularly in the spotlight. If you are unsure, do not refrain from asking a few surface questions to test the waters or, more aptly, to feel out the crowd.

It should also be noted that numerous people might give an adverse reaction to one-on-one persuasion and would start arguments to further their points. The moment you realize that your attempt to persuade a person has deteriorated into an argument, it is sensible for you to stride away. Very few disputes occurring outside law courts ever get settled. Engaging in one would be fruitless and time-consuming. That time is better spent elsewhere.

Chapter 7. How to Analyze People

Logic alone cannot help you if you want to understand an individual. To know how to analyze the non-verbal initiative cues given off by people, you have to give in to the other vital forms of information. In order to do this, you have to give up any emotional baggage or preconceptions like ego clashes or old resentments that might be stopping you from clearly seeing someone—the clue to this to receive information neutrally without contorting it and staying objective.

Whether you are trying to read your kids, your partner, co-worker, or boss, in order to do so accurately, you have to bring down some walls and surrender to any biases. You have to willingly let go of old ideas that can be very limiting. Those who can analyze other people properly are trained to read and analyze the invisible. They have learned to look further than where people generally look by utilizing their "super senses" and can access life-changing intuitive insights.

Analyzing People Effectively

In order to recognize how your mannerisms and actions can affect other people, you have to be able to comprehend the alterations between how you communicate with different people and how you act around them.

You need to note how all these people's different behavior affects you and how your actions make you appear to them. A suitable method of practicing this is by thinking about how other people might behave around you based on how they consider you in their lives. Maybe they act in a different way around you than they do around other people.

People You Do Know vs. People You Don't

How you see and behave towards someone is greatly affected by how well you know them or how well you need to know them. Your closeness to someone or distance from someone in the aspect of your relationships will define the things you need to contemplate when you are analyzing both you're and the other person's behavior while you are interacting with them. In the end, this will also help you determine how you want to make use of these insights in order to analyze what they are trying to communicate with you correctly.

Here are four examples to better elaborate on this concept:

1. You have an unstable relationship with your mother. Your relationship is long-term and intensely involved. You aim to find out the origin of the complication and fix your relationship with her. To do this, you first need to consider a few things: how she fulfills her needs, her points of concentration, comprehensive information about her personal life, the way she communicates with you, her impulses, preferences, and her body language.

2. You are in a relationship with your significant other for about a year. As it's starting to get more serious, you consider asking him/her to move in with you. The relationship is intimate and medium-term. Your first objective should be to think whether moving in together would be a smart move. You want to figure out how they might respond when you ask them the question. The essential factors that you need to consider are their past experiences and personal life, how they communicate with you, their impulses, preferences, and body language. Besides, you also need to consider how they go about fulfilling their requirements, their points of concentration, and their drive. You can also acquire more insight by consulting family and friends.

3. You are thinking about sharing innovation for a business idea with a co-worker. You have a relatively superficial relationship with this co-worker, and it is medium-term. You want to observe their behavior to determine whether the two of you are compatible to work together and whether he or she would be a suitable business

partner before expressing your idea. You want to figure out how you should approach them to get the best response. You need to observe the following factors: how they verbally communicate with you, their impulses, preferences, and body language. In addition to that, defining their concentration and having some insight into their past experiences and personal life. It could also be beneficial in this case.

4. In the initial process of meeting someone, you might ask yourself whether they are attracted to you. You are attracted to them; however, before expressing your feelings to them, you want to get to know them better. At this time, your interpersonal relationship with this other person is superficial and relatively new. In addition to that, before expressing your feelings, you want to be sure that you are correctly interpreting their signals if the feelings are not mutual. You need to pay consideration to a few things with your first encounters with this person. Some of the influences you need to contemplate are their preferences, how they speak with you, their body language, and how they convey themselves around you. You can subtly acquire some details like their history with relationships in your first few conversations and use that information to determine how you will act.

Techniques by Which You Can Analyze People

- Sense emotional energy.

Our emotions well express the energy or "vibe" we give off. Our intuition helps us register these. Some people help improve our vitality and mood, and it feels good to be around them. However, others can be draining, and you just want to move away from them. Even though this subtle energy is invisible, it can be felt feet or inches from the body. It is known as chi in Chinese medicine. It's a vitality that is important to health.

Methods to Analyze Emotional Energy

1. Notice their laugh and tone of voice—A lot about our state of emotions can be conveyed via our voice's volume and tone. The frequencies of sounds create vibrations. Try to

notice how the tone of someone's voice affects you while you are trying to analyze them. Ask yourself whether their style feels whiny, snippy, abrasive, or soothing.

2. Notice the feel of their touch, hug, and handshake—much like an electric current, emotional energy is also shared through physical contact. Ask yourself whether a hug or a handshake feels confident, comfortable, warm, or off-putting. Is the other person's hand limp, indicating that they are timid and non-committal? Or are they clammy, meaning anxiety?

3. Notice people's eyes—People's eyes send powerful energy. Studies have revealed that similar to the brain that sends electromagnetic signals beyond the body, and the eyes do this. Take time and try to watch people's eyes. Are they angry? Mean? Tranquil? Sexy? Caring? Also, try to understand whether someone seems to be hiding or guarding something or are at home in their eyes, revealing their capacity for intimacy.

4. Since their presence, someone's company is like an emotional atmosphere surrounding us like the sun or a rain cloud. It's not essentially congruent with behavior or words but is the overall energy emitted by us. While you are trying to analyze people, try to notice: Are you feeling scared, making you want to back off? Or are you attracted by their social presence?

Listen to Your Intuition

Intuition is not what your head says. It's what your gut feels. It is the non-verbal information you can perceive beyond logic, words, and body language. What counts the most when you want to understand someone is who they are from within and not just their outer appearance. With the help of intuition, you can reveal a richer story by seeing further than the obvious.

Some intuitive cues you can look into:

1. Look out for intuitive empathy—You can experience an intense form of empathy when you can feel people's emotions and symptoms in your body. Therefore, when you

analyze people, try to notice whether you are upset or depressed after an uneventful meeting or if your back hurts suddenly. Get some feedback to determine whether this is empathy or not.

2. Watch out for flashes of insight—You might get an "ah-ha" about people while you are conversing about them. It might come in a flash, so stay alert. If not, you might miss out on it. These critical insights might get lost as we tend to move onto the next thought very fast.

3. Feel the goosebumps—Goosebumps are amazing intuitive signals that tell us when we resonate with people who say something that we connect with or when they inspire or move us. It can also take place when you feel a sense of déjà-vu. Déjà-vu is a feeling of recognition that you might have known someone before, although you haven't met.

4. Honor your gut feelings—During your first meetings, try to listen to your gut. Before you even have an opportunity to ponder about it, a visceral reaction already takes place. It conveys whether you are relaxed or not. Gut feelings take place very fast as a primal response. They act as your internal truth meter and convey to you whether you can trust someone or not.

Observe Body Language Cues

According to studies, words account for only seven percent of our method of communication. The remaining is represented by our voice (thirty percent) and body language (fifty-five percent). Stay fluid and relaxed while reading body language cues. Don't get overly analytical or intense. Simple sit back, be comfortable, and observe.

1. Interpret facial expression—Our feelings and emotions tend to get stamped on our faces. The deep frown lines convey Over-thinking or worry. The smile lines of joy are depicted by the crow's feet. Pursed lips signal bitterness, contempt, or anger. Grinding teeth or clenched jaw are signs of tension.

2. Pay attention to posture—When you are trying to analyze someone's posture, ask yourself: Is their chest puffed out when they are walking, which is a sign of a big ego? Or do they cower while walking, which is a sign of low self-esteem? Or, is their head held high, confident?

3. Notice their appearance—When you are analyzing others, pay attention to their appearance. Are they wearing a t-shirt and jeans, indicating that they are dressed casually for comfort? A power suit with properly shined shoes that are indicating ambition and being dressed for success? Or a pendant like a Buddha or a cross displaying their spiritual values? Even a well-fitted top with cleavage, representing a seductive choice?

Learning how to analyze other people accurately takes time and practice, and obviously, every rule has some exceptions. However, you can improve your abilities to analyze others, communicate properly with them, and understand their thinking by keeping these points in mind while building your powers of observation.

Chapter 8. Dark Psychology Secrets

There is a concept in the world of psychology, which is called the dark triad. The obscure triad is a set of three personality traits, namely, Machiavellianism, narcissism, and psychopathy. This group of three is labeled dark, owing to the usual malignant habits correlated with certain characteristics. The dark triad's dramatic opposite is the lighter triad, which is a topic and debate for another book in itself. Although the three traits depicted on the dark triad in their studies are distinct, it is seen that they also overlap. It indicates that with blurred boundaries, a person who increases the success on the dark triad exam will likely have all these traits present. It might be hard to tell, for example, where narcissism stops and where psychopathy begins.

Discussions about the Dark Triad concept were initially begun in 1998. Three psychology experts do it. They asserted that Machiavellianism, narcissism, and psychopathology occurred overlappingly in normal samples. Two psychologists by the titles of Williams and Paulus would later invent a name for this group, in 2002: the dark triad.

There have often been discussions and debates about nature's part in seeking to comprehend the dark triad's personality traits. To put it simply, psychologists, behavioral scientists, and researchers were keen to know whether born or bred are Dark Triad persons. Are we born stupid and manipulative, or have we become so as a consequence of the things that we grow up to be exposed to? According to various research done, it has been noted that a dark triad has an important genetic basis to it. That is, some born with such susceptibility to the dark traits of the triad. However, in terms of heritability, narcissism, or psychopathy, rank greater than Machiavellianism. That is when contrasted to a parent that ranks high on the Machiavellian scale, a psychopathic mother or father is more willing to switch the characteristic to their offspring.

The dark triadic characteristics have also been seen to be underrepresented in top-level management in reports that might not be really friendly to someone working. When the dark triad elements are unpackaged in the segments below, it becomes evident why this recognition may be so.

Dark Triad: Narcissism

A narrative is revealed in the Greek myths of a young man named Narcissus. Narcissus was indeed a hunter renowned for his striking, good looks. Narcissus did not have a time of day for them, given the adoration he got from his admirers and even forced others to take their own lives to show their devotion. While there are several varieties of Narcissus's story, all of them refer to him being extremely self-absorbed, which eventually ended up in him going to die mortality that was retribution for his selfish ways. Thanks to the story of that young man, Sigmund Freud first coined the term narcissism. Freud, aptly titled On Narcissism in his famous 1914 essay.

In the simplest terms, narcissism is the increased and compulsive self-admiration which a person has towards himself and his personal features. A narcissist is always easy to recognize since they quickly offer away their behavior and values.

Asking yourself if you have a narcissist in their life? Here is what you should look for:

- Narcissists tend to feel good and always have the ability to be entitled.
- Type-A perfectionists are also narcissists.
- Narcissists have an unflagging thirst for control.
- Narcissists don't have a sense of limits.

How Do Narcissists Control People?

Now that you realize how well a narcissist looks, you're possibly curious about what the narcissist is doing to manipulate you in your life. How difficult can it be to remember, after all, that someone is attempting to manipulate you? The response is, it can be quite challenging, particularly when this person conceals their acts as only searching for you. Many narcissists are typically very clever and can fit in their daily life without drawing attention to them. They could also be very creative and talented, and the allure that tries to draw you to them will usually be that. When you're out there going to look for a narcissist-shaped monster, you might not be going to look for that skilled and super artistic friend who's always having a solution to everything. And still, she might be the only narcissist in the life who just thinks about competing or who gets injured along the way.

Narcissists are also quite keen liars, in addition to using their mentioned characteristics to the best of ability. Narcissists conduct routine the skill of deception in its various forms in a bid to be the celebrity of every show. Deception is the way the narcissist throws you off reality, so they stay in control. In either scenario, they always exist in an altered world where they are good, and everyone else is inferior to them. Hence, deceit is just a means for them to draw you through this repetitive story where they are the principal character.

Dark Triad: Machiavellianism

Niccolò Machiavelli, sometimes referred to as the founder of modern social science, was a Renaissance-era Italian who favored loads of hats. Machiavelli has been amongst others a historian, politician, poet, humanist, author, and diplomat. Machiavelli composed his most popular work, The Prince, in 1513. In this book, Machiavelli defined and advocated the usage of unscrupulous methods for obtaining and retaining political influence. The word Machiavellianism arose from this work and its endorsements, that was used to refer to the kind of politicians and tactics Machiavelli mentioned in his book. This word was later coined by psychology researchers to define a psychological characteristic marked by a lack of sympathy and a drive to succeed at the detriment of others, be it by deception, coercion, or the flouting of traditional dignity laws and morality. A person who displays Machiavellianism is, in the simplest form, willing to do almost anything if it meant playing. Machiavelli is the purpose of why the ending phrase justifies the means that exist.

Most work has been conducted since the introduction of the word Machiavellianism in philosophy to ascertain what determines the people who score highest on a Machiavellianism test, better known as high Mach's. High Mach's have been found to tend to value power, money, and competition above all else. High Mach's put a very cheap cost on things like building a community, family, and even love. Among those that score low above the Machiavellianism index, better known as low Mach's, the opposite is accurate.

Dark Triad: Psychopathy

Psychopathy is a feature of temperament marked mainly by a loss of empathy toward others. Psychopaths barely experience empathy for others and will rarely feel remorse even when other people have been hurt. There are various psychopathy views, but many of them always seem to agree on the three primary features that differentiate a psychopath from any normal individual. These three traits include fearlessness, lack of restraint, and meanness that any other person would consider uncomfortable.

Psychopaths are brave and aggressive and are not reluctant to step into new terrain even though they could be in danger. Although most individuals are usually overwhelmed by these conditions, psychopaths should be coping with such scenarios as if doing their everyday activities. Psychopaths often have a high degree of self-confidence as well as social boldness that allows them to interact with individuals without the shyness or anxiousness that others may have. Often, whenever a gruesome crime has been committed, you could perhaps hear about the nature of the investigation and shudder while going to think to yourself: how can a man live with himself for doing so? It's business as usual for a psychopath to kill someone and then grab a sunny face up at their local restaurant. It is not to say that all psychos have killed somebody. Some psychopaths instead rendered their lack of sympathy and susceptibility to other transgression and crimes.

Psychopaths show impaired regulation of the instinct, so they cannot regulate their impulses. When a regular human gets a desire of any kind, they can sometimes bring it under control and speak out of that state themselves. For instance, if you're having to deal with an irritating colleague who just won't be shutting up regarding their forthcoming bridal shower, you'll probably be able to combat the desire to slap them in their face. On the other hand, a psychopath will often be resolve by instinct and will react without giving it a second thought about the cost of everyone's decision. Psychopaths are susceptible to snapping in a simple way. Even one gets injured as they pop.

Common decency, when dealing with others, demands a certain level of decorum and kindness. It is not something of concern to psychopaths. While the majority of the people are worried about kindness and caring, the nicest person in the room will have no issue being a psychopath. Based on the situation in hand, they might be dramatic or execute about it.

The Dark Triad Practice

The dark triad test gauge how one score, as for the three practices of narcissism, Machiavellianism, or psychopathy, is concerned. The test is sometimes used in various settings, and by law courts and police in particular. The dark triad test is also used by corporations to gauge their employees. The primary reason the dark triad method is implemented is to assess an entity's personality characteristics and likely forecast their actions to prevent unsavory behaviors. It was noted that people who score high on the dark triad study are more likely to cause problems and social distress, whether in the work environment or even in their employment state. At the same time, these people will also likely have an easy time to attain leadership positions and gain sexual partners.

The dark triad test asks you to address a series of questions on a range of subjects like how you think about others and yourself, how you maintain track of details you could use to harm someone, and your general opinions on existence, death, and social experiences, among others. The dark triad test may be a nice way to gauge how you perform on the dark triad scale when self-administered. The dark triad test might not be very precise when administered by law courts and police as the respondent may purposely alter their answers to make them look better than it actually is. It is a primary drawback of the triad check in the night. If you're willing to take the dark triad exam, there are some online places where you'll be able to complete a study in minutes. Be careful to take the test results too personally—sometimes, the justifications you give are based on the kind of day you are taking and not on the type of person you are being. In any event, if you recognize yourself as a respectable human being who always respectfully treats others and never harms others, then you shouldn't worry very much about what an experiment says about you.

Chapter 9. How to Defend Ourselves of Dark Psychology

First, Identifying Them

By now, we have examined the foundations of dark psychology, the psychological profiles that make up the Dark Triad, typical forms of manipulation in relationships, and how manipulation has manifested itself in society's institutions.

First, remember that simply because you are not currently in a personal or professional relationship that could be defined as manipulative does not mean that you are free of all danger and concern. Predators have had to learn the hard way to live and achieve success using cold and calculating psychology from which they truly do not ever get any rest.

Imagine being injured in a serious accident and losing the use of one or more of your limbs. Regardless of how much you would prefer to have the use of that limb back. You will be forced to find some way to adapt. Emotional predators do the same thing. But because their injuries are invisible, and because of the business world's competitive nature, they sometimes hold an advantage over us if we fail to maintain vigilance.

Emotional predators can blend into the normal landscape because it is easy for them to go through daily living motions. They truly do not care if things don't work out because they have no value for their relationships or the things that society has established as having value.

Consider that the serial killer Ted Bundy worked on a crisis hotline while he stalked and murdered young women. He appeared successful, outgoing, handsome, and well-adjusted, but he was not. Or consider that the serial killer John Wayne Gacy, who murdered and buried in the crawl space beneath his home, almost 40 young men and boys, spent his days running a construction business, held fundraisers for local political leaders, and entertained sick children.

It may seem nauseating, especially with these extreme and dramatic examples. Still, for the emotional predator, society's important responsibilities are less a source of personal and professional satisfaction and fulfillment and more a perfect cover for their predatory addiction. As a result, you may find it helpful to develop some habits that will help you learn to classify some of the significant signs of emotionally predatory behavior.

Not everyone's life is perfectly organized or compartmentalized. Often environments and the people in them cross boundaries. Often in our daily lives, we wonder where things may have gone wrong. Quite often, the answer may be that we are trapped in a relationship with an emotional predator.

Regardless of the environment in which you meet people, you should always maintain a vigilant lookout for any of the following telltale signs of a predatory personality:

- Pathologically selfish people. They may go through friendship and love motions, but their emptiness is apparent when they fail to initiate social outings or when all encounters leave you feeling exhausted and drained.

- Emotional predators may offer lots of charm and flattery, but if there is a lack of substance to your interactions with them, you can be sure the compliments are probably false, too.

- Predators will exaggerate their accomplishments and even lie. If you call them on it, they will refuse to take responsibility or admit that they are wrong.

- A date or outing with an emotional predator may always be a high-stakes adventure. If you never seem able to engage with them simply over a cup of coffee and have a happy and fulfilling encounter, you may be dealing with a predator.

- Predators are bullies by nature and use anger as their primary means of communication. Avoid people who demonstrate a tendency to humiliate people or challenge anyone who seems to have more power or success than they do. Predators also use insults and putdowns to build themselves up. You may notice this kind of conduct directed at other people when you are out with a predator. For example, if you are at a café or restaurant, a predator may try to impress you by insulting or humiliating the staff.

- Predators are manipulative, which they often show by making promises and then not keeping them.

- Because predators lack a conscience and do not understand that their abusive behavior should make them feel bad, a telltale sign, maybe anyone who boasts about committing abusive actions or crimes

- Predators may also display parasitic behavior. If you are tangled with someone who is excessively lazy and uses you, you should find a way to end the relationship.

Guidelines

Of course, identifying the signs of predatory behavior is only half the battle. The other half is discovering a way to resolve the conflicts and repair the damage that inevitably follows in the wake of an encounter with an emotional predator.

The following are some general guidelines. Some of the tips are meant as suggestions that you should implement on a daily basis. They should become new habits that will now be part of your daily routine. It is important not to regard these tips as chores or burdensome or a diversion or interruption of your normal life. Think of these suggestions as your own personal investment in your daily professional development.

Suppose a virtuoso musician who plays violin for a symphony wants to stay at the top of his profession. In that case, no matter what else he does, one thing must remain constant: daily practice and a constant effort to stretch his repertoire by seeking out more challenging pieces, finding new forms of expression, and adding new skills to his resume. Consider a university professor in any department—being hired into a tenured position is the only beginning. The "publish or perish" mentality will soon take hold. He will find that continually refreshing his professional assessment of his area of expertise is as much a part of his daily professional routine as the more mundane tasks involved in classroom lectures.

So, it is with life in the modern world. To maintain a position of success and happiness and fulfillment, we must think like any gifted performer or professional. Constant vigilance and the continual addition of new weapons to your arsenal to fight the war against the growing threat of epidemic levels of emotional predation will keep your calendar full.

Buy a notebook, start a new spreadsheet, create a new folder in your favorite browser's bookmarks tab, and clear off a shelf on the bookcase in your office. This effort in your life can be just as much a passion and an investment in your success and happiness as the money you spent earning your college degree or the time and effort you spent building your professional network.

Most importantly, as we move down the list of tips for dealing with predators, remember that it is not unusual to find that recovery from such encounters, in some cases, may take years. Though the first step of dealing with a predator is ensuring, they are no longer physically present in your life. This step is not always easy to accomplish. And once you achieve this goal, actually repairing the damage they have caused may keep you very busy for some time to come. But relax—though the damage inflicted by emotional predators can grow increasingly worse over time, so the benefits of successfully dealing with these incursions can have increasingly beneficial returns over time.

Here are some suggestions:

Conduct A Self-Inventory

From time to time, read the details in the types of character traits that make people more susceptible to emotional predation. Look within and be truthful with yourself about your weaknesses. Don't do this as an exercise in self-abuse, though.

Consider that an emotional predator approaches you with only one goal in mind—to destroy you. You may not be entirely willing to examine yourself in an unflattering light, but an emotional predator who has made you a target may not have time for anything else.

Be Cautious

Whenever you are meeting new people, whether romantically or professionally, guard your personal information

Resist Projection and Gaslighting

When you encounter these environments, remind yourself that the goal is to defeat all genuine efforts to establish accountability.

Keep A Journal

You don't have to be eerie about it, but respect yourself enough to seriously take your personal and professional aspirations. Write down your thoughts and concerns at the end of the day, even if you can only manage a few sentences. The blank page will never pose the kind of threat to you that an emotional predator may.

By getting your complicated thoughts out of your head and on paper, you have unburdened yourself in a means that is most useful to you. A predator knows you have this need, and their willingness to listen may be designed as a trap.

Go "No Contact"

If you are in a professional or private relationship, and notice any of the signs of emotional predation, take steps immediately to end the relationship. Sometimes that may mean not replying to text messages, voice mail messages, or email messages. The predator may not like it and may react angrily, but if you try to enter into a negotiation or debate, you will be playing into their hands. Just say that you have decided not to respond any further, then stick to your plan.

Going "no contact," and in the modern world with all its digital communication, is a valid and acceptable tactic. If the predator continues to harass you, keep notes, and document their abuse. You may need to use it later if law enforcement becomes involved. Screenshots, text messages, email messages, and voice mail messages should all be saved and kept in a folder.

Get Help

Recognizing that you are in a relationship with a predator is the first step to escaping the relationship. Rescuing yourself must become your first priority. Remember that you will require professional help to solve this problem. If you are unsure how to proceed, take ten minutes out of your day, find a quiet place, and make a phone call. Don't worry about being perfect or feeling awkward. Professionals expect you to be at a loss and will know how to help.

Find A Support Network

You may need to seek the support of the law enforcement authorities. If you believe things are that bad, you are probably right. Don't let yourself be bullied or intimidated. As with a psychologist or helpline call, making the first call is the most important step. Even if things don't go exactly the way you think they should, by informing the local authorities, you will have placed yourself in a better position

Reinvent Yourself

Remember that as a victim of emotional predation, you will no longer be the person you once were and will have to restructure your thoughts and approaches to life.

Cheer Up

You have taken the first step toward defeating the predatory influences that have brought the dark cloud over your life. It is the first day of the rest of your life, not the last day of the life you used to live.

As you move forward with your new awareness of your surroundings' nature, the world may become a less intimidating place, and you will once again find the joy and happiness that seems to have been lost for so long.

Chapter 10. The Power of Hands

The hands have a power that we do not know at all, and we ignore it. They send a huge number of messages that most people can't get.

Hands have always been used in conversation, and their meaning has changed countless times over the years. An example is a handshake.

The act of shaking hands finds its roots in the past. When the ancient tribes met, they used to show their palms to show that they were not hiding anything.

The Roman Empire instead used to tighten the forearm, so both people were sure that the other did not hide anything under his sleeve. It was done because, in those days, it was normal going around with a knife under the sleeve and being safe. They adopted this habit.

But like all the customs that have passed from generation to generation, the one used by the Romans has turned into our handshake.

This gesture for us is used in a myriad of different situations. They were ranging from the classic greeting with friends to a handshake to establish a working agreement between two large multinationals.

Even in Japan, where the classic greeting has always been the bow, the handshake is widely used today.

The fact that it is now a widespread gesture does not mean that it is simple to do. Behind the handshake, there is a real-world of domination and submission.

Still, in ancient Rome, two people greeted each other with an arm-wrestling handshake, I define it.

In other words, it was not common to shake hands as we do today, but one person took the hand of the other from bottom to top and created the shape of a sandwich, so to speak. The most powerful person dominated the other.

Nowadays, this practice is not used, but the person you win always exists while handshaking. There are three different types of endings for a handshake, which are:

- Dominance
- Submission
- Equality

These attitudes are perceived at the unconscious level, and our body processes them in a particular way, and each of these can decide in which direction the conversation will go.

An example I can give you is that of a study done on some company managers.

Male or female makes no difference.

It has shown that 89% of them use the dominant handshake and always hold out their hand first so that they can control the handshake accurately.

The exact opposite is a submissive handshake. In this case, the person puts his hand palm up, granting the other person dominance. A bit like dogs do when they lie down and put their bellies to the sky.

You can use this handshake if you want your interlocutor to feel in control of the situation. You can use this squeeze when you go to make excuses, for example.

On the other hand, when the two people are in a position in which both want to turn the other's hand to dominate, a "bite" is created. It causes the people to be equal, and neither of them, in the end, gets the better.

So, if you want to create an equal relationship with the person in front of you, avoid him turning your hand, but most importantly, use the same amount of force that he uses.

Now let's use hypothetical numbers. If he applies a force of 9 out of 10 to the handshake and you apply one of 7 out of 10, you will have to increase the strength, or you will be dominated. The same thing you will have to do in reverse if you don't want to dominate.

In short, if he applies a force of 5 and you of 7, if you do not want to be seen dominant, you will have to lower the power of your grip forcefully.

But now I'll tell you a trick to never let yourself be dominated. Not even if you were to meet the president of the united states.

Indeed, with this technique, you will always and I repeat, always dominate the other. Always if in that situation you want to do it.

The technique is called "disarming the doers."

The technique consists of putting the arm outstretched with the palm facing down to not leave any escape for your interlocutor, and he will have to turn his hand and put himself in submission forcefully.

From that moment on, you can do whatever you want. You decide whether to dominate or be equal, but it will be very difficult for him to bring the situation in his favor.

A bit like it happens in games when you are three points above your antagonist, and the game is about to finish, he has to do a miracle to win; indeed, the options for him are to draw or to lose.

If you occur to find yourself in the situation where a person holds out his hand as described above, there is something you can do to reverse the situation.

Step forward with your left foot and make sure to bring his hand vertically. This practice is not simple because we tend to advance with the right, but you will see that it will come more than natural to you with a little training.

If you really can't take this step, there is another way to save yourself from domination, and that is the double catch.

When the other brings you to palm up, you use the other hand, free to return the hold to a tie. So right now, you are using two hands while he is using just one.

Staying on The Left Is an Unfair Advantage

During a handshake, your position is crucial, and staying on the left helps a lot if you want to dominate.

It happens because, on the right, you have no control over the situation, while on the left, you can actually do it.

Kennedy liked this technique very much, even if at that time, nothing was known about body language; he already applied it by intuition.

If you go to see all the photos where he meets with leaders and famous people, you will always find him on the left with the double grip.

A striking example of how Kennedy was a phenomenon with body language is when he won the Nixon election.

At that time, it was renowned that the people who only heard the two politicians' speeches were convinced that Nixon had won while those who watched the scene agreed otherwise.

It led Kennedy to win the election. Pretty important this body language, isn't it?

However, going back to the speech above, if you are on the right of the photo to be able to have an equal situation, reach out to force him to shake your hand as you want.

To conclude, I give you a summary.

Few people know what an impression they can make on a stranger, even if they are conscious of how vital it is to yield a great starting point in a conversation.

Take some time to experiment with the various handshakes with perhaps friends, relatives, or work colleagues to get familiar with it. During important moments you will know how to behave correctly.

Chapter 11. Body Language of a Child

First of all, we must dialog about why it is different from reading a child's body language. The first reason is that they are young and have not yet learned to control their emotions. If a child is sad, they cry. If a child is happy, they smile. If they are angry, they yell and make mad faces, and if they are embarrassed, their cheeks turn red, and they hide their face. Some children might even decide to tell you about the emotions that they are feeling. Children are new to the world and have no reason to hide the things they are going through.

Because of this, children have body language that is extremely easy to read. They do not distinguish how to control their emotions, so they always show how they feel. If you read the emotions of a child, you are reading what they truly feel.

Another important thing to note about reading the body language of children is that since they do not yet know how to hide their emotions, they also are unaware of the body language signs that they portray. They are not capable of sending the opposite signal of how they feel like adults are.

Their lack of awareness of their own body language can also make it easy to spot when a child is lying. A child might try to hide the truth through their words, but they do not have the wherewithal to think to conceal it in their body language as well, often allowing tells to slip through that they are not telling the truth or are omitting part of the truth.

For example, my sister has a five-year-old daughter who likes to sneak chocolate chip cookies before dinner. My sister always checks the Chips Ahoy package right before she starts making dinner, so she knows when a cookie is missing. She will still ask her daughter in the hopes that her daughter will confess on her own. My niece will most of the time try to lie about it (my personal favorite being when she claimed her father ate the cookie).

However, no matter how convincing she might think she sounds, she has one big tell that she is lying: a huge smile plastered on her face. Because she thinks she is getting away with something so mischievous, this smile appears on her face as she is so proud of her deceit. When it is clear that she will not get away with it, this smile is usually replaced by another tell, i.e., her hanging her head while looking at the floor because she is ashamed at having been caught.

Everyone has the physical tell that gives them away when they are lying. Fortunately for parents, guardians, and teachers, children are unable to hide their tells until they are older and have more experience both with lying and reading their own body language.

Today that we know how simple it is to read the body language of a child, let's look into how important it is to pay attention to the signals a child is conveying. Whether you are around children a lot or not, you need to be able to read a child's body language so that you can do your part in ensuring that our children are healthy and safe. Like reading an adult's body language can help us determine if they are in a dangerous situation, we can also use a child's body language to determine if they are in any danger. The unlucky truth is that we live in a world in which people will abuse, kidnap, and otherwise harm children. We want to help children out of such situations, but it can often be hard to tell when something suspicious is going on.

Reading a child's body language can help us determine if there is more to the state than meets the eye. Because young children do not know how to control their body language, any discomfort they feel around a specific adult will manifest in such ways as to how they hold themselves around this person. For instance, if a child exhibits such body language as standing stiffly, hunching their shoulders forward to make themselves smaller, or avoiding eye contact with everyone, including the adult they are with, it could mean that they are afraid of something. If they flinch whenever the adult that they are with reaches over to touch them, it could very well mean that this fear stems from someone hurting them on a regular basis, most likely this adult. Also, suppose they refuse to initiate physical contact with this adult while still never wandering any significant distance from them. In that case, it could mean that they are afraid to have any intimacy with this adult and of doing anything to anger them.

Mind you, none of this is a reason to call the police or Child Protective Services on someone. After all, there are multiple interpretations of any given body language. Standing stiffly, hunching their shoulders forward, or avoiding eye contact, for example, could just mean that the child is not comfortable in that particular environment or with strangers. Flinching and avoiding initiating physical contact with the adult could indicate, rather than fear, that the child has a problem with physical touch overall or that they are mad with that adult for some reason. Not wandering far from the adult, even though it is natural for a child to want to explore, could simply show that the child is well behaved or not particularly comfortable with checking out their surroundings on their own.

Like with all body language reading, what a child's body language means often depends on the context. If you know the child and adult personally, it can be easier to determine what the child's body language means. If they are complete strangers, it will be trickier. Nevertheless, spotting such body language in a child will help you to be on alert so that if suspicion arises that the child is being abused or has been kidnapped, you will be ready to take action.

Reading a child's body language will also help you to be there for them emotionally. If you have a child or take care of a child for large amounts of time, they will consider you their support system. They need you to help them learn about their lives and the world around them. It includes learning how to handle their emotions.

Sometimes, a child might have an emotion that they do not yet know how to explain. They may express this feeling through body language but still feel frustrated when they are unable to put their experience into words.

As an adult who distinguishes how to read body language, you can help in this situation. You can read the nonverbal cues that the child is portraying and use them to help the child express his or her feelings verbally. It will help the child learn about their feelings and more about who they are. It will also help the child grow up knowing that feelings are healthy and that it is okay to share your struggles with those close to you. If you can help your child in this way and teach these things to your child at a young age, they will have significantly fewer emotional struggles over the course of their life. This understanding is important to any adult who deals with children, such as doctors, teachers, and parents dealing with other kids, such as their children's friends.

Parents and caregivers need to teach their children how to express their own body language. Still, they need to teach the kids about simple body language reading techniques. You might not want to call it body language reading to them because they either will not understand or will think the topic is boring, but this skill must be taught to children in whatever creative way necessary.

You might wonder why I believe it is important for children to be able to read body language since it is a science-based topic that can be complicated at times. We will explain why this is important now.

First, if your children understand that nonverbal communication has just as much meaning as the words they speak, they will understand the people around them at a new level. Take their time on the playground, for example. If they ask a friend to play with them and the friend says no but is looking at the ground and has another child staring at them as if to tell them not to play with the child, they will know that there is more meaning behind this situation. They will either be able to speak up for their friend and encourage them to do what they want. Or they will be deprived of worrying about what other people think or be able to walk away without feeling offended because they know that there was more to the conversation than a simple denied request to play. It might even be a sign that the friend was bullied away from playing, and your child will be able to express to a trusted adult what they saw.

Also, think about if your child sees a classmate that is not saying much when they usually talk all day, every day. If your child is aware of the body language of the people around them, they might notice this difference in behavior and ask the child what is wrong. It could make a profound change in the said child's day.

You might even consider the friendships that the child already has. As an adult, you know that being able to read simple body language allows you to have better friendships. It makes sense, then, that the same is true with friendships among children.

Your child will also be able to avoid being a bully better if they are aware of their own body language. They will understand that actions like rolling the eyes or walking away from someone when they are talking to them hurt just as much as mean words. They will understand these actions and avoid them to be nice to the people around them when other children might accidentally hurt their friends with actions like these without knowing the consequences.

When a child knows body language, they are able to make sure that their friends are comfortable with them. If the child sits close to a friend, they will be able to tell if the friend is okay with close contact or not. If the friend is not tolerable and shows signs of being uncomfortable, the child will know that the right thing is to move away.

A lot of these types of body language are things that children learn through real-life experience. The only problem with this is that real feelings are getting hurt if they are learning in real life, and real friends are feeling uncomfortable. The sooner a child acquires these skills, the sooner they can use body language to their advantage.

Chapter 12. Reading People Through Their Mind

How often have you heard somebody instruct you to simply say something because they can't guess what you might be thinking?

Things being what they are, this is just half evident. The individual disclosing to you this may not know, yet they are positively equipped to guess what you might be thinking. They do what desires to be done in a more unpretentious way than they see.

A great many people can actually figure out how to guess thoughts with preparing, time, center, and a specific arrangement of abilities. It isn't something just mystics can do.

Even though clairvoyants do have the best possible ability, preparing, and "gift of perusing," it is surely something that can be figured out how to a degree.

Before I give you how everything people can figure out how to understand minds, it's essential to know some foundation data on mind perusing.

When you understand the science and the brain research behind psyche perusing, you will see that it is a reachable undertaking for anybody with the assurance to learn. And there are also a few deceives you can use to give the hallucination that you understand personalities.

Those stunts become considerably more helpful when you know the reality behind brain perusing.

Characteristic Mind Readers

The motivation behind why anybody can figure out how to guess thoughts is because we do it as of now.

Even though our suspicions are often off-base, it's not because the cycle of psyche perusing comes up short. We can reflect on the considerations and sentiments of people we cooperate with.

In any case, we often center our response around what we figure they will do rather than what they are revealing to us they will do. We often observe somebody's outward appearances and body language and effectively surmise that they are discouraged, debilitated, cheerful, irate, or content.

However, what happens when somebody has a decent poker face? Would we be able to at present guess thoughts without these visual signs to guide us?

Of course.

Required Skills

Truly is don't take those numerous aptitudes to understand minds. All you want is the drive to learn and the eagerness to incline toward your instinct when it mentions to you what somebody is likely reasoning or feeling right now.

You'll clearly require some training before your capacities easily fall into place for you. Be that as it might, you do not take to purchase a precious stone ball, an exceptional deck of cards, or an abnormal outfit to guess the thoughts of others.

You should have the option to free your brain from all interruptions before you endeavor to guess what someone might be thinking. For certain people, this will be the ability that sets aside the most effort to create.

Maybe you could take some yoga classes. Not exclusively will they assist you with centering your psyche and your energy. However, they will likewise give you some quality adaptability and exercise.

If you are searching for additional assets, these may help.

Tips for Beginners

If you need to figure out how to understand minds, you can follow some basic hints to kick you off. Widely acclaimed mystic Kiran Behara created these tips.

Behara's customers incorporate the absolute most extravagant and most well-known appearances in amusement and Broadway. You should begin by rehearsing these tips for your loved ones.

You should see snappy outcomes; however, it will take some time and practice to guess total outsiders' thoughts.

So here we go.

Open up Your Spirit

Notwithstanding freeing your brain from all contemplations and stresses, you should open up your energy to the people and potential outcomes around you. Try not to consider anything.

You simply need to be available at the time. Your psyche and soul should absorb the energy radiated by the people and things around you. Yoga is incredible at showing us how to do this. However, you can learn it all alone at home in the quietness of your room.

Simply ensure people will disregard you while you start to center your musings and energy.

Seeing and Not Seeing

Free your thoughts.

Take a couple of seconds to perceive the individual sitting close to you genuinely. Make a psychological depiction of their facial structure, hair, eyes, stance, body language, and other subtleties.

However, you likewise should see everything else around that individual.

You must have a psychological segment that isolates the individual's characteristics and the other things that don't have a place with that individual. Separate the individual from the seat they are sitting in or the divider behind them. These things must be envisioned with a particular goal in mind so you can feel all the energy being created around you.

Zero in on the Person

Presently you need to restore your concentration to that individual's face. Look at them legitimately without flinching for around 15 seconds. Try not to gaze too long, or you may intrude on the energy by causing the individual to feel awkward. Following 15 seconds pass, you will need to turn away.

Make a psychological image of their face and their eyes. What does their energy feel like? Sit peacefully now as you let the considerations and sentiments of that individual fill your psyche and your spirit. You have now really begun the cycle of psyche perusing.

Start a Conversation

It is the place you will reveal the contemplations and sentiments of the individual. You can pick any topic you like for discussion. Get some information about their work or their home life. The considerations that come racing into your own brain might be the same musings crossing the other individual's thoughts. You could promptly mention to the individual what you accept they are thinking. If you have a clad memory, you can store these contemplations for later to summarize your whole impression of their considerations in these meetings.

The key is to invite any contemplations that enter your psyche now. Regardless of whether those considerations are dull and irksome, you need to give the individual a precise perusing of their contemplations. So as to do that, you should keep your brain open to each chance.

Possibly you didn't have any sign before that your brother is discouraged, and this disclosure harms you. However, your brother should realize that you're presently mindful of his battles. And now you may have the option to support him. The capacity to guess thoughts will give you a ton of intensity; however, it's a brilliant force if you use it shrewdly.

Other Tips

There is other advice you can use to increase these tips. When you increment your capacities to zero in on others' musings and sentiments, you can use more tips to give you an away from what goes on in other people's psyches.

These tips will build your odds of progress and knock the socks off of your companions, family, and outsiders you meet in the city.

Passionate Intelligence

If you realize the individual you're conversing with, you can inquire whether they feel similar feelings you're feeling. You'll show restraint toward this. Numerous people aren't truly adept at naming their feelings. They may feel furious when they're truly simply worried.

They could feel apprehensive when they're simply prepared to proceed onward to something different. If the individual you converse with concurs with the feelings, you sense, inquire whether they can sort out any reasons they may be feeling thusly.

Finally, you can start to offer recommendations on what they ought to do close to intensify or diminish these sentiments. They will be flabbergasted at your premonition and acknowledgment.

It may sound more like psychiatry than mystic brain perusing. However, it's one of the key approaches to build up your regular aptitudes.

Create Keen Listening Skills

What do all incredible communicators share practically speaking? They should be acceptable to audience members.

When somebody talks, be totally at the time with them. Try not to tune in for having the option to react. Tune in to the other individual with the goal that you can measure and understand all that they are stating. Yet, you should likewise tune in to what they're not saying too. If somebody isn't anticipating the remainder of their day, there must be a purpose behind that. Cautious listening will assist you in revealing those reasons and make them known to the individual. So as to succeed, you'll have to figure out how to listen more than you talk some of the time. Listening is the manner in which you find out about people and their feelings.

Try Not to Ignore Emotions

The explanation people need compassion today is because they decide to. Throughout each day, we are told to disregard our emotions to complete our work. Then put on a solid face for the world.

The more we overlook our emotions, the snappier they disappear. Rather than considering the new email from the chief or what you'll have for supper later, consider how you feel. As per proficient mystics, the more you can react to your own emotions, the more you will have the option to peruse and react to other people's sentiments and considerations in your life.

Guessing thoughts is something everybody can do and isn't only something for proficient mentalists and mystic peruses. You probably won't experience a lot of accomplishment from the outset, yet you can accomplish incredible advancement with training. Absolutely never utilize your new capacities to increase a bit of leeway over another person.

If you can peruse their feelings incredibly well, you may have the option to utilize that to get your direction. Utilize your capacities to help people. Brain peruses can be extraordinary companions and emotionally supportive networks for people who simply need to vent.

You have probably thought about how things would be if you could guess other people's thoughts. A few individuals utilize their instinct for this, yet if you are not all that discerning, there is just a single decision left: reckoning out how to peruse people's body language.

We get over 55% of data through nonverbal correspondence. Allan Pease, an Australian body language master, expounded on this. Emulates, motions and other body developments can expose an individual and mention to you what they truly think or feel.

Chapter 13. Myths About Body Language

We are going to deal with some commonly harbored myths about body language and bust them to paint for you the real picture.

Body Language is Mostly Communication

Imagine having to understand what your friends say by muting your ears and simply watching their body language. Of course, you will fail at it! And odds are you will hate it too! If the world were to go mute and deaf all of a sudden and the only available form of communication left was body language. The entire planet would collapse within a matter of a few hours.

You cannot rely solely on body language to understand a person's behavior. Body language is only one form of communication and not even a major one. It is assistance to words and not the main player in the game. You cannot trust body language to help you understand what a person is saying without listening to their words. However, you can get a good or bad impression of their approach. It is a combination of communication skills that allows you to make your own decision about the honesty or reliability of the person with whom you are communicating. If you do give a clear message that you are honest by keeping your shoulders straight and looking your fellow speaker in the eye, you give a better impression than those who look downward and appear not to be taking much notice of what is being said.

Liars Avoid Eye Contact

One of the oldest myths about body language is that criminals try to avoid eye contact. Imagine if our prison system was based on the mere theory that everyone who avoided eye contact was a criminal. More than half of us would be rotting behind bars if that were the case. It is a fundamental principle of criminology and body language combined that those who lie find it hard to establish eye contact. However, an entire cult of criminals is so hardened and brazen that they have understood the art of lying and have no shame from marinating in eye contact.

They could lie about what they ate in the morning and still look straight into your eyes. Not just that, some of the notorious ones could lie to the extent of misleading and manipulating you to overthink and stress yourself out. The myth that those who have done something wrong would avoid eye contact is a thing of the past.

You can tell from the eyes the level of nervousness of the person with whom you are talking. If their eyes are constantly on the move, this is a good indication that they are not relaxed.

People Who Talk Too Fast Are Liars

Again, another one of those judgmental myths. When people talk fast, it does not mean that they are telling you lies all the way. It is true that some individuals do really talk fast when they are lying—but it does not mean the same the other way around. It depends on the context. Sometimes people talk fast because they are excited about what they are chatting about. Sometimes, that is just the way that they talk.

Maybe they are in a hurry and are trying to drive an important point home. That will force them to speak at a rapid pace and try to convey a message as soon as possible. Not all people who talk too fast are liars. The other thing to bear in mind is that some people are naturally fast talkers. They may have learned that way and may not be that articulate at getting their message across. Often, I have asked people to slow down when they talk in this way, but you will always have people whose level of nervousness comes into their speech flow. It doesn't mean they are lying or trying to hide something. It does mean that they have an inbuilt nervousness about public speaking. Use another body language in conjunction with fast speech to get a more accurate picture of the person.

Crossed Arms Is A Negative Sign

Another very commonly held myth is that crossed arms signify negativity of some kind. Generally, it so happens that in a group discussion, it is considered hostile to cross your arms and not participate in the ongoing discourse. However, crossed arms could mean a lot of other things, each as possible as the next.

Those watching a theatre play and sitting in the front row usually cross their arms in order to establish a sort of barricade between the artists and themselves. In such a case, the front row people feel vulnerable being exposed to the play from such a close angle, and crossing their arms is a form of shielding themselves. If you are in a state where those you are talking to are in a similar situation, such as a lecture room, then crossed arms can simply be doing the same thing. In a situation where manual work is being done, crossed arms may just be the speaker's way of relaxing himself between jobs. However, it still shows defensiveness and a lack of openness to other opinions for a public speaker.

Smiling While Speaking Is an Indicator of Honesty

You must have seen a public speaker employing this method. They tend to smile more when they speak rather than in other situations. Smiling conveys a feeling of security and honesty. However, most of these public speakers are so seasoned that they have mastered the art of smiling to the extent where they naturally smile while addressing a crowd. It is not plastic, but it is not genuine either. The process of smiling while speaking to a crowd has become so ingrained in their system that they cannot help but sprout a smile every time they climb a podium. However, Smiling is not a sure indicator of honesty, as is evident from development-promising politicians who are all smiles right before an election starts.

You will start to identify the difference between a genuine smile and that which would be summed up as "smarm" in order to try and charm an audience into liking a speaker who is not particularly likable. Smarm is the kind of smile that is forced, and when you are talking to others, you can generally recognize one from the other.

Fumbling Is A Sign of Lying

Not necessarily! Some people fumble naturally and have been diagnosed with the medical condition of stuttering from the very beginning. If you remember well, you will recall that we talked about how a lot of factors go into deciding the correct inference about a person's body language behavior.

While we enlisted only five of them, body language myths go on running for three miles at a stretch. It is vital to comprehend that body language is not the ultimate tool for deciphering people's true intentions and emotions. Sometimes, the tool of body language fails miserably. It is not in all circumstances that you can employ body language to give you the most accurate results.

If you assume it to be the ultimate mind reading weapon for you, you are in for a great shock. As it has been mentioned before, consider all the factors possible before applying the tool of body language to decode a person's behavior.

Body language should not be read in a vacuum. There must always be context surrounding a particular body behavior. You are undertaking it all erroneous if you isolate one instance of behavior and decode it. That is a method that will lead you to definite failure. Instead of that, try to observe body language patterns in the surroundings they are created in. Before jumping to conclusions based on one instance, understand that there may be a lot of reasons a person behaves the way they behave. Often times, it is the ongoing situation that makes a person act in a certain way.

With a female, you have to take into account the mood swings the fairer sex is subjected to on account of monthly instances of losing a reasonable amount of blood (menstruation).

There could be regional factors too. Most people have their moods on a roller coaster. Mood swings are as common as cupcakes, and you have to acknowledge that people are not constant. Change is the only constant. I may not be the same person today as who I was yesterday. It is, in fact, a good sign that people change for only change could lead to evolution, and without evolution, people would go stagnant, not just evolutionarily but also mentally. Therefore, while trying to decipher a person's true feelings and motives, try to take everything there is into account and then start decoding.

Perhaps the person that you are talking to is nervous in a situation where it would be normal to be nervous. In this case, body language can be forgiven because it's justified.

Any Nonverbal Sign Is A Message

It is one big myth that needs to be busted. Many people assume that any non-verbal sign is a basis of communication. In fact, they believe that 90% of people's communication will come from nonverbal signs. But this is not true. If you accept this to be correct, you might misinterpret things or over-rely on something that does not lead you anywhere. However, you have to practice your own skills of reading your own body language and the body language of people that you have known for a long time. Perhaps you haven't really paid much attention to this, but it's time that you did because it enables you to recognize body language that has a hidden message and that which does not.

Nose Touching Is Indicative of Lying

Nose touching is said to be a universal sign for lying. But this is not true! What if the person scratching the nose has an allergy or is on the verge of sneezing? Maybe the person is really not doing it on purpose. In fact, many people take offense when people touch their nose while speaking. If you think the other person is doing it on purpose, you can simply ask if they have a cold, which will alert them not to do it anymore.

Nose touching can mean various things. It is not a good thing to fix when you are talking to someone, although it is an area of the body that may be giving you problems. You would be better carrying a handkerchief and dealing with the problem, rather than trying to prevent it by touching your nose. Also, this area of the face may have dry skin around it, which may be the reason for the touching. You need to consider each individual case before you assume that someone is lying. In fact, this sign isn't really one of lying at all, and you would be better looking at eye movements and using them as your guide.

Chapter 14. Who Is a Manipulator?

Manipulative humans are the styles of folks that use intellectual and emotional abuse to 1-up you, normally to serve their dreams for energy or manipulate. Disdain the fact that it could be difficult to tell if a person is manipulative while you first meet them. There are numerous developments that manipulative human beings regularly show, which can assist tip you off early to this kind of behavior. It is crucial to appear out for manipulation in a relationship, friendship, or with a family member because you fall prey to a manipulator. It could become challenging to reduce yourself unfastened as soon as you have gotten exceptionally worried in their life. Even though manipulators are, in the end, egocentric, they use numerous schemes and methods to cowl this up. That is why it's so difficult to perceive a manipulative character earlier than it is too late. This list will give you an excellent knowledge of what to look out for in a manipulative man or woman. If you get one or further of these tendencies to your so-referred to as friends, you higher run for the hills. So, without ado, right here are ten bona fide developments of manipulative people you have to appear out for.

Manipulative Human Beings Play the Sufferer

Manipulative human beings are well-known for always playing the victim's function and making themselves out to be extra harmless than they may be. Frequently, they exaggerate or even make up non-public problems in order that others sense sorry for them and sympathize with them. In dating, this trait of a manipulative individual often comes out as dependency or co-dependency. The manipulator may also fake to be vulnerable or weak or want consistent assistance to pull the innocent victim profound into their existence. They do that to attract quality humans to them like a magnet, a good way to exploit later and use them to meet their own egocentric wishes and dreams. With the aid of playing the prey, the manipulator can are searching for out and damage the kindness, mortified conscience, or caring and fostering instinct of the goal. Have you ever had a pal or family member who continuously requested you to lend them money or requested you to buy matters for them, the complete time making you feel guilty for now not having completed so inside the first vicinity? You have probably been coping with a manipulative person. With a bit of luck, you determined your manner out of the entice without too much struggling.

Manipulative Humans Inform Distorted or Half-Truths

Another terrible persona trait that manipulative human beings have is mendacity or distorting reality, so they usually come outright. Fantastic instances of this behavior encompass excuse-making, suppression of important information, underestimations, exaggeration, or hypocrisy. Manipulative humans realize how to bend reality to their advantage. They'll often miss or cover facts to be able to divulge them as being a liar. Manipulators deal with all interactions as though they may ultimately visit trial, and everything they say can be held towards them. As a consequence, they frequently skirt from one place to another the problem or make unclear statements so that when faced, they are able to claim they "never stated that" or that it's miles "no longer precisely what they said."

Manipulative Humans are Passive-Competitive

A similarly demanding character trait of a manipulative man or woman is that they're more frequently than not passive-competitive. A manipulative man or woman might also use this type of behavior to get out of something or to get their manner. They may even do that to make you furious lacking outright deed of something offensive towards you. A family member or friend who frequently forgets something crucial you've got instructed them or overlooks to do something for you that you requested them to perform passive-competitive maybe to control you. It is able to seem innocent, but it's far, in fact, a form of anger, and it isn't healthful for their nicely-being or your sanity.

Manipulative Humans Will Strain You

Manipulative human beings, just like salespeople, will frequently position strain on any other individual in hopes of having you decide before you are truly prepared to. The manipulator believes that you will easily crack and deliver into their desires by using anxiety and managing them. Just like the one's actual-property schemes that stress you to behave fast with the promise of big profits that don't certainly exist, manipulative humans will do something to get you to buy into their sport or advantage a few types of aspect over you. So, be cautious of all and sundry who pressures you to offer a solution earlier than you are equipped, mainly if money is involved.

Manipulative Humans Will Guilt Trip You

A manipulative buddy or family member will often guilt journey you into doing something which you do not want to do, or vice versa, out of something which you do want to do. The underlying cause for this is there, in the long run, selfish personality. Guilt journeys encompass unreasonable blaming from the manipulator, together with concentrated on your soft spot and holding you responsible for their happiness, achievement, or disasters. The manipulator works to goal your vulnerabilities and emotional faintness to coerce you into doing what they want you to do. A manipulative person will frequently make a person they may be in close courting with feel guilty if that character isn't always available. They anticipate absolutely everyone else to assist them in coping with their issues but do nothing in return. Anyone who continually expects you to be the shoulder they cry on, however, who is in no way there for you while you want the same, is most likely a manipulative person.

Manipulative People Provide the Silent Remedy

Have you ever been given the silent remedy from a friend, boyfriend, lady friend, or family member? Probabilities are you had been managing a manipulative person. Manipulative people are bullies. One of the approaches they torment others is with the aid of alienation. Actions like disregarding one man or woman in a collection, now not permitting them to voice their evaluations, or leaving them out are immature strategies used by manipulative adults to claim their dominance. With the aid of showing these behaviors, the manipulative character believes they're coming off as self-confident and powerful. In reality, however, they've low vanity and are extraordinarily self-aware. The handiest way they understand a way to make themselves sense higher is with the aid of hurting others. The next time somebody gives you the silent remedy, don't feel horrific, approximately writing them off completely. It's miles a positive sign of a manipulator and has to be no longer taken lightly.

Manipulative People Do Not Do Anything to Remedy Troubles

Manipulators will, by no means, take the blame for anything. It additionally means that they may in no way make contributions to resolving a hassle in worry that one day they will be held accountable for their movements. A manipulator intends to skate through life while not having to step up and take duty for something. While confronted with something with the aid of a chum or family member, they will both flat out lie and say they by no means did something incorrectly or will make all varieties of justifications for his or her conduct that get them off the hook. You will frequently have many unsettled arguments with a dishonest man or woman, which isn't good. A key sign of this is that a manipulator will regularly quit a controversy or conversation that isn't going their way, without you even realizing it. It's far vital to recognize the way to address warfare well; however, the manipulator cannot do this because they're so centered on themselves and always being inside the proper. Any exact dating may be one in which each human surely needs to assist every other. In case you are coping with someone who can in no way paintings through trouble with you, there is a great hazard that they are now not the proper individual for you.

Manipulative People Choose to Play on Their Home Ground

As we have already set up, the character of a manipulative man or woman is very controlling. A manipulative character will generally insist on assembly or interacting with you in an area in which they feel extra powerful and in control of the situation. It could be their workplace, automobile, domestic, or any other residence where the manipulator senses awareness and ownership. The manipulator, in the long run, does this for two motives. One, they want to hold the upper hand with the aid of being in their consolation sector. And two, they want to weaken you via taking you out of yours. It ought not to be just bodily, both. A manipulator will attempt to take you from your comfort area emotionally and financially as well. Be cautious of everybody who's in no way willing to come out of their comfort zone for you or meet you midway. It's far never an amazing sign.

Manipulative People Rationalize Their Conduct

If ever approached about their manipulative phrases and deeds, a manipulator will make it appear as if it is not a great deal or will shift the responsibility onto someone else, someway making you sense horrific for them usually. However, it's miles, the manipulator who makes a big deal out of things. Until you say something to them approximately it, and then they fireplace every cannon they have got back at you to distract you from the principal subject matter at hand. Manipulators also don't have any empathy for the humans who've helped them and could even pass up to attack those humans, need to experience protecting, or want to cowl up one among their actions or deeds. The manipulative man or woman commonly knows that they have trouble but make it out to look like it's miles the world towards them, instead of the alternative way around. To the manipulative man or woman, not anything they do is ever wrong. Instead, it is always a person else's fault, and there's usually an excuse to rationalize why the manipulative individual said or did what they did.

Manipulative Human Beings Shake Your Confidence

Manipulators regularly cross overboard messing about with different people with the aid of the use of little blow jabs and abuses. Genuine friends ought to sense relaxed poking a laugh at each other harmlessly, but manipulative human beings continually take it a step too some distance. They try this, particularly in groups or social conditions, to undermine others and set up their dominance. Suppose you have a pal that continually leaves you feeling much less than brilliant approximately yourself. In that case, they will be a manipulator, and you ought to cease your friendship with them without delay.

Chapter 15. Dark Psychology and Women

Dark psychology is usually linked with the exploited behavior of people. These types of behavior are perceived very negatively. They often complete successfully for power and resources, and it usually highlights for men, but the samples of women with diversities can also not be neglected. The women's associative behavior that is very antisocial and the trade that hypnotizes and underestimates women's ability to receive and be evil is often taken in very fewer women exploit others. Yet, all of our population don't expect a woman to be threatening. They are often taken very positively, softly, and non-threatening. Even if the women harm, it is minimized, and women are very less responsible for the reactions. Also, they are very less held responsible for the actions, and because of the reason women even have done because the behavior is so unexpected.

It is the reason women think whatever they do, they can always gain sympathy in front of society, which is not necessary but somehow true.

Not everybody knows this dark psychology horror. It would benefit the women, or if they are aware of themselves' darker side, they are afraid of the headed monster. They often don't like to talk about this Complex topic where it is often said that women are the worst Enemies of other women and themselves.

It is very weird to listen to this and talk about it where it is. It is one of the highest growths in society nowadays. Women's empowerment is stronger than any other Era. People are more liberal and more vocal about women's empowerment.

They talk about it more openly. The topic of feminism is so wide and addressed and portrayed in such a beautiful way that everybody comes ahead to give their part and add; however, there is something inside every woman that reacts against their kind goes against their own will.

How it may not look wrong; however, the journey is not so easy, which is a lot of people say that it's a woman who breaks down another woman. Downgrading other Downgrading by Downgrading by life can be hard sometimes anywhere pulling Each Other back. We don't think of it often, and it is a very innocent reality that we are not aware of. It remains in their selves. Town selves' personality is negative, but it is demeaning and taken as negative because that is how we perceive. We know it is a fact that we experience space at every stage of life, but we don't discuss that. We should not discuss that women's empowerment is all about human behavior should be controlled. The women's darkest psychology should also be understood and taken in charge as it is taken in charge of the men. With men, women can also be harmful when it comes to this as compared to men.

Gossiping

There is no boundary set by dark psychology for the people. That's the same with the woman. The backbiting and the gossiping nature are the women's basic nature; it has no boundaries that are defined fun in doing so ever they don't care if anybody sentiments are being hurt. In contrast, they are being hurt. Women tend to talk so disgustingly about other women they find entertaining; however, it is very shameful because they don't understand how much attention-seeking. It is often taken as a trait of women; however, they don't understand how attention-seeking and how embarrassing it gets, no matter if people are enjoying it, but it still looks really bad. Gossiping might look fine but can ruin another person's reputation because nobody is born a perfectionist, and nobody is born Evil. They are good on the inside; however, if a person is spreading rumors about someone, it can ruin the reputation and affect them similarly, it can of the people themselves.

It is right to be fully solved. They are being offended because if a person is gossiping, for example, if they are gossiping and confronted about their bad habit, they lose control. It does not mean that they stop doing it because it is not bound. They won't do it that openly but they would still do it is because they feel there is nothing wrong with it, and once they are pinpointed for it, they would start to pull away from people instead of abandoning this habit of themselves. They are not that trustworthy to give out secrets to them, and they can also forget someone. When women gossip, they don't know when to stop and what to say, and it can hurt someone genuinely. It gives out negative energy from them. One of the biggest things that women associated with dark psychology give out so many negative Vibes from them that are not our society is used to looking at the home. When they have them too, they always think that they would be that sweet child of people when they are not.

Bad Wording

Usually, females criticize others without giving it a thought, which doesn't take charge of everything. A woman is working to make another woman let down, and they don't feel sorry for it. Older women are bringing down the younger ones; younger ones do it to the old ones. It is an unhealthy practice overall. The funny thing is that whatever they say is so easily digestible to the people that they don't even ask them to shut up then and there. The most common practice of this is in every household between a mother in law and daughter in law relation and even the value educated people tend to do it and the thing that is the part of human nature. However, they don't understand that it can lead to something very aggressive, and still, they don't stop or refrain from doing so.

Glaring

Women are born with the most beautiful eyes, and so are men. The woman is praised for the eyes throughout their life, but it is one of the women's most typical characteristics. They glare others to their soul and give out dirty looks to everybody around them, and it is an incoming threat in general.

We often talk about bringing changes in women's empowerment forever. They can do anything that brings joy to them, and they would judge another woman by clearing at the measure; it would make them feel any better.

But they do it so the other person can feel very uncomfortable and they find betterment in doing so and they would laugh out loud, later on thinking about it. It is a very belittle characteristic of every woman; however, they don't want to help the darker side of the personality, so as a result, they don't stop doing it.

Insecure and Jealous

Women are extremely unconfident as compared to men. The same thing arises when they fear losing anyone they are attached to or something they want badly. They are very fragile, and in that situation, they suffer more emotional jealousy than any other, and it is found in any age of the women regardless of how old they are, and they can do anything to for it. They don't want to lose someone they love no matter what happens. Women react to certain situations, and insecurity and jealousy are quite common in them; however, insecurity becomes an extreme obsession if it is not taken care of.

Comparison and Competition

It sometimes happens that people are very competitive. These are the words in the personality that bring out the best outcome in people, especially women. It gets negative when they demoralize and destabilize and push Each Other down when there is a cold war among them.

It just comes with a very competitive nature and then compares them with other women irrespective of any relationship and friendship. It happens quite frequently, which is why we live in a place where there is so much competition going on. Everything is going so digital the competition becomes natural; however, there are two types of competition.

There are one healthy competition and one unhealthy competition among competitions, and women are competing against Each Other. They don't look at the outcomes and what it will bring, which is why it brings out an unhealthy competition between them that brings out the worst in them. It is always necessary to hold the Horses of the hidden and powerful demons, working on the dark side. They are always competing, and they need to know that everything is temporary, and harming anybody while working to get something is not something great to do.

Belittling

The darker side of every human being gives them the feeling that they are superior to others, and they have nothing to do in their life. When that happens to them is that they start thinking that the world revolves around them. They try to belittle others because it is very easy to do so instead of showing gratitude to them, and they do anything to make others wrong. When they are criticized or shown the reality, they won't do anything to make it better. Instead, they always put other people down and want to preserve their superiority over others. They always want to have a high status in front of everybody, so what they think is necessary to do so to look better and everybody, whereas they are just making a fool of themselves, which is quite toxic.

Women cannot usually understand this behavior. People must admit and examine themselves, which is the above dark psychology because it can disturb women's life and people around them because not every woman is like this.

But there are certainly some women whose darker side is more powerful than the other side of their life. Every human being has a dark and light inside. It happens women's approach is how they see different things. Similarly, when feminism has become the town's talk, women should understand that there is a light side of feminism and a dark side of feminism. There is so much more related to the community, especially when their traditional ideas on the concept of femininity. It targets women in a particular way of living in a particular way of acting; however, some women do not agree with the feminism idea and its criteria. They never oppose their beliefs, which are that living like a nice girl is not enough. It may be a pleasant experience to see what it takes to take the whole of the darker side. Still, they need to understand that feminine energy is such a beautiful gift for women to experience by the substrates woman to be only the underside of themselves. They are unaware of how the direct energy works, but they keep falling into a pit hole.

Chapter 16. Techniques of Dark Psychology

Reverse Psychology

A first tactic that a dark persuader can use is reverse psychology. This technique consists of assuming a behavior opposite to the desired one. It is with the expectation that this "prohibition" will arouse curiosity and induce the person to do what is desired.

Some people are known to be like boomerangs. They refuse to go in the direction they are sent to but take the opposite route. It works better when someone else is educated and chooses instinctively rather than thinking about things. They can introduce the intention to do X thing when they suggest the 'do not do X.' When you claim that you will do it, you may wonder whether you will do so.

A dark persuader can use this type of behavior because it is a weakness that the victim has. Take an example of a friend who loves to eat junk food at any opportunity he gets. The dark persuader knows this and will suggest that they eat because it will be good for him, knowing that the friend will choose fast food, anyway.

Reverse Psychology can be used in sales techniques when dealing with a difficult customer.

In this case, the seller can say: "this is a product for rich people. I don't know if it can work for you because it costs a lot of money". So, the seller is like saying: "I don't want to sell it to you. It's not the right product for you since you can't afford it," just because reverse psychology leads the person to want the product even more.

Masking True Intentions (Door in the Face)

Masking true intentions is another tactic a dark persuader will use to get what they want. A dark persuader will disguise their true intentions from their victims and can use different approaches depending on their victims and the surrounding circumstance. One approach a dark persuader can use is using two requests consecutively because people find it hard to refuse two requests in a row. Take this example; a manipulator wants $500 from their victim. The dark persuader will begin by explaining why they need $1000 while stating what will happen if they cannot come up with that amount. The victim may feel guilt or compassion but will kindly explain to the manipulator that they cannot lend the amount because, quite frankly, it's more than they can manage to give when the persuader lessens the amount to $500, which was what they wanted from the beginning. They will attach the amount with some emotional reason where the victim will be unable to refuse the second request. The dark persuader walks away with the original sum, and the victim is left confused about what took place.

The Blame Game

If the manipulator wants to make you do something against your will, he will have a better chance of getting that behavior by making you feel guilty. Blame is one of the most powerful manipulation techniques known to humankind. Guilt can be used to manipulate people by making them feel inferior to the help and support they have received, or it can also be used to make others feel inadequate for a "condition" they have. Think about all those times you hear people say, "things would be different if I weren't sick." It is one of the most rudimentary ways to make someone feel guilty, but it is very powerful. Besides, you might hear others say things like, "remember when you need my help? Now I need your help." It is a clear attempt to convince someone to follow the manipulator's intentions.

Putting the Other Person Down

Through this technique, we try to make the other person feel less capable than he is. For example, you find every pretext to point out to the victim when makes a mistake, and you do it repeatedly to throw off his self-esteem. A person with low self-esteem is manageable and controllable, therefore manipulable. This way, the manipulator will feel in control of the situation.

When a person tries to manipulate you with this technique, remember that they will attack your identity, telling you phrases like "you are incapable" instead. They will never tell you, "you are behaving like an incapable person." To react to this technique, you have to detach yourself from this psycho-trap. Instead, you need to think that the person is judging your behavior at that moment and not your identity.

Leading Questions

It involves the dark persuader questions that trigger some response from the victim. A persuader may ask a question like, "do you think that this person could be so mean?" This question implies that the person will be bad in one way or another. An example of a non-leading question is, "What do you think about that person?" When we use leading questions, dark persuaders ensure that they use it carefully. Dark persuaders know that when the victim feels like they are being led to trigger a certain response, they will become more resistant to being persuaded. When the dark persuader feels that the victim has to be aware that he or she is being led, they will immediately change tactics and return to asking the leading questions only when the victim has come down.

Fatigue Inducement

The impact of mental fatigue on perceptual, emotional, and motivational factors are complex. In exhaustion, special effects can be assumed to rely on the operation's essence that causes fatigue. This study investigated the impact of exhaustion on different activities based on working memory demands on brain function and efficiency. The results showed that driving quality was not impaired by exhaustion. The effects of fatigue on novelty therapy depended on the mental requirements for the task that caused fatigue.

Creating an Illusion

Create exaggeratedly high or unrealizable expectations. But presenting and selling them in such a powerful, persuasive, and tempting way for you that you'll end up believing it.

With this technique, it is likely to make the victim see the most beautiful future so that she will be willing to do anything to make it happen, even spend a lot of money. The goal is to make people "daydream" to give them the hope of living their lives to the full.

Commitment and Congruity

Highly skilled and sophisticated manipulators know that building trust capital is essential, especially when building a long-term approach. Think about the most sophisticated conmen you can imagine. These are individuals who take time, often years, building up trust around them through congruent behavior so that others can tumble into their trap.

At first, no one suspects the least bit in this individual as they have earned everyone's trust. As they gain more and more trust, they can use that trust capital to deceive others. It gives them some leeway in case they slip up. Given their track record, they will always have the benefit of the doubt.

This tactic is not common in less-sophisticated manipulators as it requires a great deal of dedication. Impulsive individuals will never be able to pull this off as they focus more on short-term rather than long-term gain. Through this type of tactic, many manipulators can build a name for themselves in their chosen domain. However, they are often exposed. When this occurs, the world is shocked to learn that who they thought was a pillar of their community was actually a manipulator.

One good example of this is a cheating spouse. An individual may cheat on their spouse for years without them noticing what's going on. Then, one day, the manipulator makes a mistake, whatever it is, and they are exposed. The shock that comes to the victim is overwhelming.

The reason why this tactic always backfires is due to the fact that the manipulator doesn't know when to stop. The longer they go without getting caught, the more they think the con will last forever. History has taught us that everyone gets caught eventually.

Reciprocity

It is the classic "quid pro quo," in other words; you scratch my back, I'll scratch yours. However, the victim doesn't know the extent to which they are being manipulated.

A great example of this can be found with informants.

When a manipulator wishes to extract information from someone, they may offer tidbits of information of their own in the hopes of motivating the victim to furnish the information the manipulator is looking for. However, the key to making this tactic work is that the manipulator must give information of little or no value while extracting information that may be profitable.

Manipulators also use this tactic when doing favors. They build up capital and then "call-in" favors. While this may seem like it's perfectly reasonable, it is a manipulation tactic as the manipulator doesn't do favors out of the goodness of their heart. They do it so that they can have people they can rely on in times of need. Alternatively, they can resort to guilt or even blackmail if the other party refuses to cooperate.

Scarcity and Demand

Often, manipulators realize that they have something, or at least have access to something, that people really want. When this occurs, they can manipulate those around them by creating a false illusion of scarcity.

Earlier, we talked about how advertisers generally use phrases such as "limited quantities available" or "while supplies last." These phrases have become so cliché that no one really buys into them anymore.

Yet, manipulators can make this work by creating a sense that there really is a scarcity of a product or service. Some of the more outright, devious ways of pulling this off are by planting fake informants who spread lies. When these lies spread, people may begin to panic and flock to get the products and services in question.

Another way of pulling this off is by spreading rumors on social media. Some people fall for it, and some don't. In the end, the goal is to create enough confusion so that no one is able to tell the difference.

Lastly, manufacturers may go as far as hoarding supplies in order to create an artificial scarcity. It has worked well throughout history. In fact, it's worked so well that it is illegal in most countries. Still, manufacturers can pull this off by controlling the entire supply chain of their products. So, any disruption along that line will cause scarcity, thereby creating panic in people. The manufacturers themselves are not responsible for the scarcity as they are not the ones who technically caused the issue.

Consensus

This tactic consists of setting situations in such a manner that people will agree to them regardless of what it is. Governments do this all the time. For instance, they know that no one will ever agree to a tax hike. Yet, they frame the situation in such a manner that if people wish to continue receiving government benefits, they need to accept the tax hike as there is no other way to fund it. So, people reluctantly accept the tax hike out of fear of losing their benefits.

Chapter 17. Practical Exercises For Mind Control Prevention

The real question here is why, in the first place, would anyone want to control your mind? Some people may not want to check out some of these exercises because they feel like there would be no reason for a person to try to control their minds in the first place, but you must know that there are many reasons people may want to control your mind. Some of the reasons why people would want to control your mind include:

- They want you to get something for them: It may be money, documents, or any other thing. They have chosen you because they know you are the only one that can get it for them. As such, you become their mind control project. There are even stories of people that say that they were robbed one way or the other, but when they checked the security tapes, the people who called the police were the robbers. Sounds strange, right? A professional can get you to rob your own house and plant a bomb in there by yourself, even if you have no bomb training.

- They may want information: This is another reason why someone would want to hypnotize you. You do not necessarily need to have money for someone to need something from you. They may need access codes or maybe the names of people in a place. What they want to do with the information is a total mystery, but the thing is that you might have succeeded in telling them things that you would not normally tell them if you were not hypnotized in the first place.

Exercise 1: Do Not Keep Your Eyes in One Position

People who tend to control the minds of others can be very skilled at times. Some of them would want to use everything they can to get your attention to persuade you and control your mind at all times. When you notice that you are in the presence of someone that wants to control your mind, try as much as possible to keep your eyes in random motion. Do not let your eyes focus on one thing simultaneously, especially if that thing is something they are holding.

There are various ways a person can control your mind, and your eyes are a good gateway for that to happen. You do not want your gateway to be wide open and for you to be defenseless when someone is trying to get into your mind. When someone is trying to control your mind, and you notice, all you have to do is avoid any kind of eye contact with them.

Do not let them think that they can get to you with your eyes because when they do, they will use that technique against you almost every single time. When people like that find your weak point, they tend to exploit it no matter how many times you try to hide it. It is why you mustn't let them know what that is in the first place.

You should not do certain things when trying to avoid eye contact with the person trying to control your mind. These things are said to be very important and should not be taken for granted. Some of these things include:

- Don't let them know: You should never let the person that is trying to control your mind know that you know what he or she is doing and, most importantly. Do not let them know that you are aware of their technique because when they know that you are aware of their technique, they will tend to change it immediately, and they might still be able to get you one way or the other. If you want to be able to get out of that problem, all you have to do is act oblivious.

- Don't get distracted: Getting distracted around a person who is trying to control your mind is the last thing you want to do when it comes to avoiding them. When you want to avoid something like mind control, you need to make sure that you are alert at all times. When you are avoiding the eyes of the people who are trying to control you, you mustn't forget and mistakenly gaze at them again because that might be your downfall.

Keep your mind and body alert at all times because the moment you let your guard down, they would not hesitate to take advantage of you.

If you can keep your eyes in constant random motion and at the same time avoid all these pointers, there is a good chance that no one would be able to get into your mind no matter how many times they try. You should know that some professionals would go out of their way to get to you, but if you stick to all that you need to do, you would be one of their biggest challenges. If you play your cards right, you may be able to confuse them to the point that they would have to leave you alone and go for much easier targets. How do you confuse them? When they try to get to you with your eyes, let them get to the point that they think they have almost gotten you and make them know that they are still a long way from penetrating your mind. Once they notice that the closer they are to getting to your mind, the harder it gets; they would get confused because you would become a harder nut to crack.

Exercise 2: Don't Let People Copy Your Body Language

It is probably something that you thought was far from important, but it is. If you are in the presence of a person trying to control your mind and find out the person is sitting in the way you are seated. Even the person is mirroring your movements in any way, keep it in mind that the person is somehow trying to get inside your mind. It is why it is important to mind your surroundings at all times because they could get to you just by mirroring your hand gestures.

You may not notice them doing this because they can be subtle as they possibly can. If you even come in contact with the professionals, there is a huge chance that you will not be able to find out what they are up to until it is too late to go back. It is important to know that you may figure the person out if they are new in the game.

The thing is that professionals are very clean in their game, so clean that you may not know what they are doing until they are done. Still, when it comes to a rookie, you can be able to spot what he or she is doing almost immediately because they are not as clean as the professionals. A professional would mirror your movements and gestures very quietly, meaning that you would never catch them doing it. Still, a rookie, on the other hand, may tend to change his or her gestures immediately. You change yours. That's right; there is a huge giveaway. When you notice something like that happening around you, know that the person you are dealing with is a big-time rookie, and all you have to do is to mess with them and have fun with it. You can change your gestures and movements as often as possible and watch them get confused and break down.

There are certain things that you do not want to be doing. Especially when a person is trying to mirror your movements in any way at all, these things include:

- Never sit in one place: This is probably the last thing you want to do, especially if the person trying to mirror you is right in front of you. When you are in the presence of someone like that, all you have to do is keep moving around. You do not need to move around like a mad person. If not, they would know that you have made them.

Just move around casually like you have no idea what is going on around you, and if you can be in as many places as possible and still make as many gestures as possible, there is a good chance that they are not going to be able to see where you are going. Some of them may get so frustrated. Even decide to get your attention by subtly standing in front of you. It is so that you forget what exactly you are doing. But when they do, you can always change your gestures over and over again. It is to mess with their heads.

- Mind your surroundings: This may be hard for some people because many people find it hard to mind their surroundings, no matter how long you try to teach them. They are more focused on the things happening right in front of them and fail to see the things happening around them.

If you are that kind of person, getting into your mind would be a piece of cake because if you want to notice someone trying to get you, you have to be aware of your surroundings with every chance you get. Do not see something strange on the road or in your house and just let it go like that. Try as much as possible to investigate even if you do not get there by yourself.

- The bottom line to all of this is that if you know what is going on around you, you would be able to tackle and address it before it becomes too late, and when you address it early enough, there is absolutely no way that a person can easily control your mind.

It is imperative to know that these tips would not work for everyone, and you must also know that you would not be able to get the best results out of this if you practice it repeatedly. You need to practice in this context because there are many skilled mind control specialists out there, and you need to be on your game at all times. You do not need to sit down thinking that no one can get into your mind just because you have succeeded in successfully spotting one or two of them coming your way. There is a good chance that you will meet a person that is more than a professional. These mind control specialists do not need to get close to you to know what you are doing and control your mind.

Some of these kinds of people can come to you, and the only thing they have to do is to say a word to you, and that word may be able to trigger some series of events, and before you know it, you are under the control of someone you just met.

Chapter 18. Touch As a Form of Body Language

We engage in touching routinely. We commonly shake hands as greetings or assign to signal shared understanding. Touch, as a form of communication, is called haptics. For children, touch is a crucial aspect of their development. Children that do not get adequate touch have developmental issues. Touch helps babies cope with stress. At infancy, touch is the first sense that an infant responds to.

Functional Touch

At the workplace, touch is among effective means of communication, but it is necessary to keep it professional or casual. For instance, handshakes are often exchanged within a professional environment and can convey a trusting relationship between two people. Pay attention to the nonverbal cues that you are sending next time you shake someone's hand. Overall, one should always convey confidence when shaking another person's hand, but you should avoid being overly-confident. A firm pat on the back communicates praise and encouragement. Remember, people have varied reactions to touch as nonverbal communication. For instance, an innocent touch can make another person feel uncomfortable or frightened.

Touch can become particularly complicated when touch is between a boss and a subordinate. Generally, those in power will utilize touch with subordinates to reinforce the hierarchy of the workplace. It is usually not acceptable for it to occur the other way around. For this reason, you should make sure to be careful even in the instance of using the most trivial of touches and resolve to enhance your communication techniques with your juniors. A standard measure is that it is better to fail but remain on the side of caution. Functional touch includes being physically examined by a doctor and being touch as a form of professional massage.

Social Touch

In the United States, a handshake is the most common way one engages in social touching. Handshakes vary from culture to culture, though. In some countries, kissing one or both cheeks are more common than a handshake. In the same interactions, men will allow a male stranger to touch them on their shoulders and arms, whereas women feel comfortable being touched by a female stranger only on the arms. Men are likely to enjoy a female stranger's touch while women tend to feel uncomfortable with any touch by a male stranger. Equally important, men and women process touch differently, which can create confusing and awkward situations. One should be respectful and cautious. For instance, while you stand close to a stranger on an elevator, it is not acceptable to stand so close to them that you contact him or her.

Friendship Touch

The types of touches allowed between friends vary depending on the context. For instance, women are more receptive to touching female friends compared to their male counterparts. Touch is different depending on the closeness of the family and the sex of the family member. Displays of affection between friends are almost always appreciated and necessary, even if you are not a touchy person. One should be willing to get out of their comfort zone and offer their friend a hug when struggling. Helping others enliven their moods is likely to uplift your moods as well.

Intimacy Touch

In romantic relationships, touches that communicate love play a critical role. For instance, the simplest of touches can convey a critical meaning, such as holding hands or placing your arm around your partner, which communicates that you are together. According to recent communication studies, adults place more emphasis on nonverbal cues than verbal cues when communicating. In the earlier stages of dating, men tend to initiate physical contact in line with societal norms, but in later stages, women initiate contact. Women place more premiums on touch compared to men, and even the smallest of gestures can help calm women. They were upset.

Arousal Touch

Arousing touches are elicited by intense feelings and are only acceptable when mutually agreed upon. Arousal touches are meant to evoke pleasure and involve kissing, hugging, flirtatious touching, and are often intended to suggest sex. One should be careful about their partner's needs. One can greatly improve their communication skills and relationships by considering the nonverbal messages you send via touching behavior.

Additionally, our sense of touch is intended to communicate clearly and quickly. Touch can elicit subconscious communication. For instance, you instantly pull away from your hand when touching something hot even before you consciously process. In this manner, touch constitutes one of the quickest ways to communicate. Touch, as a form of nonverbal communication, is an instinctive form of communication. In detail, touch conveys information instantly and causes a guttural reaction. Completely withholding touch will communicate the wrong messages without your realization.

Ways of Improving Touch in Appropriate Contexts

Pat Someone on the Back When You Grant Them Praise

If your colleague or friend has graduated, earned a promotion, or married, then pat them on the back. Giving a pat suggests that you are happy with the person and are encouraging them. Touch has a therapeutic value that relaxes the mind and the body and helps an individual feel secure and appreciated. At school, you must have felt valued and loved if you were patted on the back.

Initiate Discussions with a Touch to Create Cooperative Relationships

Studies have established that touching a person increases their willingness to cooperate and work with others. They were establishing physical contact with an individual that you wish to initiate a conversation with can help. Sometimes the target person may not realize that you touched them but will register subconsciously and establish a bond.

Extend the Handshakes

Shaking hands shows confidence and simplicity in interacting with others. Touch helps build trust between two people. Make your handshakes firm when shaking hands with people. It is also necessary to remember that some health conditions may make one shy away from shaking hands, and this includes hyperhidrosis, which makes the palms of the person sweat. With sweaty hands, the individual is likely to shun handshakes, and this has little to do with the context of the conversation.

Adjust the Touch-Type Concerning Context

As indicated, touch is highly contextual. For instance, the Japanese do not favor shaking hands, and a person in this environment will avoid shaking hands at all costs. In the American context, shaking hands is encouraged. For this reason, one should adjust their touch-type depending on the contexts. It might be welcome to continuously hold your partner's hands while the same is creepy when talking to a stranger or to a colleague at the workplace.

Another form of touch is tickling, mostly reserved for lovers, parents versus children, and peers. For instance, a mother may tickle her baby, which is a therapeutic touch and is permissible. On the other hand, children of the same age set may tickle each other, which is permissible. However, it is inappropriate to tickle an adult when you are not lovers, or the relationship between you and them is formal.

Touch as a Form of Abuse

Expectedly, there is a thin line between permissible touch and physical abuse. If not, certain one should avoid initiating touch unless fully certain its meaning to the target person. Pushing someone or pinching someone is considered a form of physical abuse. Kicking or striking someone as well as strangling, are forms of physical abuse.

- Touch as a game

In some contexts, a touch is a form of the game, especially teasing. Touch as a form of the game should only happen where the participants are peers and are receptive to it. For instance, your friend or classmate may blindfold your eyes with the palms of their hands from behind. The participants in this tease may touch each other. For instance, the blinded person may try to feel your arms or head to guess the person's identity. In this form of touch, the scope of teaching allowed is large and may be equivalent to that of lovers.

Chapter 19. Facial Expression As a Form of Body

Facial Expressions and Physiognomy

We want to understand by facial expressions all phenomena that we can observe in the face of a human being. By this, we mean both facial features, eye contact, and viewing direction, as well as psychosomatic processes, such as pale. Finally, we also include entire head movements with such. As a nodding, oblique (the latter, depending on the context, of course, the attitude can be assigned).

In general, we are concerned with the evaluation of congruence signals. As long as the facial expressions match the verbal utterances, we usually do not take them very well. When the incongruity is strong, it attracts even the most inexperienced. But the experienced can take note of a variety of facial expressions to perceive even slight disturbances or incipient incongruence (or, of course, first signs of relief, approval, etc.). Often only a barely perceptible grin indicates that someone is making a joke. Or it may be that a (questioning) raised eyebrow is the only indication of contradiction when the other one says, "Yes, I understand what you mean."

At this point in the seminar, the question often arises of how far one can manipulate his non-linguistic signals to what extent z. For example, it would be possible not to let it be noted whether one grasps or approves of something?

Answer: Of course, anyone can learn to influence his body language to a degree.

However, it is particularly difficult to get the facial muscles under control. So, you can often observe that someone looks outwardly calm because he has learned to control his hands (for example, by intertwining his fingers to prevent him from playing around nervously). Nevertheless, an inner restlessness (if any) will express itself, and most likely, in the face. Why is the manipulation of our facial muscles so difficult? The word "manipulate" includes the word manus (lat., The hand). However, to be able to handle something skillfully, you have to know it well. We do not know enough about our facial muscles to get a grip on them. In general, we do not know how we look or how we affect others. Try it (right now) yourself! Check your facial expression.

A real experiment on this would look like this: You get a small pocket mirror, which you always have at hand shortly. Now and then, you will try first to feel your expression and then immediately see it in the mirror. Ask yourself before and while you look in each case: "How do I look now? How do I now seem to others?" (Or how would I act on others now?)

You will experience very exciting surprises, although they are not positively fascinating for everyone. Some people are horrified when they realize how often they have a discontented, disgruntled look around their mouths and eyes that they did not even realize! However, the less you know about his facial expression, the less you really know him, the less you can, of course, also manipulate him. That is, you have it.

A second mini-experiment that you can do immediately confirms this. After reading the instruction, close your eyes briefly and try to relax your face, especially the lips and chin, as much as possible. Observe and feel consciously what it feels like.

Stop.

Now three questions:

- Have you achieved relaxation?

- Have you got a feel for feeling your facial muscles?

- Were your lips laid together loosely?

If you answered yes to the last question, then you have confirmed what FELDENKRAIS (29) means when he says:

"How is it that such an important part of the body as the lower jaw is constantly held up? Muscles that work while we are awake, without even the slightest sensation that we are doing something to hold the jaw up?

To drop it, you even have to learn how to apply the muscle inhibitor. Suppose one tries to relax his lower jaw so much that he falls through his own weight and opens his mouth completely, so you will wonder how difficult that is. If it finally succeeds, one will notice changes in the facial expression and in the eyes. It will probably also be noticed later that one usually presses his lower jaw upwards or keeps his mouth firmly closed. "

Did the little experiments teach you a little about how little you normally know about your facial muscles? Every actor who deals (or mainly) with pantomime knows the difficulties associated with the conscious creation of a desired facial expression.

Knowing the difficulties of manipulating one's facial expressions is essential if we want to control our facial expressions. With too much control, if they succeed, resulting in a robotic, non-living expression! But Information is also essential if we want to interpret the signals of others. Since the other person is just as unaware of his facial expressions, one can rely on the facial expressions in general quite well.

By the way, the study of the facial expression is divided into two areas, the facial expression itself and the physiognomy. Under the latter, one understands not the momentary, ever-changing expression but the facial features that a person has in general. I call that the "facial expression." If a person often expresses displeasure by squeezing his lips and lowering his mouth's corners, it does not surprise him if he has so-called mis-wrinkles after years. These are deeply scored "lines" that run down from the corners of the mouth. Anyone who looks at the young SCHOPENHAUER's face and then compares it with the old image can clearly see this (see also: "the compressed mouth").

The physiognomy also includes an interpretation of the facial or nasal form. Although the separation from the phrenology, which GALL (94) founded, is not clear. We will not practice physiognomy or phrenology.

Nevertheless, we cannot help but, for example, to register deep scored wrinkles when we consciously perceive. But even such a signal alone has no significance. To be sure, the wrinkling itself is unmistakable, so that we know that this man must often have his lips pinched and the corners of his mouth lowered, but we do not know why this happened. Of course, it may be that this human being is a "Griesgram" who does not like anything. But it may just as well be that this person has suffered a serious illness or a hard fate. Think of persons who have lost a loved one, to people who have spent years in concentration camps or to those who have been tortured (as is commonplace in certain parts of the world today), etc.

It has become customary to assume the following subdivision:

- Forehead area (including the eyebrows)
- Midface, i.e., eye, nose, and cheek area (for most authors, including the upper lip)
- Mouth (or lower lip) and chin area

The Forehead Area

It is believed that the forehead, with its wrinkles and eyebrows, provides information about processes of thinking and analyzing. Although this opinion seems to be a remnant of GALL's phrenology (94), I still hold the forehead's statements applicable. Nevertheless, of course, there is the demand for caution on the part of "scientificity" of such interpretations.

The Midface

The eye, nose, and cheek area are also referred to as the sense of sight. Most authors include the upper lip because they make more nuanced detail statements than we do. We usually only speak of the Lips or from the mouth, so that it is not so important in our frame, where you want to draw the border exactly.

The sense of sight is said to give us clues about taking on the outside world. It is because the eyes are the "window to the world." But they are rightly called the "window to the soul." So that we see that information from the inner life can also be seen in this area. It should also be borne in mind that the mouth also plays a key role in environmental uptake processes.

The Mouth and Chin Area

The mouth has developed from the Ur-Maw, which already has a very simple organism. It represents the relationship to the environment, in that the organism absorbs as well as eliminates it. It is easy for small children to see that they put everything in their mouths to grasp it. Therefore, it is not surprising that the mouth plays an essential role, both when it comes to not "let in" information from the environment and when one does not want to or is not allowed to express.

Next, assign the chin part (including the lower lip) the emotional and intuitive life, and, especially the chin, the assertiveness. A person who is about to assert himself vigorously will push his chin as a mimic signal. (While the assessment of the chin shape regarding the character traits of assertiveness belongs to the field of phrenology.)

And now, let's look at the interpretations of the three facial area turns.

Since we do not want to analyze the forehead's shape, we are concerned with the mimic expressions of forehead wrinkles, horizontal and vertical. Usually, horizontal wrinkles are accompanied by a lifting of the eyebrows. But there is also a barely noticeable lifting of one or both brows, which does not wrinkle.

Horizontal Forehead Wrinkles

As a rule of thumb, we can say that the horizontal forehead wrinkles indicate that the attention has been drawn heavily. However, this strong attention can have very different occasions. For example, Zeddies (94) calls the following:

- Fright.
- Anxiety.
- Obtuseness.
- Astonish.
- Amazement.
- Confusion.
- Surprise.

Again, it becomes clear that individual signals (usually) must be seen in association with others. It also applies within a category, such as facial expressions. For the forehead, wrinkles are automatically associated with the face's other muscle movements, which open eyes (or an open mouth) can lead to. Such a combination provides, for example, the following:

Horizontal wrinkles and open eyes. According to ZEDDIES (94), the two mean signals interpreted together: "The mental attitude lies in a waiting, attentive attitude to any circumstances that offer themselves to the consciousness."

Another possible combination of two mimic signals would be horizontal forehead wrinkles forming in conjunction with half-closed (= easy squinted) eyes. This combination can be observed if someone goes to great lengths to listen; in the case of the hard of hearing, for example, or in situations in which the volume of the transmitter (including technical sound sources such as a radio) is not sufficient. The vernacular describes this with the expression "the ears are pointed." However, this formulation not only describes "in a figurative sense" but also indicates physiological processes. In fact, when we tip our ears, we actually move our severely stunted ear muscles in a reflex that is pronounced in dogs, cats, and rabbits. An additional gesture and attitude change will often accompany the effort to "play" our "spoons."

Chapter 20. Manipulation In a Relationship

The culture romanticizes deceptive relations so much when talking about the love that it can be hard to recognize them for what they are. We have lots of literature suggesting that genuine relationships are about fixation, that pure love is all-out, and that infatuated people have no boundaries or separate lives.

While many people romanticize the concept of a deceptive relationship, we have to realize that it is not real love. Sometimes it may trigger a dramatic storyline and tension that keeps the reader engaged, but there is no fun living through a deceptive relationship that is romantic.

You may have been warned of manipulating people and the fact that coercion and mistreatment are worrying; the facts are that being in a relationship of control and manipulation that never develops into ill-treatment can also be terrifying and dangerous. Just because somebody does not harm you physically does not mean you cannot feel pain from their actions yet.

Being dominated or put down by a partner can damage our faith, make us feel fearful of relationships in the future, and leave us feeling lost rather than comforted, with various mental and emotional injuries with which we should not be burdened.

You may be familiar with the symptoms of a negative relationship. You might have met a partner, for instance, who required you to wear only certain clothing items or did not want you to visit your friends and family.

This person might want to know where you are going, what you are doing, and why you are just a couple of minutes late. Manipulators are frequently very anxious people, allowing nervous thoughts to pass through their brains and control their actions. We channel their intense fear and anxiety into hallucinations about what you might do if you are not around them. They will think about their worst fears and what you can do to damage them, so they will assume you are doing these things when you are not around.

Such things may spur them to hate you if you are not around. Sometimes it may seem flattering to have someone so concerned about you. You might think, "It is so sweet that they always want to know where I am, and I am safe," but it is not their intention when someone is going to take great steps to control you.

Unfortunately, they are not concerned about your well-being. Therefore, the manipulators are thinking, "I need to make sure I know where this person is at all times, so they do not do something that I do not approve of." Your presence is their assurance that you are not meeting their worst fears about the bad things that you are doing to them when you are not both of you together. In this case, they will not be addressing your needs. The manipulator behaves only to serve the interests of his own.

A manipulator will never tell you that but will only be worried about improving the way they look to you. They are always going to use this technique to make sure you feel guilty. They will make you feel guilty if you do not respond for 20 minutes, instead of admitting that it is acceptable for a person not always to write back immediately. They would view you as if you did something wrong or disrespectful to them because, at the time, you were not around your phone or too busy to answer first.

Marriage should feel better, not confining, scary, or distressing, and having an accomplice will make you happier, not more sorrowful. There will be hard times in life. Your mate may not be understood, and they may not understand you. On the way to making you stronger, these challenges should be pure obstacles. There shouldn't be a healthy relationship that continuously drains you and tears you down, making you feel constantly exhausted.

Signs of a Manipulative Relationship

Most of us have had terrible things happening in our lives—enough terrible things that the prospect of a hero sweeping us off our feet and protecting us from any problems for whatever remains of our lives can sound extremely tempting. For this reason, we are sometimes looking in the wrong places for security, empathy, and care.

Reconsider whether your partner's support thoughts include stopping you from making your own decisions and living your own life. This partner secures you by assuming responsibility for your maxed-out accounts. Or perhaps speaking to a partner you have been struggling with does not pay special attention to you; they are trying to make you have no choice but to put all your faith in them and no one else.

A true partner knows they cannot protect you and what it holds from everyday life—they can just support when you need them. If you run into a money-related issue at some point, a trusted partner can help you pray an overabundance of unopened bills—give help, but do not take control of the situation. They will not take your passwords or insist that only a small amount of money per month be allowed until you have paid off all of your current debt. A right partner is going to offer help yet realize you need to manage your problems.

One typical manipulative relationship is making us feel guilty when we see friends and family members. Suppose we imagine someone trying to cut off their partner from their emotionally supportive network. In that case, we envision something similar to the contemptible husband in a movie made for TV that threatens his better half that she will never talk to her closest friend again. Nevertheless, deceptive spouses can also inconspicuously isolate you from your support network.

A shrewdly manipulative person will not outwardly discourage you from seeing your family because it can be an obvious sign that you should be running in the opposite direction. We will make the coercion more subtle, rather than slowly dragging you out of your life, rather than an outright ban. If your partner can convince you to apologize for an action that you know you have not done wrongly and that you are doing, your manipulative partner will realize that he or she can force you to do whatever they want you to do.

Each time you go out with your buddies, your partner can sulk until you blow off other friends just to save the tension. Perhaps your partner will make negative remarks about your loved ones until you begin to believe that the thoughts they have about these people are valid.

You may even have a hobby or an event you enjoy trying to get your manipulator to stop doing it. They will ensure that you know that your interest is idiotic and will ridicule you until you give it up.

The scrutiny of a controlling partner may not always appear as such. It can be framed reasonably and rationally, implying that your partner is just trying to help you. They might even tell you they are trying to help you.

At school, they will research your decisions. Some of their sentences may include: "Why do you choose to use it for your presentation? You are not thinking about what the boss will think? They are going to question your spending habits and how you are going to buy things with questions like, "Did you have to buy another shirt?" Manipulators are going to spin their words, so it is not clear that the choices you make are wrong, but a seed of doubt and insecurity is being planted.

All partners, however, examine each other periodically. Our loved ones are still supposed to look for us, and sometimes we need others to help us make choices or point out bad habits. Remember, always test this person's true purpose and determine why they had wanted you to change your actions.

Sometimes a manipulator may ask for access to your personal belongings in a relationship, but they will not grant you the same rights. We may know all your secrets, but we rarely trust you.

They are not just less likely to share, and they are not helping you.

This type of behavior demonstrates that the other person dominates. Your partner does not reserve the right to search your emails or texts or asking for your passwords because they say they are concerned that you may be cheating. There is a distinction between having insider facts and having healthy independence from your partner, and when you are in a relationship with someone, you do not have to surrender that.

Every so often, sincere couples healing from a disaster would require the weakened spouse to view each other's messages as a form of transparency. If this is not an agreement you have worked out directly with your partner, it is incorrect.

By emotional influence, coercion is all about influencing the way someone else thinks and acts. Coercion is veiled with emotion, or at least what appears to be a sort of empathy. Most of the time, this is a calculated attempt by the manipulator concerned to relate to the victim.

We must recognize the impact it has had on us to overcome this manipulation completely. If you want a healthy relationship with someone, we must look at all the ways we have been affected by their relationship. It may be the first sign that there is a manipulative relationship if that impact is negative.

Most manipulative people have four standard attributes: they know the weaknesses.

- They use your vulnerabilities against you.

- They persuade you to surrender something of yourself to serve them through their quick plots.

- If a controller triumphs in manipulating you, he will likely repeat the crime until the mistreatment is stopped.

- They are going to have a lot of different reasons for keeping you around and controlling you.

One might just be because a past relationship damages them. We may have confidence issues that have made it difficult for them to be transparent and consider other partners. This situation can make them feel like they need to manipulate you to keep you loyal to them.

Understand Your Rights in a Relationship

It can be difficult to understand how to get out when someone is in the midst of an abusive relationship.

Manipulators are good at creating uncertainty, so they can also avoid blame for trying to control others instantly. Recalling your rights is the way to ensure that you are safe.

These are the things you completely have the right to take away and should never allow another person to take away. If you can remember these consistently, manipulation will be easier to confront as it happens, and it will be easier to recognize when a conversation may be toxic.

Then again, you may give up these rights if you convey vulnerability to other people. Our common, main human rights are the following: you deserve respect from others, especially those you respect.

Your thoughts, feelings, and emotions can be expressed.

You reserve the right to understand your own needs, share them with others, and do what you need to do to meet those needs, as long as you do not take anything away from others.

Chapter 21. How to Know if Someone Is Lying Through Body Language

Psychology of Lying

Almost everybody tells a lie once a day or gets lied to. Lying is a part of being a human being with the motive to protect himself against certain situations or to praise oneself. The reasons for lying are endless. Can you remember the very first time you realized that you were lying, or you were lied to?

There is a series of ideas as to why people lie, ranging from saving the hurting of oneself or something else, or with the motive to achieve personal gains. However, science has a different perspective on why people tell lies and the different types of lies. Nobody likes to be lied to, and it's not surprising to find that most liars do not like to be considered as liars.

You wouldn't have any trouble in believing anybody in a perfect world, but unfortunately, it's not perfect, so you need to be cautious about whom to believe and who not to. There are professionals primarily in law enforcement that are trained to detect liars. You don't have to have access to the polygraph machines so that you can understand who is lying to you and who is not. There are many behavioral clues that you could use to know who is telling the truth and who is not.

Detecting deceit will give you the rare opportunity to choose your associates wisely without having to say a word. The body goes into an immense ball of anxiety when a person lies. The trained eye will be able to detect these small variances that occur. Although words may speak their version of the truth, the body never lies. Deceit is the act of covering up the way you truly feel through seeking control. Often, that control is executed in a sloppy manner, thus leading to dominant cues that signal deceit. Whether it's a large lie or a little white lie, the results of dishonesty come with a variety of consequences.

Essentially, people lie as a subconscious form of protection. They are either hiding their negative behavior or protecting their reputations. Even when used to exaggerate a story, they may be attempting to protect the fact that their life is truly boring. They want others to find them enjoyable. Thus, various lies are told.

In general, lying requires more cognitive effort rather than telling the truth because you must work harder and strain to make your information or statement sound authentic. After you have settled on the path of lying, you must remember all the facts, but how? You already changed all facts. Having presented you with the small background about detecting lies, the following are now the various ways you could identify a person lying to you.

Some Liars Are Always Tense and Nervous

It takes a great deal for a liar to pull together fake points to convince you. However, this is not the case with professional liars. These know how to do it just right. But for those who are not used to telling lies, you will quickly notice that their body language is betraying them. On the other hand, a person who tells the truth looks relaxed and happy as far as the story that she is telling is not a sad or painful one.

Some Talk Unusually Slow

If you have ever observed or listened to somebody telling a true story, you might have realized that his or her speech is normal. However, some liars would tend to take quite long before they can respond so that they have a chance to edit their story. They act as if they are trying to be consistent and avoid negative comments. But for other people, it might be hard to detect when they are telling lies, especially salespersons; this is because they have recited lines they keep on mentioning every day with their numerous encounters with customers. You need to keep check of these factors when you are speaking to a person so that you can analyze them and determine when they are telling a lie.

The Hands of a Liar

When people are gesturing and using their hands while telling their stories, this is often seen as a truth-telling sign. However, if the gesturing comes after telling the story, this is often a sign of lying. The mind is so preoccupied with coming up with a story and realistic details that make sense that the mind is too preoccupied to gesture with their hands at the same time that they are talking. Granted, not all people use their hands when talking, but many people do, and this is a simple tactic that the FBI uses and focuses on determining whether someone is lying.

Breathing

Another good indicator if someone is lying is if their breathing suddenly changes. If you ask someone a question and their breathing changes while answering, this is a good sign that they are lying. When somebody is lying, their heart rate upsurges and they turn out to be nervous. It makes them breathe quicker and harder.

Too Still

Another good sign that someone is lying is if they are too still. It is normal for us to move around a bit while talking. It could be shifting in our seat or from foot to foot. Glancing around, hand movements, etc. However, when someone is noticeably too still, this can be a sign of deception. People are often aware that their body language can give them away if they are lying. They think that being fidgety and moving around will give them away. Instead, they do the opposite. They focus very hard on remaining very still so as not to seem fidgety. However, this has the opposite effect than what they were thinking.

Gut Instinct

Lastly, but most importantly, follow your gut instinct. It is probably one of the best ways to figure out if someone is lying to you. People are often very distracted when trying to determine if someone is lying because they focus too hard on the little signs that are supposed to tell you if someone is lying. Frequently, just listen to that other person and then ask yourself if you believe them. We instinctually know when something is "off" about someone. Sometimes we can't even accurately explain what it is or why we feel that way, but we know when something is not genuine. It could be the pitch of their voice, their facial expressions, etc.

Watch the Eyelids

If someone closes his or her eyelids for a long time, it means the person is trying to avoid eye contact. If the person blinks more than three times, it is a sign of nervousness and apprehension that you will catch him or her. If someone uses the hands to cover their eyes, this is another sign that they want to 'block-out' the truth.

Pointing of Eyes

Our eyes point at things we find attractive or where our body wants to go. If you are talking to someone lying, the person will continuously look at the door or watch, signaling the desire to cut short the conversation because they are fearful you will catch the lie.

Avoiding Eye Contact

Breaking eye contact is the most basic way to identify a lie. Someone who has complete confidence about what he or she is saying will never avoid eye contact. However, if someone is lying, he or she will avoid eye contact.

Facial Expressions

Observing facial expressions can help you detect a lie. The most common facial expressions observed in a liar are, dilated pupils, the appearance of lines on the forehead, narrowing of the eyebrows, and blinking eyes. Sweat on the forehead and an angry expression are common with these facial expressions.

Dilated Pupils

Pupil dilation indicates tension and concentration. When someone gets worried about exposure, the pupils unconsciously dilate as they think of ways to hide the lie. If you are talking to someone but unsure if the person is honest or not, look at the person's pupils for answers.

Several key facial indicators may tip you off to whether a person is lying to you. Though none of these are necessarily conclusive in and of themselves, learning to notice these indicators will be your ally when determining if someone is less than trustworthy.

Lines on Forehead

Someone lying may have lines on the forehead because of the stress the person has to bear as they seek ways to cover the lie.

Apart from the facial expression, we can also observe many other gestures in a liar.

Clearing of Throat

If someone is lying to you, he or she will probably clear his or her throat more than once as a nervous tendency to distract from the stress of telling a lie.

Backward Head Movement

When someone is telling a lie, the head could possibly move backward. This gesture occurs as the lying person tries to avoid the source of anxiety because people tend to distance themselves from things they dislike.

Hard Swallowing

The throat of someone who is lying may become dry, and additionally, they may become self-conscious of their swallowing and breathing so as not to give away their deception.

Therefore, it is common for a person to swallow hard to bring moisture back to avoid clearing their throat. It is common for people trying to hide a lie.

Statement Analysis to Determine Lie

Analyzing someone's lie through his or her statement is the last step in lie detection. Sometimes what people say does not support their body language. It allows you to detect lies. People often stammer or talk at a fast pace as a way of trying to avoid discovery.

For instance, if you suspect your classmate stole your money and ask her about it, you notice darting eyes and nervousness in her tone. Her body language does not support her statement that she did not steal the money. It means she is lying and has stolen it or knows who did.

No matter how good a person is at lying, if the person's body language is not supportive of their statement, that person is lying. To identify a liar, analyze someone's body language and determine if it matches the person's statement. If the two contradict, you may have a liar on your hands.

You now have a complete idea of analyzing your target by studying body language, expressions, and gestures. It is just one way, however, to analyze people. If you wish to analyze people more efficiently, then you can use the information you gathered from your body language observations. It will give you a complete understanding of your target's state of mind, personality, habits, tendencies, thought patterns, and general operation mode.

Chapter 22. How Body Language Improves Your Mindset

Our body language is the way we speak with our outside world—and the more significant part of us don't understand, we are doing it! Body language phenomenally affects the center of who you are as an individual. It impacts our posture and physiological well-being, yet it can likewise change our psychological viewpoint, an impression of the world, and others' perception of us.

How Our Body Imparts

We utilize our body language to communicate our musings, thoughts, and feelings; we synchronize body developments to the words we express. We impart purposefully through activities like shrugging our shoulders or applauding just as through inadvertent correspondence like twisting in on ourselves or guiding our feet an alternate way toward the individual we talked about. Before spoken language was made, our body language was the primary technique for correspondence. Our body is our major method to speak with life!

How Can It Influence Our State of Mind?

Our body language is how we interface with our outside world, yet it is likewise how we associate with ourselves. How would you treat yourself? Do you slouch over when you walk, or do you walk tall and satisfied? It is true to say that you are thankful for each development that your body makes for you?

Most likely not; we regularly underestimate our body; we frequently decide to condemn it. Body language can impact our physical body and posture. However, it can likewise change how we are feeling. Having a great attitude can affect misery and cause us to keep up more elevated levels of confidence and energy when confronted with pressure.

An up and coming field of psychology, known as installed comprehension, asserts that the association between our body and our general surroundings doesn't merely impact us. However, we are personally woven into the way that we think.

Four Different Ways You Can Change Your Body Language

The followings are four ways you can change your body language.

Flip Around That Glare!

Grinning and snickering is infectious! A complete report on smiling found that a grin which draws in the mouth and moves the skin around the eyes can enact the cerebrum examples of positive feelings. So, grin and grin frequently! Regardless of whether you are having an awful day, grin at any rate! It may very well assist you with turning the day around!

Collapsing Your Arms

The intersection of the arms is a resistance system to ensure the heart and lungs. We regularly do it when we feel shaky, anxious, or disturbed. The physical obstruction gives others the feeling that we are cut off and detached from them.

The intersection of the arms is a broad idea to be an antagonistic body posture anyway. A few investigations have indicated that crossing the arms can cause individuals to progressively industrious when they feel like stopping.

If you believe you need a little additional lift to take a stab at making some regular mindset boosting homegrown cures like Hyperiforce. It contains concentrates of the bloom hypericum frequently utilized as a treatment for low mind-set and gentle nervousness.

Force Presenting

One of the significant specialists in the zone of body language is Amy Cuddy. She made members remain in high force stances and low force models for two minutes before sending them into a top weight talk with the condition. She estimated levels of the pressure hormone cortisol and the predominance hormone testosterone. The outcomes demonstrated that those remaining in high force present had expanded testosterone degrees and lower cortisol levels than those in little force presents.

Quit Slumping

It may appear glaringly evident; however, slumping not just influences your spine. It can likewise change your state of mind! Indeed, slumping can prompt back agony and an irregular spine arrangement. Intellectually, it can leave you feeling miserable, lacking vitality, and shut off from others. Sitting and standing up straighter can assist with settling back torment just as lift your life and state of mind.

Changing your posture can be trying for your body from the outset, particularly on the off chance you are accustomed to slumping over for significant periods! You may feel muscle hurts in the neck, back, and bears—don't stress, this will pass! Meanwhile, I'd suggest utilizing Atrogel, a natural relief from discomfort cure containing new concentrates of arnica blossoms.

Improve Your Posture to Improve Your Temperament!

Body language likely isn't the first sport you'd think to look at when experiencing a low state of mind. However, investigating our body language can reveal to us how we are truly feeling. Our body language has an immediate connection to our temperament, similarly that our mindset influences our posture.

Simple ways you can fix your posture to adjust your state of mind:

- Smile when you are having a terrible day!

- Unfold your arms when you feel anxious and permit yourself to be available to circumstances.

- Turning the palms of your hands forward when you walk will urge the shoulders to unwind back as opposed to moving advances.

- Power present before pressure instigating situations like prospective employee meet-ups.

Body Language Signs When Someone Hides Something from You

Untrustworthiness. It happens in many connections—and a great deal of the time, it accomplishes more mischief than anything. It's once in a while ever astute to keep insider facts from your accomplice in a relationship. You never need to keep your accomplice in obscurity about a lot of things in your lives together. That is simply out and out insolent. It shows that you don't regard your accomplice enough to recognize that they are deserving of reality. You are saying that they aren't sufficient to be determined what's genuine—and that is, in every case, terrible in a relationship. You generally need to confess all to your accomplice, particularly about vital issues encompassing your relationship.

Be that as it may, a considerable deal of us are childish. Here and there, reality can be difficult to stomach. Now and then, a fact can place us in an extreme condition of a burden once it's uncovered. So, a great deal of us will turn to lie just to spare our butts. Your man may be blameworthy of doing as such. He may be keeping you out of the loop about something that he ought to be opening up to you.

What's more, that is hazardous for a relationship. You can't hope to make your link work if you're not being taken care of the entirety of the best possible realities. You generally need to ensure that you know all that is going on to don't wind up getting tricked or bushwhacked by anything.

Men aren't generally the best verbal communicators. You may likely know this at this point. Be that as it may, he consistently communicates through his body language and physical developments. His intuitive may be disclosed to you many things about himself without seeing it in any event. You simply need to willingly volunteer to ensure that you spot out the signs when they present themselves. You need to ensure that you keep steady over things in your relationship.

Getting and Understanding Nonverbal Signals

Lauren murmured. She'd quite recently gotten an email from her chief, Gus, saying that the item proposition she'd been taking a shot at would not have been closed down. It didn't bode well. Seven days prior, she'd been in a gathering with Gus, and he'd appeared to be extremely positive about everything. Of course, he hadn't looked, and he continued watching out of the window at something. In any case, she'd recently put that down to him being occupied. Furthermore, he'd said that "the task will most likely stretch the go-beyond."

On the off chance that Lauren had discovered somewhat progressively about body language, she'd have understood that Gus was attempting to reveal to her that he wasn't "sold" on her thought. He simply wasn't utilizing words.

The Most Effective Method to Read Negative Body Language

Monitoring negative body language in others can permit you to get on implicit issues or awful emotions. Along these lines, in this area, we'll feature some negative nonverbal signs that you should pay individual minds to.

Troublesome Conversations and Defensiveness

Troublesome or tense discussions are an awkward unavoidable truth grinding away. Maybe you've needed to manage an annoying client or expected to converse with somebody about their terrible showing. Or then again, perhaps you've arranged a significant agreement.

In a perfect world, these circumstances would be settled tranquility. Be that as it may, regularly, they are entangled by sentiments of apprehension, stress, preventiveness, or even resentment. However, we may also attempt to shroud them; these feelings regularly appear through in our body language. For instance, on the chance that somebody is showing at least one of the accompanying practices, he will probably be withdrawn, uninvolved, or miserable:

- Arms collapsed before the body.
- Insignificant or tense outward appearance.
- The body got some distance from you.
- Eyes depressed, keeping in touch.
- Keeping away from Unengaged Audiences

At the point when you have to convey an introduction or to work together in a gathering, you need the individuals around you to be 100 percent locked in. Here are some "obvious" signs that individuals might be exhausted or unbiased in what you're stating:

- Sitting drooped, with heads sad.
- Looking at something different, or into space.
- Squirming, picking at garments, or tinkering with pens and telephones.
- She was composing or doodling.

Step by Step Instructions to Project Positive Body Language

When you utilize positive body language, it can add solidarity to the verbal messages or thoughts you need to pass; on and help you abstain from imparting blended or befuddling signs. In this segment, we'll portray some fundamental postures that you can embrace to extend fearlessness and receptiveness.

Establishing a Confident First Connection

These tips can assist you in adjusting your body language so you establish an extraordinary first connection:

- Have an open posture. Be loose; however, don't slump! Sit or stand upstanding and place your hands by your sides. Abstain from remaining with your hands on your hips will cause you to seem more significant, conveying animosity or craving to rule.

- Utilize a firm handshake. However, don't become overly energetic! You don't need it to get unbalanced or, more regrettable, excruciating for the other individual. On the chance that it does, you'll likely seem to be impolite or forceful.

- Keep in touch. Try to maintain eye contact with the other person for a couple of moments, one after another. It will give her that you're right and locked in. Be that as it may, abstain from transforming it into a gazing match!

- Abstain from contacting your face. There's a typical discernment that individuals who contact their appearances while addressing questions are being untrustworthy. While this isn't in every case valid, it's ideal to abstain from tinkering with your hair or contacting your mouth or nose, especially if your point is to seem to be reliable.

Chapter 23. Proxemics

Now, imagine that you are standing in front of someone. You can see that they are crossing their arms with hands hidden behind them, their eyes shifting nervously from you to veer off to the left now and then. They shift their weight from foot to foot and struggle to maintain eye contact. Something about the body language of this person makes you uneasy, but you cannot place it. They keep their distance from you, and every time you approach closer, you notice that they are likely to move away.

Body language is good at giving us feelings that tell us to be on edge, offended, or relaxed, but if you do not know what you are reading, you will struggle to understand why you feel that way. It can be difficult to know what someone intends to not put meaning to what they are doing. You can have a general idea of how you want to respond, but it can be incredibly beneficial

Proxemics refers to the distance between yourself and someone else—it is the usage of space between yourself and the world around you. Naturally, people put varying degrees of space between themselves and others. When you are looking to understand proxemics, the best way to do so is to consider it a judgment of the relationship between yourself and those around you. You can also judge others' relationships based upon the distance they put between each other, both vertical and horizontal.

The Use of Vertical Space

Vertical space is what it sounds like—it is the space relative to your position height-wise. When someone utilizes vertical space, they attempt to make themselves taller or shorter, depending on the context. Those who want to make themselves taller may want to be an authority or otherwise as someone that is deserving of respect and compliance. They may even use this space when they are trying to look at others who are taller than them—they simply tilt their heads back to look down their nose at the taller person to create the same impact.

When you make yourself smaller, you typically want to be seen as less dominant for some reason. You may be attempting to shrink down to speak to a child to be understood truly, for example, or you may be lowering yourself to make yourself seem more submissive. In particular, people will pull their chins inward when they want to be smaller because they will then be required to look up through their eyelashes at the other person, even if the other person is taller.

The default, eye level, is deemed to be the most respectful—it marks you and the other person as equals deserving of the same respect and consideration.

The Use of Horizontal Space

In horizontal space, you are looking at how near or far people are to each other. You will use this when you are picking apart the relationships of others. There are four distances used between each other, ranging from intimate distances to public distance.

- The intimate distance: This refers to being as close as possible to the other person. When you are in this position, you are usually touching without trying or close enough to do so. It is typically for young children and parents, or for lovers that are comfortable being this close to each other. Generally speaking, this zone is only about 18 inches away from you.

- The personal distance: Slightly further away than the intimate distance, the personal distance covers about 18 inches away up to about 5 feet around you. It is what people are talking about when they say that you are invading their personal bubbles. This zone is usually reserved for those you like or feel comfortable with, such as friends and family members or children who are too old to be within the intimate zone. The closer you can get to the center, the closer your relationship with that other person.

- The social distance: This is a bit further out. It is the distance you naturally try to maintain with strangers around you or interacting with someone else you do not know. Typically, this is between about 5 and 10 feet. You will use this when you are out and about unless you have no choice otherwise. When you are forced to encroach on this distance, you will most often make it a point to ignore the other person in an attempt to ignore the fact that they are violating those personal boundaries, such as sitting on the bus.

- The public distance is even further out. It refers to anything beyond 12 feet and is reserved for instances in which you speak out toward a crowd. You want to be loud enough that everyone in the crowd can speak, so you want to ensure that people are a bit further away from you so they can see and hear you easier. It is reserved for lectures in classrooms, for example, or in performances.

Chapter 24. Muscular Core, Posture, and Breathing

The best way to find out is to copy your subject's muscular core state. Just look at how their muscles are arranged and try to set yours the same way. There's a good expression, "to carry oneself," and your goal will be to carry yourself just like them. Your copy doesn't have to be identical, just close enough. Hence, you feel close enough to themselves. Imitate them as close to perfection as your present acting skills allow (to be a good judge of character, a good analyst, you don't have to be a good actor, but it helps—remember Sherlock Holmes and his transformations?) It isn't hard—just contract whatever they have acquired and kept it that way!

Now, as we learned to carry ourselves like our subject of study, we must learn to walk like them and breathe like them, or at least pretend to do it, deep inside.

Much can be learned from a human posture and walk: people with bad eyesight recognize and spot their relatives and friends by their silhouette, their stance, their walk in the crowd of hundreds of people, alone, as easy as a person with keen eyesight would. Can you stand or sit as your subject does and feel as comfortable as they seem? Can you breathe like them, at the same rate, with the same depth, following the same intervals?

Try and practice it alone at first, looking at a video of someone else. Soon you'll be able to perform it mentally, running the process almost entirely in your imagination. As soon as your musculature and posture imprint feels identical to that of your subject, as soon as your collective breath sounds like one, it's time to analyze their non-verbal message.

Are they demonstrating the will to move closer, shorten the distance between you—or are they trying to distance themselves from you? Is their posture open towards you (face, chest, and groin unobstructed by limbs) or closed from you? (Folded arms, crossed knees, etc.) If their posture is closed, don't jump to conclusions: they may position themselves this way merely for comfort, not because they'd like to lock themselves away from you. If your object's posture is closed and is comfortable—they are likely an introvert. With extroverts, expect abrupt changes in posture, quick movements ahead (lean towards the person they're speaking to, or reach for them), meant to shorten the distance between them.

Body language is a nation-specific feature of communication—in some countries, it's hardly used, while in the other two conversing's, people may resemble two windmills. Still, you can generally detect the heat of discussion by the amount and smoothness of gesturing, even when watching the speakers from a distance. The rougher, sharper gestures become, the less controlled they are, the higher the conflict's likeliness.

A conflict is something often provoked by the opposition, or a third party, with intent to unsettle us, upset us, or make us lose our temper and act out. Our goal in this situation will be to retain control of ourselves. It doesn't mean suppressing our anger or bottling our frustration. It means dissolving the heat of emotions in the cold presence of our reason. It means starting with controlled breathing, restrained posture, and slow relaxation of the muscle core, resetting it to absolute calm.

A person in control is not someone gritting their teeth, holding reins back—it's the person showing calm restraint and conscious choice of their words and actions. Remember the monkey and the computer? The last one is the analyst; the first one lives for battle and spots a good fight mile away. There's a good use for this quality, too: your instincts will tell you when the situation is about to heat up a bit too much, so your reason could be there in time to prevent unnecessary drama before it has a chance to happen!

The point is neither of the two parts of one's consciousness must be restrained or removed from the interaction. When the reason is cast aside, no civilized communication is possible: any conversation will quickly derail and devolve into something childish, silly, and virtually useless for any purposes but socializing itself. If the moving part is suppressed, the person starts feeling discomfort.

It is a significant point. It happens to be twofold: whenever you spot manifestations of discomfort in yourself or your object, you will know it happens because the primal part, the emotional aspect, is subdued by reason. It may occur when the person's reason doesn't want to give something away, yet their body—heartbeat, breathing, perspiration—seems eager to betray them. Hence, they try and shut it off using reason, forcing themselves under control for some time, after which their animalistic part will inevitably act out. You must have seen how leaving the room after a difficult meeting. Usually, people will be overly childish and agitated. They even exclaiming loudly, pushing each other. At the same time, others are craving some sort of physical gratification. It is all the backlash of self-control imposed by reason. Then it is lifted.

Hence, to stay comfortable, to remain in full control of oneself—which is something you want to practice to become a good restrained analyst—one must never suppress their inner feelings! It's hard to give advice on how your computer could keep your monkey in check, as this is a personal thing, inherent to your character. There's a huge number of venting and confidence-building techniques out there, and you're free to try them all! Just remember this simple rule: by indulging a specific whim of your animal, you grow it, not reduce it. For instance, aggressive behavior does not deplete aggression. On the contrary, it increases your aggressiveness—the same as being afraid will not deplete your fear.

Still, techniques help you drop the level of aggression and overcome fear, from the essential things like counting to ten, naming objects around you mentally, or drinking a glass of water—down to counseling and transcendental meditation. In this book, we'll merely say the solution is out there, and self-control is essential if you want to stay an involved yet unbiased party.

On the other hand, this is what you want to notice in the behavior of your subject: not their controlled, reasonable actions, but their slips, their subliminal telltales, the small movements, expressions, and changes in posture that happen without the subject noticing. How to interpret this body language? The problem is that it's inherent to a particular culture and varies from one individual to another.

Many sources claim they're able to teach you some kind of universal list of telltales. One that enables you to tell the truth from lies, present you with recipes of telling an act from the real deal. But these sources are at best-generalized information. It is sometimes applied to many people. Enough to make it seem true, but not to be applied to just everyone. The truth is, only your own experience, attentiveness, and insight will help you to read another person's body language, for there are as many body languages as there are different people.

For instance, when someone is trying to touch or hide a part of their face—lips, the nose, an ear—it's typically considered a sign of secretiveness, the telltale of a person lying or trying to hide some information from the listener. In many cases, it's indeed so—and still, be careful not to call someone a liar just because they tend to rub their three-day stubble while they're thinking.

Another popular facial feature to be pointed out as a telltale: a genuine smile would cause crinkles around eyes, while a fake smile normally wouldn't. Yet again, in many cases, it may be true—we often hear about "someone smiling while their eyes remain cold." Then again, the experiments show the "smiling eyes" can be faked more or less quickly, and if you were to encounter a sociopathic person, someone good at mimicry—you'd never catch them faking a smile.

Approach tendencies in your subject's posture may mean aggression—or they could mean affection, and only your judgment may discern between the two. If your issue demonstrates avoidance tendencies—this, yet again, could mean an entire spectrum of emotions: apathy, fear, disgust, mistrust, submission, meekness, and so on.

A good analyst would always view the non-verbal signals of their subject as a part of the bigger picture, applying to them the knowledge of this person as a whole. Even a habit as simple as biting one's fingernails—are you sure I bite mine when I'm nervous? It may happen a person tends to stick their thumb in their mouth while they're thoughtful, relaxed, their attention directed inward—miles from feeling nervous!

Always remember: what you see is only half of the picture. Another half, no less important, is what you hear.

Chapter 25. Hand Gestures and Arm Signals

It is important to read gestures in the context of other aspects of body language, but we will explore ways of reading gestures. We all talk with our hands often. For some people, the gesturing matches their message well. Some people do not deploy hand gestures while others overuse hand gestures. Most hand gestures are universal. A person that does not use hand gestures may be seen as indifferent.

For this reason, the audience may feel that one does not care about what the other is talking about. If your hands are hidden, then the audience will find it difficult to trust you. If one's hands are open and the palms wide enough, the individual communicates that they are honest and sincere.

Furthermore, randomly throwing hands in the air while talking may suggest that one is anxious or panicking. Extreme anger will also make one throw their hands in an uncoordinated manner. For further understanding, take time and watch movie characters quarreling, and you will note that most people being accused of something will randomly throw their hands in the air. It is something that they have little control over because most of the body language happens at the subconscious level of the mind. Randomly throwing hands in the air indicates that one is overwhelmed with emotions or has given up defending their position in the argument and has left the argument to the individual who started it.

Additionally, one may point at an object or a person. Pointing as a gesture helps the focus of the speaker and the audience to the focused area. During your school days, you probably saw your teacher's point in a particular direction without speaking until the talking students had to stop. As such, pointing at specific students drew the entire class's attention to their direction, making them become the center of attention, and they had to do a quick self-evaluation and stop talking. All these illustrate that body language communicates tone and emotions just as verbal communication.

Furthermore, pointing while wafting the index finger indicates a warning. When one points the index finger at someone and wafts it up and down, then you are denoting a stern warning and judgment to the individual. It is the equivalent of saying, "this is the last warning." Your parent or teacher may probably have a point and waft gesture to signal a warning that what you are doing is wrong and that you should stop. You might have observed that the police or the lead actor uses the index finger to warn someone in movie characters. The finger signal singles out the individual and reduces the focus to just one aspect of behavior that the speaker wants the target person to understand.

If one spreads all the fingers and holds them together against those of the opposite hand, it indicates strong personal reflection, such as praying or remembering the departed soul. The same gesture can be used when one is focusing the mind during meditation or yoga. The holding of each of your fingers against their peers. On the other hand, it may also indicate feeling humble and thankful for everything. For instance, followers of the Catholic faith frequently use this gesture when praying. The gesture shows humility and thankfulness.

Sometimes one may tap on the head once or continuously. When one taps on the head using a hand or a finger, it indicates the individual is thinking hard or trying hard to recall something. For instance, when speaking and you try to remember what another person said, you might use this gesture. Children often tap their heads once or continuously using one finger or the entire palm to signal attempts to recall something. The gesture is equivalent to saying, "Come on, what it was?" or "Come on, what was the name again!" It is a prop to recall hard.

Similarly, a fully raised palm with fingers spread may indicate that one should stop. When stopping the vehicle on the roadside, one raises one of their palms high up, and it is taken as a sign to stop. The same is true in the sporting environment where raising one palm high up commonly communicates that the playing should stop. When arguing with your partner, if they raise one of their palms, it signifies the other to stop arguing or stop whatever action they are doing.

If one claps, the palms together may indicate applauding the message or the speaker. When the speaker is done speaking, the audience may clap their hands together to mark the message's appreciation or both the message and the speaker. However, when the hands are spontaneously and violently clapped, then it is a message that the audience should stop because what they are doing is unethical or irritating. At home, one of your parents probably clapped their hands suddenly and violently to make you stop as well as draw attention to their presence, especially where you were playing loudly around the house.

Relatedly, if one interlocks one hand against those of the other hands and folding them. The application of this gesture indicates that one is attentive but unease at the same time. During an interview, meeting, or a class session, the audience is likely to interlock their fingers and fold them. In a way, the interlocking of the fingers is supposed to offer assurance to the affected person that he or she is safe. One is likely also to use this gesture when he or she is mentioned negatively. Think of how you reacted when you were mentioned among noisemakers or workers having challenges following the company's rules. Most probably, you interlocked your fingers and folded them.

Additionally, if one feels shy or uncertain, the individual is also likely to interlock their fingers and raise the interlocked fingers when speaking. The gesture in this context appears to give some prop for the affected individual enabling them to navigate the anxiety. The gesture in this context is not just about communicating the affected person's physiological status but as a coping mechanism of sudden anxiety and discomfort of the individual.

Still on body language and focusing on gesture, if one raises both hands behind the head and interlocks the fingers, it acts as a cushion for the head. The gesture indicates that one is feeling casual, tired, or simply not tasked by the current conversation. The gesture may also suggest that the individual is feeling tired by the discussion or the activity. Think of how you react when feeling exhausted when talking to a friend or after watching a movie. You probably raised both of your hands behind the head and interlocked the fingers to act as a headrest. In most cases, when one invokes this gesture, the individual is likely to let the mind allow other thoughts to escape from the current conversation.

Correspondingly, there is the gesture where one lets one of their palms to brush down their faces. The gesture is used to signal deeper thinking, process new contradictory information, or accept humiliation in front of the audience. The gesture suggests surrender. It indicates yielding to inner thoughts or views from the audience that one may have initially opposed. At one point, the class or your friends cornered a speaker facing the speaker to pause and take a minute to admit that he or she may have overlooked some facts about the issue. Probably, the speaker used this gesture to indicate defeat.

On the other hand, to indicate rejection or strong disagreement. It is with both hands with palms broad are waved in an alternating manner to create the letter X. You probably drew the letter X using both hands to indicate that you disagree\what is being proposed in class. For instance, as a kid or as a student, you probably drew letter X to signal rejection that you will not follow instructions when the teacher sarcastically indicated that you should not follow his instructions. The sign also indicates retreat to your inner world to avoid listening or watching what the speaker wants.

For accentuation, when hands are open with palms down, at that point, one is communicating that he or she is certain almost what they are talking about. In case your palms are confronting each other with the fingers together. At that point, you're communicating that you just possess the skill around what you're talking about almost. At that point, there's the approximation gesture performed by holding the hand horizontally with palm down and with fingers forward. After that, tilting the hand to the correct and the cleared out. The guess signal shows that an explanation is to be taken a near appraise of the truth.

Equally important, the gesture with a gentle rocking from left to right means that it is not so good or not so bad. The same gesture indicates that an event is equally likely to end in one of the two ways suggesting that it can go either way. The gesture can signal the other person when a match is going, and the friends are watching in the house, and they do not want to wake up the child through loud talking.

Similarly, the beckoning sign has the index finger sticking out of the clenched fist and palm facing the gesture. Then the speaker's finger moves repeatedly towards the gesturer as to invite something nearer. The beckoning sign has the general meaning of commanding someone to where you are standing. The beckoning sign is often performed with the four fingers using the entire hand, depending on how far the sign's recipient is. Depending on the circumstance, when performed with the index finger, it can have a sexual connotation.

If one feels that the speaker is not making sense, they are likely to keep their fingers straight and together while holding them upwards with the thumb pointing downwards. Then the fingers and thumb snap together to indicate a talking mouth. The gesture suggests contempt for a person talking for an excessive period about a topic that the gesturer feels is trivial. In Asian cultures, the gesture is used as a reaction to a dry joke. The gesture may also indicate that one is blabbering.

Also, there's the check signal that's caught on by servers around the world to flag that a supper supporter wishes to pay the charge and get out. The signal is showed by touching the record finger and thumb together and signifying a wavy line within the air associated with marking one's title. Drawing a checkmark within the discussion utilizing the fingers communicates that the person needs to pay the charge.

Chapter 26. Different Types of People and How They Fit In the Social Circle

All of us are full of different flaws that make us feel ashamed. We do have strengths that we want to brag about in front of everyone. Some of us prefer to stay natural in their everyday life while others love to take up their favorite persona to get through different hurdles in their lives. Some people like to make their way by deception, lies, and manipulation, while others prefer to face stumbling blocks but refuse to deviate from the right path. Whatever our choice of being a person in our lives is, the goal mustn't be of hiding our weaknesses and dark spots if we have any. We must allow our flaws to be a part of our personality. We should celebrate our flaws. It is what being human is about. When a person takes up a fake persona, he forgets that the people loving him are loving that persona that he has taken up and not that person who is in hiding under the fake personality. The real success is that people start loving us because of what we are and not because of what we are trying to become.

The Joker

The first category is a joker. The foremost feeling on hearing the word joker is of a person who is cracking jokes and laughing his heart out even during sober conversations. Jokers love jokes, costumes, and makeup. Each makeover gives them a new look and personality. They love to hide their real looks and nature from others. Generally, jokers are considered harmless, but things get different if we bring to mind batman's joker. A scary and nutty person comes to mind who is evil personified. That joker is always bent on inflicting the greatest pain on the people surrounding him. Can you think of a person who fulfills the above personality traits? Do you know anyone who laughs too much, always cracks jokes or tries to tease others while laughing it out? Beware! Jokers are masters of disguise.

The Smart One

Smart people can mold themselves according to the situation. They learn or are naturally gifted to adapt to changing circumstances. Smart people always remember to read other people's styles to gain more knowledge about them. They tend to see through the motives behind their acts and their hidden desires to work with them and gain benefits. Smart people are good at conveying their messages in an effective manner and without making the slightest buzz. They know how to express their feelings clearly, which is the most important thing when it comes to building and strengthening a relationship.

Similarly, smart people are very successful in their businesses or jobs. They work hard to learn how to read people, and the rest gets automatically easy for you. You can tell if a person is smart by looking at how they behave with you and other people around him. One important point to note is that smart people are very good at taking care of their interests, even at others' cost.

The Worker

Workers are the people who belong to a specific social class that is known for doing jobs for low pay only to live hand to mouth in their lives. The jobs they do low demand skills and labor and also have low literacy requirements. This category of people also lives off on social welfare programs. Working-class people mostly remain preoccupied with their day-to-day expenditures. They don't have time to take up different personas and disguises. Also, they are not smart enough to get a job done in the easiest way possible. Their brains are generally wired to do it the hard way. These people typically wear their hearts on their sleeves. They are easy to predict and are simple to understand.

The Loyal

These people are hard to find but exist. They are reliable as well as truthful. If a person is loyal to you, he shares affection with you and will not leave you when life gets hard for you.

Loyal people think from their hearts and always work to benefit the people who are close to them. Just like the working class, loyal people are easily predictable and trustworthy.

The Strong

Physically strong people generally have a happy temperament. A strong person has higher levels of physical and mental strength. They don't have self-pity; that's why they are confident and good at judging people and dealing with them. Before they judge other people, they try to judge themselves. Besides, they have higher levels of self-restraint. Their nerves are powerful; that's why they are patient. They also are good listeners and observers. Their physical and mental strengths make them very good at reading other people and reaching an educated judgment. They don't hesitate to ask for help when they are in need, and also, they are open to helping others.

Different Types of Personalities

People are driven by their nature when they do this or leave you wondering why they did something that looked unwanted to you. It is perfectly normal if you think you need to understand someone a bit more than you already do. This someone can be a loved one or a person at our workplace. We have to accept the reality that people are not perfect. We are different, and it is this difference and diversity that makes this world a colorful and interesting place to live in. When people stay true to their role, they tend to contribute their bit to this diverse world. Imagine if we were all created in the same way, how the world looks like then. It would be boring.

Take an example of diversity. When a car hits a motorbike in a road accident, many people gather at the site. Most of them are on-lookers who are just investigating what happened. Some mourn the wounds of the injured while some call the ambulance. Only a handful of them step up and help the injured recover their senses. They try to administer to the first aid and take care of them until the ambulance arrives at the site. It is not that those people leap into a house on fire without thinking about their lives. We react differently to different situations. Our fears and desires trigger these reactions. Sometimes they motivate us, while at other times, they just demotivate us.

In analyzing people, you should know the people around you. What they do and how they react to different situations. Knowing their personality types and the fears that guide their behavior can improve how you interact with other people. It helps you read people more efficiently so that your interaction with them becomes smooth and your analysis of people broadens and deepens. Besides, you can track down your personality traits as well as faults. Let's roll on and take a look at different types of people in the world.

The Reformer/Idealist

The Reformer is a perfectionist. They have principles and are conscientious. These kinds of people have specific ideas to follow, and they come down hard on themselves and other people. They just love to keep them at pretty high standards. They are dedicated and responsible besides having perfect self-discipline.

They are usually successful in life because they tend to get lots of things to happen in a short time, and that too in the right way. They are always looking forward to setting themselves on the right path by eliminating their weaknesses. (9 Personality Types—Enneagram Numbers, nod)

The Performer

As the title suggests, these kinds of people will always be setting goals for themselves. They are highly target-oriented individuals, and they believe in doing rather than sitting on the couch and thinking day and night. They are always striving for success. This drive makes them pretty excellent at doing things right. You can find them in a big company, a shop or on the street selling vegetables or fruit. Wherever they are, their eyes are always on the horizon. They have dreams of success, and they are in the world to make them happen. These kinds of people are considered as role-models by many other people.

They have the fears that drive them toward the top. What makes them perfect is their urge to become somebody. The fear of dying as nobody makes them state-conscious. Instead of discouraging others, they respect the opinion of other people. (9 Personality Types—Enneagram Numbers, nod)

The Observer

These kinds of people spend time thinking and are of an introvert type. Their focus always is on gaining knowledge. They also prefer reading their personality instead of reading others. They remain absorbed in themselves and love to play with different types of concepts. They usually despise worldly attractions like big mansions, cars, and social status. They are always busy searching for themselves. They prefer to observe what is happening in their brains. You can see that these people will lock themselves in their rooms for hours as they love to understand how things go. This exclusive behavior allows them to concentrate on what they do. That's why they are usually considered experts on what they do. As they don't have the social skills needed to keep relationships healthy, they get overlooked most of the time.

The Adventurer

These kinds of people are fun-loving people. You will see them engaged in enjoyable pursuits, and also, they are often in an upbeat mood. They thrive on pleasure and adventures, which makes them a positive person. They tend to avoid negativity at all costs, which helps them fight off pessimism and stress well. They are also very optimistic and don't let tough challenges mar their optimism. They are the ones who always find that silver lining in dark clouds. They stick to that silver lining and turn negative situations fast and well. (9 Personality Types—Enneagram Numbers, nod)

Also, they are highly inconsistent. As they are fun-oriented, they remain in a particular work until the fun factor is alive but shoot out of it once they are bored, no matter if the work is complete or not. Completing projects poses a big challenge to them; that's why they struggle to succeed in the practical world.

The Warrior

As the name suggests, these kinds of people love to throw and take the gauntlet. They are strong and have dominating personalities. You can say they are born leaders and are confident. They are real alphas. They hate to depend on other people and also don't like to reveal their weaknesses. Instead, they use their strengths to cover those people who are around them as their family and friends. They are always ready to take charge of any situation, no matter how thundering and dreadful it is. They love to be the masters of their fate, and they also prefer to take control of people and circumstances.

Chapter 27: Conclusion of Body Language

If your mind is reeling from all the information shared so far, brace yourself. You see, this is an exceedingly vast topic. It is an essential topic because communication is one of the essential parts of our lives. How we communicate impacts our relationships, whether private, personal, or professional.

As with anything else, the impact can be positive or negative, so knowing what your body is saying on your behalf is of the utmost importance. The value in this book is not in learning all you need to know about this subject. It is in understanding that there is so much to know and that you can learn it over time by paying attention and putting in some effort.

Imagine that you are a very shy person who has amazing ideas for inventions or songs or movies, or whatever. Now, imagine how hard it would be for a very timid person to get those great ideas across to the right patent attorney, the right musician, or the right producer if they could barely speak above a whisper when they were nervous.

If they finally did get a meeting with their target audience, how would it look if they averted their eyes and crossed their arms over their body the whole time? Do you think they would be taken seriously? What is the possibility that they would win an influential person in a position of influence over under those circumstances?

There is nothing wrong with any personality type, but if you have a timid personality, know what your body language is saying on your behalf. If that is not what you want to convey, you can learn better behaviors that reflect what you want to say.

What of the person who is the opposite? What if you were naturally loud, bordering on boisterous, and the more nervous you became, the louder you seemed to get?

Being aware of how your volume affects others, you might try to tone it down a bit, but those who are naturally boisterous tend to have "big" body language as well.

If you walk into a room and begin to grip and shake hands as if you were arm wrestling, you would naturally start your event with mistrust and wariness as to your motives though you said very little at a modified decibel.

Here is one last word of caution about becoming a student of body language; never to use one cue to determine what a speaker means. Several factors are involved in each person's dynamic, and all must be considered before making an important determination.

Factors that could possibly affect someone's body language might include a physical or mental disability or limitation, a person's culture or background, or even a current health crisis.

Be aware that you can be influenced by body language with or without your consent, and you can influence others by your own body language, whether you are aware of it or even whether or not you mean to.

Body language is a powerful tool. Understand it and that understanding thoughtfully.

Chapter 28: Dark Psychology

It is the study of the human condition because it involves people's psychological nature; that is, they prey on other people with criminal activities and criminal motives. Illegal reasons and unlawful purposes lack instinct and social science theories. All human beings may harm other humans and creatures. Although many people have suppressed or sublimated this trend, some have acted on these impulses. Dark psychology attempts to understand the thoughts, feelings, perceptions, and subjective processing systems that lead to predatory behavior contrary to the contemporary understanding of human behavior. Dark psychology assumes that crime, deviance, and abuse are purposeful and have rational, goal-oriented motivation 99.99% of the time. It is the remaining 0.01% of the dark psychology part of Adler's theory and teleology. Dark psychology assumes an area in the human mind that enables some people to perform cruel behavior without a purpose. In this theory, it is called a dark singularity.

Dark psychology believes that all humanity's malicious intentions towards others vary from minimal ambiguous and short thoughts to purely psychotic deviant behavior, without any rationality of cohesion. That is called a dark continuum. Dark psychology calls it the confounding factor. The mitigating factor is the promoter and attractant close to the mysterious singularity. The heinous behavior of people falls on the dark continuum. A brief introduction to these concepts is as follows. Dark psychology is a concept that the author has struggled with for fifteen years. It was only recently that he finally conceptualized the human condition, philosophy, and psychology definition. Dark psychology covers all the people who connect us to the dark side. All cultures, all faiths, and all humanity suffer from this well-known cancer. From the moment we are born to our death, there is a latent side within us, which some people call evil. In contrast, others define it as crime, immorality, and pathology.

Dark Psychology introduces a third philosophical construction, arguing that these behaviors are different from religious teachings and contemporary social science theories. Dark psychology believes that some people will act the same, not for power, money, gender, retribution, or any other known purpose. They commit these terrible acts without aim. Simply put, their use does not justify their methods. Some people assault and hurt others because of this. There is this potential in all of us. The area the author explores may be to harm others for no reason, no explanation, or purposelessness. Dark psychology believes that this dark potential is very complicated and even confusing to define. Dark psychology assumes that we all have the potential for predator behavior and that this potential can enter our thoughts, feelings, and perceptions. As you will read through this manual, we all have this potential, but only a few of us will make a difference. All of us once had the thought and feeling of acting cruelly. All of us have thought about hurting others seriously and without mercy.

You are honest with yourself. You have to agree with the thoughts and feelings you once thought about committing heinous behavior. Given this fact, we consider ourselves to be a kind species. We want to believe that these thoughts and feelings do not exist. Unfortunately, we all have these ideas, and fortunately, no action has taken against them. Dark psychology constitutes that some people have the same thoughts, feelings, and opinions but act deliberately or impulsively. The apparent difference is that they operate independently, while others only have brief thoughts and feelings about it. "Dark Psychology" believes that this predator style is purposeful and has a specific rational, goal-oriented motivation. Religion, philosophy, psychology, and other dogmas have made convincing attempts to define dark psychology. Most human behaviors related to evil practices are indeed purposeful and goal-oriented. Still, dark psychology believes that persistent behavior and goal-oriented motives seem to be blurred in a particular field.

From thought to pure psychosis, dark psychology has suffered continuous damage without any apparent rationality or purpose. This continuum, the dark continuum, helps conceptualize the philosophy of dark psychology. Dark psychology addresses human psychology or the general human condition that allows or might even promote predatory behavior. In many cases, this behavioral tendency's specific characteristics lack the rational motivation of universality and predictability. Dark psychology believes that this general human condition is different or an extension of evolution. Let's look at some basic principles of development. First of all, consider that we have evolved from other animals. At present, we are a model of all animal life. Our frontal lobe makes us apex creatures. Now let us suppose that being advanced creatures does not entirely separate us from animals' instincts and predatory nature.

Chapter 29. What Is Dark Psychology?

The idea of psychology is to help people by helping them understand themselves. Dark psychology is about using the mental weaknesses that people have to get people to do what you want them to do. I know it sounds cringe worth to many people, but this is not nearly as bad as you think it is. The fact is that everywhere around, the tools of dark psychology are chipping away at your mind. Facebook ran a test on its users by curating their content and measuring their mood. They wanted to see how showing people more negative content would affect their news by showing them more positive content. Magazines and advertisements like to play on your need to keep up with the Joneses or not lose something. In doing so, you are drawn into whatever they are selling. The news feeds a looping heap of controlled opinions to try and make you agree with the viewpoint you already share. The world is full of psychology being used darkly, and most of the time, you are on the receiving end of it rather than getting the benefit of it.

That is about to change. Dark Psychology is about recognizing the compulsions, needs, and desires that we all have, which can be used to get what we want.

What Do We Mean by That?

Whether it is a fear of loss, a desire to keep up with the Joneses, or a need to feel wanted or feel right, these things guide our decisions and impulses, whether we like them or not. Alternatively, whether we want them to or not, people act against their interests every day simply because they are in an emotional state that guides your actions. When someone finds out these emotional triggers, it is a matter of time before they can start to guide your actions, control your behavior, and even manipulate you.

There can be nothing worse when people have figured out your emotional triggers and begin to play them. Whether it is a parent or a stranger, you can feel yourself often taking action and not even certain why you feel drawn to taking action just knowing that you have to, or want to, or that it is something that must be done. No, you cannot wait and Dark Psychology is the tool that sets this into action. It is the tool that shines a light on finding all these mental triggers in yourself and others.

It also recognizes that as amazing as our brains are, they take many shortcuts in the name of efficiency, which leaves them vulnerable to some of the simplest attacks. Ideally, our minds should not make us feel sad simply because we had a negative thought, and yet, this happens all the time. We're wandering around, having a good time, a good day. Someone says something or does something, maybe even inconsequential, and yet suddenly, our mood is shifted, and we have to fight to get back to balance. Our brains, however, are just working to be efficient; they are not working to be perfect. And when you understand that, you know that there is a huge opportunity to be had when dealing with people. More importantly, you understand that there are something's that you need to learn to safeguard yourself.

You have desires and wants, needs, and how far you are willing to go to have those things met. Do you know? What are your buying triggers? What are your emotional triggers? You have them, but are you completely aware of them. What makes you stressed, confused, angry, happy, and excited? All of these things are inside your mind? They are inside everyone's mind. When you know how to access them, you will suddenly have greater freedom, happiness, excitement, and possibility in yourself and others. Because finally, you will be bringing your desires to life by getting others to see and want to help.

We are going to address manipulation—one of the keys to dark psychology. Manipulation is different from persuasion, influence, sales, and other such things. It is often about getting people to take action by playing on their weaknesses. We will talk about the ethics of manipulation, what you need to think about, and the "Right now" is essential to set the stage for what you can expect and learn the handful of psychological techniques and methods that will allow you to control people.

Dark Psychology is a tool, like a hammer. You can use it to build things or use it as a weapon to hurt people. We are making no moral judgments and go about using these skills. But the most important thing is for you to learn these techniques to make sure that you have a better understanding of yourself and what people are using against you.

The world can be a dangerous place knowing these techniques and understanding how people can manipulate you or fundamentally transform how you respond to people and how you engage with them. You will recognize when people are trying to use your emotional states and trying to take advantage of you. You will also learn how to use these techniques in ethical ways so that you can guide people to take the best action for themselves or the action you think they should take. Beyond everything, you will discover through the dark psychology what exactly is triggering your behaviors and, in part two, how to change those triggers if they are not going to be helpful or serve you in the way that you want them to.

Dark Psychology involves the use of mind tricks, which is in between deception and persuasion. The psychological mind tricks might sound outrageous, but it works well. They are being used to mislead people to think that what they know to be right is wrong, and what they believe to be wrong is right.

In a simple term, dark psychology allows humans to be willing and deliberate to harm others through their decisions and actions; sometimes, this might not be physical. However, some emotions are groomed from a very early stage of an individual's life. For example, a child grows to learn how to cry so that the adults around will make themselves available for their bidding. We can call this crying a manipulative tool for the child to be enabled to control people around. As a child grows up, if such as a child is not being cautioned on what he's doing, the so-called innocent childish behavior would now become a dark way of controlling people to do what he/she wants.

Dark psychology is the study of how a person thinks and sees a need to understand the intent behind actions and words. In general, it illuminates the dark side of human nature. In dark psychology, the effect is experienced by both the victim and the perpetrator. The personality traits which are considered as dark include narcissism, psychopathy, and Machiavellianism.

In a simple term, an excessive admiration of oneself in an obsessive manner towards appearance is referred to as narcissism. Narcissists usually feel superior. They do not subscribe to the rule of giving and take in a normal relationship. They are good at blaming others whenever there is an issue. A common feature is to be an extremely self-centered individual. Narcissists have a public appetite for control and power. They control people by making them think that they are looking out for them. They are also very smart such that they get involved in your day to day activities in life without being noticed. Above all, they are Keen liars and master is the lie skills.

Psychopathy is a trait that is associated with not being sensitive to other people. A psychopath will almost not have empathy for other people. Psychopaths are usually bold, confident, and fearless. They are risk-takers and extremely charming.

On the other hand, the third personality trait is known as Machiavelli's; the term is used to describe someone who lacks emotions and desire to achieve something at the expense of other people's feelings. This can be done through deceit, manipulation, or going against some moral rules. An individual who scores highly in Machiavelli's test is usually referred to as a "High Mach." These people are always around us, sometimes in our workplace or as a neighbor. They are hard-working people who are smart and are unapologetic about stepping on other people's toe. This set of people are opportunists and can emotionally detach themselves from situations they are in. Due to this ability, they are capable of involving themselves in several sexual several encounters. They can stand a chance of being good teammates but certainly not a good friend.

This knowledge of dark psychology is to protect yourself from those personalities when you come across them. Dark psychology cuts across all human conditions in which are universal. It studies how the state of humans relates to their thoughts, feelings, and perception. The general assumption here is that every human has the potential to be violent. Learning this concept is of two-folded benefits. First, it helps individuals accept that they tend to become evil, so the knowledge of this will prevent it from erupting. And secondly, it gives everyone a reason to struggle to survive.

The following concept I will be talking about is Neuro-Linguistics Programming (NLP). This is a technique used in restructuring people's minds on how to get rid of bad habits, how to become productive, and how to make them effective in general. You can use this technique to connect sense, mind, behavior, and language. This method is designed so that you tend to control people without them even being aware of what you are doing to them.

Neuro refers to the nervous system, which is made up of the mind and all other senses. Your nervous system functions when you interact with your environment or people. That's why when you listen more to people, you get to understand what is being said. When you pay more attention to what happens around you, you know and see more things about people around you.

Chapter 30. Explication of Dark Psychology

Several skills are essential in analyzing people. The first and perhaps most important skill is having an understanding of human nature and normal human behavior. If you do not understand how humans behave under normal circumstances or what motivates most people, you are unlikely to interpret others' actions and intentions correctly. Just as a judge relies on their sense of how people typically behave and what motivates them in their judgments, so too must you develop an understanding of the typical spectrum of human behavior to analyze someone properly.

Of course, human beings can behave in highly original ways, making analyzing them difficult at times. Although human beings frequently behave in typically human ways–like being jealous of others' success or envious of a colleague who just married a beautiful wife–sometimes people can surprise you. Indeed, some people never feel jealous or envious of others. Most poor people do not steal even though they may need this because it is not part of their character. Frequently the most significant, most flamboyant thief is the person who already has all that they need.

To analyze people, you are going to have to start with knowing how humans are generally. It includes understanding the spectrum of human emotion, the behaviors linked to these emotions, and the things that motivate people to do this. Everyone wears a mask, which means that sometimes the intentions of others are not always clear. But even with this mask, people can reveal their emotional state to you, the things that make them happy, and the things that make them sad.

We all wear a mask, but perhaps only FBI agents are so skilled that they never give you some clue. A spontaneous laugh, a twinkle in the eye, a giddy tapping of the foot: These are unconscious signs that men and women give of how they feel. Analyzing men and women will require understanding human behavior and interpreting what people say and do.

Non-Verbal Communication

Non-verbal communication refers to the little clues that others give us that convey essential information outside of language. Human beings are social animals, meaning we evolved in settings where we were generally close to one another rather than alone. For this reason, we developed the ability to perceive and interpret the signals that others send to indicate their emotional state, thoughts, and motivations.

It is easy to pay attention to words when we are attempting to analyze others. Still, because language is not always an accurate indication of how people feel, it is essential to pay attention to the non-verbal cues others send. These cues can include facial expression, body distance, and the position of hands, quick movements of the hands or the feet, and the like. These non-verbal cues are not specific to human beings. Non-human primates are excellent examples of how animal societies can be built without speech. From bearing of teeth to the tail position, apes have a language comprised entirely of non-verbal cues.

Differentiating Fake From Real Emotion

Analyzing others will require developing the ability to distinguish exact sentiment from a false one. Human beings know that others observe and interpret them, at least the intelligent ones do, so they have become adept at hiding their feelings. A typical example of this is someone who smiles even though they are not happy. Still, this hiding of emotion can mean angry when one is hurt or vulnerable. Human beings wear masks to protect themselves, as you must if you plan on defending yourself from practitioners of dark psychology. But protecting yourself also means analyzing people appropriately, and this means determining which emotions are real and which are not.

The practitioner of dark psychological tactics perceives you as prey, so they pay very close attention to your words, actions, and non-verbal cues: virtually anything that indicates what's going on inside. You may put a wall to make your emotions more difficult for the predator to access, but you will most likely say or do something to reveal the truth. This is just as true of the predator as it is of you, the prey. They can put on a façade of smiles and pleasantries, but sometimes all it takes is one fierce look to reveal that their intentions are not so friendly.

We see this all the time in films and television shows. The new neighbor seems nice, but the camera shot reveals their subtle change in expression when your back is turned. They are not so neighborly. Their goal is to steal your husband and wreak havoc in your life (in the case of the standard Lifetime Original Movie). To protect yourself, you need to use your understanding of human nature and analyze it to figure out what is going on. Is there a discrepancy between the surface emotion and the events taking place? Perhaps the other person is smiling, but you heard that they lost their house and are short of funds. Would most people be so giddy in this situation?

An essential part of distinguishing real from fake emotion is deciding whether the surface or "fake" feeling makes sense, given what you know. Human beings are good at being emotionally aware by dint of being so communal. A person can hide what they feel, but it may only take a brief glimmer of real emotion for you to establish the rule of what is real in this person and what is not. The other person drops their mask for a second and notes what the natural person beneath looks like.

Tips to Identify a Liar

Anyone who has spent time around a pathological liar knows that little tricks can be used to tell when fibbing. Pathological liars are often highly friendly people who love to talk and always have something to say. It is this still having something to say that gets them into trouble. If you are suspicious that the person you are speaking to is a pathological liar, pay attention to the factual aspects of the things they say. This will become natural in time as you become aware the person is lying. You will make a mental note about facts like a specific monetary amount of something, a date, or a restaurant's name because you know these things may potentially be false.

Paying close attention to the details is the first step in identifying a liar. The second is knowing when to face the liar with the facts. It may not be a good idea to confront them pointedly, as you may decide. If they said they went to a particular restaurant, ask them what they had to eat—baked chicken and mixed vegetable stir fry. The next day, s/he asks them how the steak was. If they say, it was beautiful when you have caught them. They did not go to the restaurant at all. A pathological liar tells so many lies that they cannot keep track of them.

Chapter 31. How To Use Dark Psychology

How Can Psychology Improve Your Life?

The following are some of the top ten realistic uses for psychology in regular life:

1. Get Prompted

Whether your purpose is to stop smoking, lose weight, or examine a new language, psychology training provides pointers for buying motivation. To grow your motivation while drawing close to a project, make use of some of the following tips derived from research in cognitive and educational psychology:

- Introduce new or novel factors to hold your interest high.

- Vary the series to help stave off boredom.

- Study new matters that build on your present understanding.

- Set clear goals that might be at once related to the assignment.

2. Enhance Your Management Abilities

It doesn't count number in case you're an office supervisor or a volunteer at a neighborhood teenage activity group; having true leadership abilities will, in all likelihood, be vital sometime in the future for your existence. Now, not all of us are born leaders, but some easy suggestions from mental studies can improve your leadership capabilities.

One of the most famous research papers on this topic looked at three distinct management styles. Primarily based on the findings of this look at and subsequent studies, practice several of the following when you are in a management function:

- Offer clear steering but permit group contributors to voice opinions.
- Communicate approximately possible answers to troubles with contributors to the group.
- Focus on stimulating ideas and be inclined to praise creativity.

3. Come to be a Better Communicator

Conversation involves a whole lot more than just the way you speak or write. Research indicates that nonverbal indicators make up a big portion of our interpersonal communications

Some key strategies encompass the subsequent:

- Use proper eye contact.
- Start noticing nonverbal indicators in others.
- Learn to use your tone of voice to boost your message.

4. Learn To Better Understand Others

Just like nonverbal communication, your capacity to apprehend your emotions and the feelings of those around you perform an important role in your relationships and professional lifestyles. The time emotional intelligence refers to your potential to apprehend each of your emotions in addition to those of other human beings.

What can you do to emerge as more emotionally stable? Recall a few of the subsequent techniques:

- Cautiously assess your very own emotional reactions.

- Record your enjoyment and emotions in a journal.

- Try to see situations from the angle of a different person.

5. Make Extra Correct Selections

Studies in cognitive psychology supply a wealth of statistics about choice making. By making use of those techniques for your lifestyles, you can discover ways to make wiser choices. The following time you want to make a huge decision, strive the usage of several the subsequent techniques:

- Try using the "Six Thinking Hats" technique with the aid of searching on the situation from multiple points of view, including rational, emotional, intuitive, creative, advantageous, and Dark views.

- Recall the capacity prices and blessings of choice.

- Appoint a grid evaluation approach that offers a score for how a selected decision will fulfill unique requirements you may have.

6. Enhance Your Reminiscence

Have you ever wondered why you can remember the precise information of childhood events yet forget the call of the new customer you met yesterday? Research on how we form new reminiscences and how and why we forget has caused some of the findings that can be implemented without delay in your daily life.

What are some methods you can grow your reminiscence of electricity?

- Awareness of the data.

- Rehearse what you have discovered.

- Do away with distractions.

7. Make Wiser financial decisions

Nobel Prize-winning psychologist Daniel Kahneman and his colleague Amos Tversky performed a chain of research that looked at how humans manipulate uncertainty and danger while making decisions.

One looks at located that workers could extra than triple their financial savings by making use of some of the following strategies:

- Don't procrastinate. Start investing savings now.

- Commit earlier to dedicate quantities of your future profits to your retirement financial savings.

- Try to be aware of non-public biases that may result in Dark money choices.

8. Get Higher Grades

The subsequent time you are tempted to whine about pop quizzes, midterms, or finals, consider that research has confirmed that taking checks helps you better consider what you have learned, even if it wasn't on the test.

Every other study discovered that repeated check-taking might be a higher reminiscence aid than studying. College students who were tested repeatedly have been able to remember 61% of the content while looking at the group recalled the most effective 40%. How can you observe those findings to your lifestyles? While seeking to research new data, self-check frequently to cement what you have learned into your memory.

9. Become More Effective

Occasionally, it looks as if there are hundreds of books, blogs, and magazine articles telling us the way to get more completed in an afternoon. However, how much of this advice is based on real studies? For example, think about the variety of times you have ever heard that multitasking can help you become more productive. Studies have discovered that trying to carry out multiple missions at the same time severely impairs pace, accuracy, and productiveness.

What classes from psychology can you operate to boom your productivity? Consider several of the following:

- Avoid multitasking while running on complex or dangerous obligations.
- Cognizance at the venture at hand.
- Eliminate distractions.

10. Be Healthier

Psychology also can be a useful device for improving your ordinary health. From approaches to encourage workout and better nutrients to new remedies for melancholy, the sector of fitness psychology gives a wealth of beneficial strategies that can help you to be more healthy and happier.

Some examples that you may practice at once in your very own existence:

- Research has shown that both daylight and synthetic mild can reduce the symptoms of seasonal affective sickness.
- Studies have demonstrated that exercise can contribute to more mental well-being.
- Studies have determined that supporting people apprehend the dangers of bad behaviors can lead to healthier choices.

Chapter 32. Delving Into Dark Psychology

Some of the best science fiction that has ever been written has surrounded the subject of mind control and its ability to control our world. However, it can still sound like a futuristic event. However, many neuroscientists are continuing to create a digital interface specifically designed to connect to the brain, which has continued to make progress in recent times. Even though this advanced technology is still unreachable, it has made plenty of headway where we could see mind control gadgets popping up everywhere shortly.

Currently, a technology known as brain-computer interfaces, or BCIs, has only been in the development stage for individuals who have fallen victim to injuries, debilitating such as being paralyzed. A great example of this is a paraplegic by the name of Dennis DeGray. Neuroscientists at Stanford University assisted DeGray in creating a major breakthrough and a typing world record involving mind control.

DeGray's success partially stems from the assistance of Jaimie Henderson. Henderson, a neurosurgeon at Stanford, successfully implanted two electrodes arrays the size of a tic-tac into DeGray's brain. DeGray's brain activity is then monitored by the electrode arrays, which helps decode electrical brain signals that neurons fire deep in the brain's motor cortex. The results achieved were beyond impressive and allowed for the early steps of achieving independence for many currently fully or partially paralyzed people. With a lot of interest pointed towards this ability to control the environment through a BCI, many researchers hope that future demonstrations can further the technology in the future ahead. It could even be as soon as the next 5-10 years that we could see more of it being integrated into people's lives.

Besides the research and development being conducted at Stanford, another company seems to be taking it one step further. Neural ink, founded by Tesla and SpaceX CEO Elon Musk, has become dedicated to creating BCI that they have labeled as "neural lace." To date, Neuralink has already raised close to $30 million for funding the project.

Nevertheless, like anything connected to the internet, one has to be extremely careful and diligent in the security and safe handling of all devices so that the device's security does not become compromised. We saw this occur when the Mirai botnet practically destroyed many internet areas that created attacks that used Denial of Service. Once a person's brain is implanted and connected to an internet device, this is when an entirely new level of security issues could occur, including a possible 'brain jacking.' Not only for security purposes, but it also could lead to many questions about ethical responsibility. For example, if a brain-controlled machine breaks the law, then who is arrested for it? Problems like this would need to require in-depth discussion before our future becomes a place where mind control is used for everything. However, in the short-term, an interface that is a less invasive brain-computer is already in use and which have significantly lower risks.

Many headsets have been developed and used in many drone races successfully as well as controlling Mind Desktop, which is a brain interface that is generalized for the use of Windows. With these devices, they bring less of a risk than implanting a chip into your brain. Not only that, but they do lack a few things too, especially with performance. This is seen with Mind Desktop, where a character is typed in 20 seconds. Regardless of that, they are still pretty cheap because of their use of electronics that have been modified. Therefore, if you currently have Mind Desktop, you are using an $800 "electroencephalogram" (a medical device used to measure brain activity) for a fraction of the real machine's cost.

When it comes to external BCI challenges, they mostly surround the skull, brain coverings, and scalps density and thickness. These characteristics prevent us from snooping on the brain's neurons with accuracy, which is what we think is essential for a BCI system to be high performing. As far as the future is concerned, we can only get remotely close to the information found on neurons is if we get an implant placed inside.

With many researchers making attempts to build a better BCI, other researchers have continued with their BCI implant technology. However, they have been experiencing technical issues of their own, which they will need to overcome. First, they hope to obtain an increased amount of views from their sensors, which will increase their ability to decode faster brain signals a lot more accurately. Plus, there remains the question of getting these outsides of the laboratory so people can use them.

These BCI's need to be constructed not to require a technician or some third-party intervention is of high importance since the main goal includes restoring people's independence while being paralyzed. This is why researchers are continuing to address these issues actively.

The erasing and implanting of memories seem to be only capable in movies such as Total Recall, Dark City, and Inception. But this idea no longer sounds as farfetched as we once thought since many people do not even lose sleep over the fact that it could happen someday. But now we can begin to see a brighter future with ontogenetic and how it continues to tamper with memory to bring it to light eventually. Although ontogenetic is still a relatively new procedure in the experimental stage, it has broken some laboratory ground. It uses light to activate or inactivate neurons that are highly specific by way of light-sensitive channels. For these to be used, they also require sensitive proteins. A few of these proteins include halorhodopsin or channelrhodopsin, which are added to the subject. These proteins are found naturally in many organisms. They need to be inserted genetically into an organism like in a rat or mice in the laboratory. Once injected, the neuron will fire every time the light is activated. When the light is on, the light enacts discretionary particles' progression, such as calcium or sodium, making the neuron produce an activity potential.

This system has been utilized in mice to control their eating or drinking propensities. The mice are hereditarily built to have these light-touchy proteins, and a wire is embedded into their cerebrum. Specialists demonstrated that the mice would keep eating while the light is turned on, regardless of whether they do not feel hungry. The best way to prevent the mice from eating is by killing the light. By basically turning on or off a light, one can control a neuron from terminating, bringing about certain and automatic conduct changes. This procedure can be utilized to figure out which neurons are required for specific activities. Likewise, researchers would now be able to figure out what capacity a neuron has by initiating it or deactivating and watching the impacts.

There have been a few speculations that caffeine may avert memory deficiencies by restraining the adenosine A2A receptor. A recent report demonstrated that the actuation of adenosine A2A receptor in the hippocampus, utilizing ontogenetic, was sufficient to weaken spatial memory in mice. This investigation not just exhibits the relationship between caffeine and abatement in memory misfortune; however, this additionally demonstrates the likelihood of erasing and hindering recollections in mice utilizing ontogenetic. Another investigation demonstrated that if neurons in the thalamic core reunions were initiated utilizing ontogenetic, the working memory in mice indicated deficiencies. As this system turns out to be further developed and used, researchers will frequently have a superior comprehension of which neurons influence memory and how they influence it.

Ontogenetic was utilized to take a gander at the impact of core cucumbers (NAC) on the "cocaine-setting related" memory guideline. They found that when the NAC neurons were enacted, the mice basically "overlooked" that cocaine was situated in that district. The researcher likewise saw that the actuation caused a diminished number of c-Fos+ cells in the VP, which has recently been related to a "decline in medication chasing." They presumed that these neurons were significant for the directing prize looking for conduct brought about by cocaine. This might be significant for deciding how a habit is shaped and maybe helping expansion issues.

This demonstrates the significance of certain natural triggers for medication addicts. If ontogenetic can help cancel the recollections engaged with the situations, it can have exceptional consequences for how we treat chronic drug habits. Not exclusively would memories be able to be deleted, yet false recollections can likewise be included. A recent report demonstrated that when dentate gyrus neurons were enacted, mice solidified in a spot where they had never been stunned, indicating dread. This dread was not there earlier, yet after the light was demonstrated, these mice had recollections of dread in a novel spot.

Even though ontogenetic is genuinely new, it is rapidly being consolidated into numerous tests. It is enabling us to all the more likely comprehend what impact enacting or deactivating neurons has on conduct. Unmistakably it is conceivable, at any rate in mice, to cause a mouse to do certain things utilizing optogenetics; we can even eradicate recollections and "make" new ones. One day those science fiction films may not look so inconceivable.

I do not mean the enthusiastic control intentionally used to get our particular manner. I mean the capacity to get others to figure out how we do and concur with us, just by the sheer quality of psyche.

Consider despots who can bewilder hordes of individuals with quality of speech while on the ascent to control. Analyze the content sometime in the not too distant future. You think it is difficult to see in what capacity numerous individuals moved toward becoming influenced around then. Consider a well-prepared canine or horse and the association with their proprietor. A steed is more grounded than the proprietor, and a canine normally increasingly deft, yet they obey directions. Consider the impact of "charm." How does a specific entertainer hold a crowd of people while similar words or activities by another entertainer are less captivating?

Are these things the aftereffect of the idea structure billows of extraordinary power, created by a solitary individual who empties their feelings into the conveyance and into that idea structure cloud? Rather than a few contemplations, social events to cause a solid cloud can include a solitary individual who has excellent conviction and self-conviction blended with crude feeling produce their cloud that overwhelms the psyches in the crowd?

In most close to home connections, there are fluctuating degrees of control, some favoring one individual one minute and the other the following minute. Equalization is accomplished at the point when intense feeling bolsters amazing personalities.

Chapter 33. The History of Dark Psychology

Human mythology is riddled with tales of ghosts and creatures that behave in such drastic ways. The very description sends chills down the adults' length that listened to such stories as relayed by past musicians and bards. The creation of monsters advises us that perhaps the universe is not as secure as it might seem from within our window. Beasts live among us and render our lifestyles as something to be protected against, as anything to be covered.

Maybe a creature crawls out of the closet while you rest in your room or slips in from a backdoor that you failed to lock. Perhaps you assumed you were over there, but as it enters your door, you listen to footprints crackling upstairs and a soft voice roaring. You see a bushy, tail-like foot poking out beneath the bed or a claw. You notice a massive, vicious laugh while running for life. You sprint into the shower, and the door is locked. It's not necessarily a stellar exit strategy as there is no window in your toilet, but you didn't know where to get off. Maybe the beast is on the escalators. You don't know where everything is. But after that, you push the above head bathroom light chain and see that you are the monster.

Monsters exist among humans and are medically related to as H. Sapiens... sapiens. Aliens from some other world did not commit actions of murder, theft, and ruin. They were living things who decided to commit these crimes, and today they also live among us. There is indeed a term in behavioral genetics, the so-called dark chord. Applies to the three characteristics of psychopathy, narcissism, and sociopathy, such as factors are deemed especially harmful, so distinguishing such people from the general public is necessary, or would it be?

Since ancient times, an argument could be made that human beings accept their character's horrific components. Today we believe in everyday practices of ancient history, such as orgiastic religious practices, human sacrifice, and ritualized murder as brutal acts of the past that indicate a better forgotten time. Still, it has been argued that these acts represent social and cultural outlets for the black universe that lies beneath the beautiful surface of the human outside.

Societies were then explicitly organized. This would be up upon you to determine whether things are more comfortable today or bad. As tacky as the past, as mentioned earlier, practices may have been, their career status within their living area represented an acknowledgment. That human being had a wrong side to their personality. It was great to give outlets to this dark side than to let it explode and simmer in unexpected ways. For what do today's gang stalking, serial murder, cybercrime, and narcissistic and antisocial acts portray, but living things give in to ends of themselves because they have already expressed themselves in other ways?

The argument is not to assert that living things must consider to give in to their so-called dark tendency of singularity, but to recommend that the contemporary art of mind control represents a variety of activities expressed in ancient society in unique ways. Although the conversation of societies' tradition of providing into their character's dark sides may seem incidental to the discussion of mind control, few things could be essential. A significant phase in planning for defense lies in understanding anyone, you know, maybe the perpetrator of these black arts. It could be someone you already understand.

History of Dark Psychology Study

The 2 social scientific patterns that proactive solutions-day dark psychology are undoubtedly abnormal psychology and psychology for individuals. Irregular psychology is a psychology experiment concerned with psychological illness-related habits of behaviors, emotion, and behavior. These emotions, thoughts, and actions can precede a psychiatric disorder and are usually thought abnormal. As psychology tends to construct a relatively linear dichotomy between normal versus strange behavior, a sociological factor will come under the scepter between irregular or atypical behavioral forms instead of actions assumed to be inside the usual spectrum.

In the early late nineteenth century, person psychology was founded on human conduct driven by the purposeful activity compared to latent libido and sex impulses that describe Freudian psychoanalysis. While we have already addressed in some depth the degree to which individual acts are not consciously driven. May thus be viewed as non-purpose, person psychology allows for implicit or involuntary motives. It just appears to recognize them when non-Freudian, benevolent, and even not always implicit.

For example, as a motivating factor for action, Alfred Adler focused many of his texts on superiority complexes. He found that people who handled the situation in angry or otherwise unbecoming ways were generally inspired by a sense of inadequacy, which is a certain sense caused them to "act out." Now in some people, an inferiority complex as an enthusiastic may lie beneath the surface. However, others may be fully aware that they have a feature of themselves. They are not completely satisfied and trying to compensate.

When creating dark psychology as an outgrowth of internal mental ideas compared to Freudian psychoanalysis concepts, it may be simpler to assume. That human beings usually act with conscious, deliberate motivations instead of being consciously or unconsciously inspired by sexual urges, such as the well-studied complex of Oedipus (the desire for a man to kill his father and sleep). To truly comprehend the historical growth of dark psychology as a research field, it is crucial to realize that individual psychology's philosophy requires non-completely aware motives to explain why human beings tend to act in such a cruel fashion. Even so, the theory of dark psychology supposes that humans are capable of a dark universe, engaging in harmful actions that have no purpose at all.

The research and therapy of psychological disorders have been around as a field of study since the Ancient Egyptians. We have more data from the Greek period, partly because we are closer to the Greek philosophy period in time than we are from the Egyptians. This group just seems to reach the concept of pathology with a fascinating avidity. The research of what we term pathological psychology today existed in the 18th and 19th centuries and earlier in asylum and hospices that diagnosed people and women with rare mental disorders, but the discipline as we now know it dates from the 20th century.

Indeed, in the 19th century, trepanation, exorcism, and being burnt on the stakes as a witch were the standard remedies for pathological mental conditions. Trepanation relates to drilling a hole in the brain to expel malignant spirits from their grip over the head. It is claimed by others to be the earliest surgical technique we have historical evidence. Trepanation was already performed in the 19th century. Today, there are proponents of the procedure, though their appeals usually fell on deaf ears.

Exorcism also looks at how society viewed odd habits and emotions in the current age. Indeed, many practices that we consider to fall inside the normal range today have been considered mental diseases up till the early 1980s. Exorcism, although maybe less brutal than trepanation, represented the perspective that an evil force or demon inhabited the individual who possessed the weird thoughts and actions. All this has been a transmission from the individual's malevolent encouragement to anything else, whether something else was an informant of evil or an agent of evil.

One line of thinking recognizes Satan as the manifestation of human potential to act in a manner "strange" or, more accurately, evil or cruel. It is hard to say whether their ideas of ghouls, demons, values, or even of Satan himself embody that people beings were produced to commit acts of possession. They could be better described as stories intended to fool children or teach them valuable life lessons of good and evil. Of course, exorcisms are still happening today; individuals who assume evil acts come from ownership.

If you believe that the evil committed by human beings comes from a source outside the human being, then the dark psychological theory because it currently stands may be somewhat contrary to what you believe. However, a locally crucial in dark psychology is the idea that humans can behave without purpose in a remarkably violent and cruel manner, only as an augmentation of something obscure that dwells inside us. It is up to you to ascribe this type of conduct to Satan as a component of your religious views.

Of course, 19th-century and later abnormal psychologists did not fully recognize this idea of an independent factor for the conditions they were seeing. So treatments such as trepanation or exorcism would've been disturbing or at least pointless to them. As we commented on earlier, scientists shifted away towards the dogmatic beliefs that dominated their careers, ideologies that mostly had more to do with theology than with the professions' empirical compendia. There is nothing intrinsically inconsistent with religious belief, of course. Still, a practitioner who is inexperienced with human anatomy if he is not permitted to examine q cadaver is probably to follow a religion that is not advantageous to him (or herself) or you.

Abnormal psychologists started to question why humans were inspired to behave abnormally. The Devil or the Demons were not entirely acceptable responses. Most of these research groups in psychological disorders were psychiatrists and psychoanalysts who undertook detailed studies of these subjects based on a new, more free understanding of health matters. Though the word dark psychology did not emerge until later in the mid-twentieth century, narcissists, sociopaths, and those who we might identify today as possessing mental illnesses were conducted already throughout the 19th-century studies.

Abnormal psychology of that time would have followed the trend of what we now understand as Freudian psychoanalysis, with Alfred Adler's writings representing one of Freudian's first significant departures. Although Adler is a virtually unknown figure today, his biographies from the generations 1912-1914 provided the basis of many concepts that permeate today's psychological field. His writings were translated into English in 1925. And his personality beliefs and where they derive from predominate in advance psychotherapy and psychoanalysis.

Adler focused on resignation, compensation, and over-compensation as the 3 external factors that shaped personality development. His theories parallel those of another essential psychologist, Abraham Maslow, who acknowledged Alder's influence on his work. Although Adler himself didn't even write about "dark psychology," his theories helped shape this topic's development as a departure from pre-existing psychoanalytical theories.

The analysis of dark psychology can be new. Still, it reflects a spectrum of habits that have been associated with individuals from the very start. The dark area of psychology provides the illusion of a transient research domain. The word and the principles connected with it are more widely available to the people. This has turned dark psychological into a topic that remains beyond the radar of those who may be victims of perpetrators exploiting their resources to damage impact.

Chapter 34. Advanced Techniques to Manipulate Human Psychology

Sources tell us that it is concealment—hiding in the shadows, knowing when to strike. It is also a false front, hiding true intentions. When we are talking about this level of deception, we are talking about hiding aggression. When we take, there is a certain level of aggressive behavior that happens. A small part of manipulation is hiding that aggressive behavior so that the victim sees only good nature.

This is accomplished in various ways and means, one being knowledge. When we allow another to know us, we display vulnerability along with strengths. The experience of these personality traits can give the manipulator the ability to maneuver around without any alarms going off.

- The effectiveness of manipulating those strengths and vulnerabilities arrives when the dark practitioner knows what is vulnerable and inspires pride.

A reoccurring ideology that drives us to war takes into consideration that the action is more negative than positive. We want to avoid it. The manipulation process sees pride in all of us and plays to that pride. It is our strength. For example, when used to drive an army to slaughter others, the intention of our satisfaction has been manipulated to enforce the agendas of others.

- Often, the practitioners of dark psychology use aggression and fear to drive us. The less dark side still falls into the category of knowing what weakness is. That weakness leaves the individual open to control.

How the manipulator uses that control determines the severity of manipulation. There are positive versions of manipulating others, like convincing someone that they are not doing well and needing help. We, however, are looking at the darker side of this. The manipulator uses their control skills to get what they want—and the cost does not apply.

- There are many ways to move another into a place of being controlled. From the positive to the negative, psychological manipulators utilize all tactics.

When positive reinforcement is used, the charm is displayed. A forced smile or laughter can trigger laughter in all of us. As when we were infants, we copy what we see. When we see tears, we want them to stop. When we see a smile, we find ourselves smiling as well. Using positive reinforcement, the manipulator can shower money, charm, and gifts to get us to feel something. The usage of these things allows control of us on an instinctual level. We follow those who tell us what we want to hear.

- Psychological manipulation can also implement negative reinforcement. This is a form of deflection—the substitution of one thing for another.

Often, we have things we need or have to do, and we do not want to do them. The psychological manipulation of negative reinforcement uses that power of negativity to lure the subject from their original need, pushing them toward something they want to be done instead. The long game, a slow play of putting tasks into another's life and then controlling those tasks so that the manipulator can get what they want, is an extraordinarily useful and subdued tactic. Sometimes only partial reinforcement is required to gain control. We are talking about elevating the fear or doubt regarding the tasks needed to be done. The partial is the extended play. It knows that in the end, the victim will lose. It knows that by planting small seeds now, victory will eventually happen. It knows that we all have our weaknesses and that by planting even a tiny seed, we can take someone to that weakness. An individual trying to work toward something they already were shaky on or had doubts about will listen to the lie and flow with that idea, and use it to their destruction.

- The partial manipulator only needs to put the thought in mind, knowing the weakness is already there, and utilizing it will take their prey to a destructive end.

Psychological manipulators flat, outright punish. From an actual physical lashing to the victim's passive-aggressive playing, punishment is beneficial when one wants to control another.

- We skulk and cry and yell and nag and go completely silent. This is the blackmail of the manipulator. It inspires guilt in us. That "wanting to be the better person" rises to the front, and we do what the manipulator wants. When the manipulator sets free the crocodile tears, we have no idea if they are real or not. The degree of crying is not up to us to determine. Only the manipulator knows if the tears are legitimate or not. In this case, the trap is often sprung from the victim's side. They walk up to the hurt individual to help, only to find that the manipulator is just lying in wait to strike.

- One extreme version of manipulation is violence.

Violence triggers something inside us. We often do anything to avoid it. The manipulator knows that power strategically applied can make us go into a state of avoidance. There incites the control, physical violence can have mental scarring, and the manipulator causes the scarring. It places power in tactical places to get the result they want.

Some would say this is the darkest of the dark. Taken to the individual, this can mentally damage them for an extended period, if not permanently. Placed on a world stage, it can lead up to the physical conflict of genocide.

- Mostly, it is about gain. Manipulators of the dark want to gain something. When we speak about improvement, we are talking about power and influence, control and manipulation over others. The trophy is up to the individual. This can be everything as to gaining affections, to money, and even to life itself.

It is about gaining for their reasons and gratifications. The taking of others and making the power and control their own. Selfishness to the extreme. The mind of the dark practitioner sees the ultimate win as the gain over others. They have power. Superiority is the power over another, and taking of someone else's power makes them feel superior. This is a tremendous driving force behind the manipulator. Often, in the case of immature individuals driving manipulations toward superiority, any is pushed aside for just the feeling of being superior. In relationships, it is about control. The manipulation of power can put one in control. Although we have looked at the vampire and energy role, we know who has control.

This feeling of control can be overwhelming to the mental state of the dark. Almost drug-like, it is a feeling of emotion that is more logical. Management is one of the most straightforward manipulation tactics to achieve with only logic to guide. It drives not only the victim but the manipulator as well. Psychological manipulation can also be about self-esteem. The self of the manipulator is always in question. This is one of the reasons they manipulate, to define themselves. How easily they can manage, another can tell the dark that they are better than others. That weakness and strength can be measured in the tactical playing field of the hustle.

- The dark psychological manipulator is bored most of the time, more than most. The psychological manipulator will often use manipulation to determine the validity of feelings and emotions.

This boils down to that manipulation applied in relations with others helps the manipulator regulate reactions to validate or not validate their own emotions. The manipulator measures the self and their self-esteem by how others handle their self-questioning. This happens when the practitioner does not have a grasp on what emotions are. They look at their feelings as invalid and manipulate the situation in such a way as to validate them. We are stuck with ourselves, and we cannot get away. Psychological manipulators validate or invalidate themselves by the tactical controlling of others. It is an exciting way of viewing life, although we all idolize one form of manipulation.

- **The con aspect.** One common form of manipulation is the convincing of another to make their money's yours. This is a hidden agenda of the criminal. This form of mental manipulation preys mostly on the elderly and the rich. However, we all can fall into this form of manipulation. We choose to spend on, and we do not respond to a state of psychological manipulation.

Something happens when the buck is passed over, we go from manipulation into action, and something drives us. It is within us, and it is outside forces that drive. What causes this drive and the drive itself is called Persuasion.

The manipulation process in dark psychology usually is not a single move. It is a complex series of actions, often with the outcome only known by the manipulator. The motivations of manipulators are as convoluted as human nature.

Chapter 35. Mind Control

Mind control is an aspect of manipulation that is similar to brainwashing. The main difference is that the individual might only want to control your mind at the moment. Maybe they want to get you to do something that will benefit them temporarily because they are opportunistic individuals. Since there is not much time to take over a person's mind when you are engaged in a simple conversation, there are some very detailed techniques that a manipulator will use to attempt to gain control of your mind. As you explore these techniques, you will also learn how to combat each of them. The stronger your reason is, the better you will ward off the people trying to harm you.

Compensating for Lack of Physical Prowess

Someone might try to control your mind because you secretly intimate them. Because someone does not appear physically threatening, a manipulator will be quick to move forward with mind control by seeing how much they can change your thoughts. The mind control gives them the same type of satisfaction they would receive if they were physically controlling you. Because the latter is a lot more prominent, the idea of controlling your mind is also a lot more appealing. You will find that manipulators are very discreet about this.

They might remark on how strong or tough you are, building you up based on your physical characteristics. Even a simple comment about you being tall can be enough to let you think that they respect you because you have more physical prowess than they do—this is what they want you to think. Instead of backing down, which you will think they are doing, they make you more vulnerable by making you comfortable.

When you believe that someone sees powerful traits in you, you will be less likely to assume that they have bad intentions. Surely because they appear to respect you, they won't deceive you, right? Always make sure that you remind yourself anyone can fool you at any time. It is hard to keep track of everyone's true intentions, especially when they have mastered the art of mind control.

What You Can Do: Remain firm in your core beliefs. Even if you believe that the individual respects you and what you stand for, always remind yourself of what you hold dear to your heart. Staying true to who you give you little reason to change your opinions on a whim. Remind yourself that the person trying to control your mind is very insecure.

Using Hand Placement as a Decoy

Have you ever noticed that people normally place their fingers on their heads when thinking very hard? In moments of concentration, you have probably done the same thing. This is a subconscious mind control technique that is often used by manipulators. When they want you to rethink something, they might place their fingers on their head to coax you into doing the same. With the help of muscle memory, your brain will be receiving a message that it needs to think harder.

It is an interesting technique because it is so subtle. You surely would not notice it if you were not looking for it in the first place. As you become better at reading body language, you will become more aware of moments when the person you are talking to is merely using a decoy movement as an attempt to control you. Do your best to break the mirroring effect that typically happens during a conversation. Keep your arms in a neutral position by your side.

Manipulators get nervous. They probably get very nervous and will do the best they can to hide this from you. As soon as you notice their fingers move up to their head, imagine that they are nervous that they won't be able to pull off this attempt at mind control. Pride yourself in your ability to pick up on it before it affects you—this will keep you strong.

What You Can Do: In an attempt to break their cycle, you can make a comment that indirectly refers to them concentrating. Something like, "Oh, is that what you were thinking?" is a way to make manipulators second-guess their abilities. If you let them know from the start that you are not automatically going to agree with what they are saying, this will be your way of standing your ground.

Convincing You of Psychic Powers

The person who is manipulating you is not any more powerful than you—repeat this to yourself often. Even though many mind controllers are portrayed as psychic beings, this is not the case for most. A successful manipulator is usually just very good at picking up on your body language and context. There is nothing psychic about it, though it can feel that way at times.

Being misinformed that someone is psychic and can read your mind at any time is intimidating. These are your private thoughts, and you do not want anyone intruding upon them. The good news is that you never have to let this happen. You are still in control of your inner thoughts, and what you share with the world is always going to be your decision. Anyone who tries to force you or to coax you into sharing something you do not want to does not have your best interest at heart.

The mention of psychic abilities might come up as a joke. For example, the manipulator will joke around with you while mentioning that you don't need to say much because they already know what you are thinking. You can laugh this off, but you can also remain firm in believing that this isn't true. With the way you portray yourself, you can get them to think anything you want.

What You Can Do: Always be aware of your intention during every conversation. If you are presenting yourself in a certain way, the manipulative person will pick up on it. Try your hardest to practice standing neutrally and speaking neutrally. When you can master this concept, it will be a lot harder for them to read you.

Surrounding You with Other Manipulative People

This is an incredibly dangerous mind-control technique because it closely ties in with the idea behind brainwashing. The more people that you believe are on the same page about something will make you want to agree with them, too. If a manipulator can find other people who want to manipulate a vulnerable person, you might become an easy target for a bad situation. They will gang up on you in a way that is subtle yet effective. You do not have to put up with this. Knowing who you are as a person will protect you in many ways.

There will be times when a manipulator will only "scout" for like-minded individuals that believe in the point they are making. Unknowingly, they might recruit innocent bystanders to further lead you into thinking that you must agree with them. The people that also fall victim to these traps might be people you love and respect. This is why it might be tempting to give in and to just "go with the flow." It is what the manipulator wants you to think. They want others to know that it is easier to go with a mass opinion than form their own.

What You Can Do: Speak up when you disagree with something. This is difficult because you do not want to cause conflict or controversy, but it becomes necessary to protect yourself. A disagreement does not always have to turn into an argument. If you approach the situation maturely, you can simply speak your mind to get your point across without requiring validation. You can provide this for yourself. Remind yourself that it is not other people's opinions that matter most. Your view of yourself dictates your self-esteem.

Believing it Won't Happen to You

Because a mind controller works hard to use other people, you might assume that they would instead do this to strangers or bystanders. One of the most challenging realities to face is that these individuals are more likely to attempt the act of mind control on a loved one. This happens because the task seems a lot easier—they already know you well. Instead of having to figure out the things that get under your skin, they have an idea of what to say and how to persuade you. Realizing this can be very hurtful, especially when you have many trusts invested in the person.

"I would never do anything to hurt you" is a promise that is often broken by a manipulator. With mind control, they are directly going against that promise, even if it doesn't feel hurtful at the moment. When someone does not respect you for who you are, they will do anything to change you. Suggesting you should get something else to eat or that you should shop elsewhere for clothing are two simple examples of how manipulators can use their conviction to change you.

You might not believe that these little changes mean much, but when you add them up, they can completely transform who you are as a person. It is not a great feeling to realize that you no longer recognize who you are. As upsetting as it is, you have to work on rebuilding yourself and getting back to your roots. It is normal to feel betrayed because this is what the manipulator has done to you—betrayed your trust.

What You Can Do: Never let your naive thinking get in the way of your rational thinking. You are not immune to the mind control that goes on around you. Your strength does not necessarily protect you from the intentions of all manipulators. By keeping yourself humble, you will always be on alert for the red flags presented by those who wish to change your mind.

The Blank Stares of Intimidation

Making a statement to someone and receiving a blank stare in return is intimidating for many reasons. One of the most prominent is that you do not know what they are thinking. It scares you because you might not know what to say or do next. A manipulator will use this technique to control your mind after you have said something vulnerable or profound. This will make you second-guess if what you said was "wrong" or incorrect somehow. You will end up prioritizing their feelings over your own.

They might follow this instance up with a statement that seems wise or all-knowing. When you combine the two actions, you are sure to believe that they can read your mind or that they know something you don't know. Both possibilities are unsettling in their ways. When you feel a negative emotion, understand that this is what your manipulator wants you to feel. They want to catch you off-guard and make you question everything that you have confirmed in your reality. By slowly breaking you down and staring at you blankly, you will get the idea that you came to this conclusion independently. It becomes maddening when you do not realize what is happening to you.

Chapter 36. Mind Control Techniques

Mind control involves using influence and persuasion to change the behaviors and beliefs of someone. That someone might be the person themselves, or it might be someone else. Mind control has also been referred to as brainwashing, thought reform, coercive persuasion, mental control, and manipulation, just to name a few. Some people feel that everything is done by manipulation. But if that is true to be believed, then important points about manipulation will be lost. Influence is much better thought of as a mental continuum with two extremes. One side has respectful and ethical influences and works to improve the individual while showing respect for them and their basic human rights. The other side contains dark and destructive influences that work to remove that human rights from a person, such as independence, rational thought, and sometimes their real identity.

When thinking of mind control, it is better to see it use influence on other people to disrupt something in them, as their way of thinking or living. The influence works based on what makes people human, such as their behaviors, beliefs, and values. It can disrupt the very way they chose personal preferences or make critical decisions. Mind control is nothing more than using words and ideas to convince someone to say or do something they might never have thought of saying or doing on their own.

There are scientifically proven methods that can be used to influence other people. Mind control has nothing to do with fakery, ancient arts, or even magical powers. Real mind control is the basis of a word that many people hate to hear. That word is marketing. Many people hate to hear that word because of the negative connotations associated with it. When people hear "marketing," they automatically assume that it refers to those ideas taught in business school. But the basis of marketing is not about deciding which part of the market to target or deciding which customers will likely buy this product. The basis of marketing is one very simple word. That word is "YES."

If a salesperson asks a regular customer to write a brief endorsement of the product they buy, they will hopefully say yes. If someone asks their significant other to take some of the business cards to pass out at work, they will hopefully say yes. If you write any blog and ask another blogger to provide a link to yours on their blog, they will hopefully say yes. When enough people say yes, the business or blog will begin to grow. With even more yesses, it will continue to grow and thrive. This is the very simple basis of marketing. Marketing is nothing more than using mind control to get other people to buy something or do something beneficial. And the techniques can easily be learned.

The first technique in mind control is to tell people what you want them to want. Never tell people to think it over or take some time. That is a definite mind control killer. People already have too much going on in their minds. When they are told to think something over, they will not. It will be forgotten, and then it will never happen. This has nothing to do with being stupid or lazy and everything to do with just being way too busy.

So the best strategy is to take the offensive and think for them. Everything must be explained in the beginning. Never assume that the other blogger will automatically understand the benefits of adding a link will be for them. Do not expect anyone to give a demonstration blindly. And merely asking for a testimonial, while it might garner an appositive response, probably will not garner a well-formed testimonial to the product. Instead, be prepared to explain the blog, show examples, and offer compelling reasons why this merger will benefit both parties. Have the demonstration laid out in great detail with notes on what to say when and visuals to go along with the letters, so all the other person has to do is present the information. Offer the customer a few testimonials that have already been received and ask them to choose one and personalize it a bit. Always be specific in explaining what is desired. Explain why it is desired. Show how this will work. Tell the person how to do it and why they should do it. If done correctly, it will feel exactly like one friend advising another friend on which is the best path to take. And the answer will be yes, simply because saying yes makes so much sense.

Think of the avalanche. Think of climbing all the way to the top of the highest mountain ever. Now, at the top, think of searching for the biggest, heaviest boulder on the mountain. Now, picture summoning up superhuman strength to push this boulder, dislodging it from the place it has rested for years and years. Once this boulder is loosened, it rolls easily over the edge of the cliff, crashing into thousands of other boulders on its way down the mountain, taking half of the mountain with it in a beautiful cascade of rocks and dirt. Imagine sitting there, smiling cheerfully at the avalanche that was just created.

Marketing and mind control are very like creating an avalanche. Getting the first person to answer yes might be difficult. But each subsequent yes will be easier. Always start at the top, never the bottom. Starting at the top is more complicated. It is more likely to come with more negative responses than positive responses in the beginning. But starting at the top also yields a much greater reward when the avalanche does begin. And the results will be far greater than beginning at the bottom of the mountain. Yes, the small rock is easier to push over. Then it can be built upon by pushing over another small rock, then another. This way can work, but it will take much longer than being successful at the top. No one ever went fishing for the smallest fish in the pond or auditioned for the secondary role just to be safe. Everyone wants that top prize. Do not be afraid to go for it.

On the other hand, never ask for the whole boulder the first time. Ask for part of it. This may seem directly contradictory, but it is not. Always start with a small piece. Make the beginning easier for everyone to see. Let other people use their insight to see the result. When the first bit goes well, then gradually ask for more and more and more.

Think of writing a guest spot for someone else who has their own blog. By sending in the entire manuscript first, there is a greater risk of rejection. Begin small. Send them a paragraph or two discussing them with the idea. Then outline the idea and send that in an email. Then write the complete draft you would like them to use and send it along. When asking a customer for a testimonial, start by asking for a few lines in an email. Then ask the customer to expand those few lines into a testimonial covering at least half a typed page. The customer will soon be ready for an hour-long webcast extolling the product's virtues and your great customer service skills.

Everything must have a deadline that exists. The important word here is the word 'real.' Everyone has heard the salesperson who said to decide right away because the deal might not be available later or another customer was coming in, and they might get it. That is a total fabrication, and everyone knows it to be true. There are no impending other customers, and the deal is not going to disappear. There is no real sense of urgency involved. But everyone does it. There are too many situations where people are given a fake deadline by someone who thinks it will instill a great sense of urgency for completing the task. It is not only totally not effective but completely unneeded. It is a simple matter to create true urgency. Only leave free things available for a finite amount of time. When asking customers for testimonials, be certain to mention the last possible day for it to be received to be able to be used. Some people will be unable to assist, but having people unable to participate is better than never beginning.

Always give before you receive it. And do not ever think that giving is fifty-fifty. Always give much more than is expected in return. Before asking for a testimonial from a satisfied customer, be sure to make numerous acts of exceptional customer service. Before asking a blog writer for a link, link theirs to yours many times. This is not about helping someone out so that they will help you. This is all about being so totally generous that the person who is asked for the favor cannot possibly say no. It might mean extra work, but that is how to influence other people.

Always stand up for something much bigger than average. Do not just write another blog on how to do something. Use a critical issue to take a stand and defend the stance with unbeatable logic and genuine passion. Do not just write a how-to manual. Choose a particular idea and sell people on it, using examples of other people with the same idea living the philosophy.

Never feel shame. This does not mean being extremely extroverted to the point of silliness or having a total lack of conscience in business dealings. In mind control, shamelessness refers to a full, complete belief that this course of action is the best possible course. Everyone will benefit greatly from it. This is about writing the best possible blog ever and believing that everyone needs to read it to improve their lives. It is about believing in a particular product so deeply that the feeling is that everyone will benefit from using it. Knowing deep inside that this belief is the correct belief ever and everyone should believe it.

Mind control uses the idea that someone's decisions and emotions can be controlled using psychological means. It uses negotiation or mental influence powers to ensure the outcome of the interaction is more favorable to one person over the other. This is what marketing is: convincing someone to do something particular or buy something in particular. Being able to control someone else's mind merely means understanding the power of human emotion and playing upon those emotions. It is easier to have a mental impact on people if there is a basic understanding of human emotions. Angry people will back down when the subject of their anger is not afraid. Angry people feed upon the fear of others.

Chapter 37. Influence People With Mind Control

A mind controller approaches the victim with the sole intent of cloning themselves, making the other person think like them. This is a complicated thing to do, so, to achieve it, one has to possess an inflated ego, lack doubts about themselves, and have a high sense of entitlement. All of us are susceptible to manipulation, and what matters is how much effect the mind control will have on us.

Psychologists studying mind control have found out that the entire process seems to adhere to a typical structure. This conclusion was made after a study was conducted on multiple marketing and networking companies which used mind control to persuade clients to purchase their products. One of the remarkable similarities is that all new members joining the companies underwent pre-planned training to recruit more people and convince potential customers to buy their products. The training sessions are meant to make the employees think like the company wants and use a mind twist to convince people.

Let us now look at the mind control process in detail:

Step 1: Understanding the target

Before anything else, the manipulator will seek to establish a bond or connection with their potential victim. Good intent, or friendship, will be the first step because it makes the victim lower all their social and psychological defenses. Once the controller gains the target's trust, they start reading them to devise the most effective method to invade them. The reading aims to tell whether their victim is susceptible to their manipulation. Just like any project manager, they do not like wasting time on a subject they suspect might outsmart them and lead to failure.

Multiple clues are used to scan the victim. They include vocal style, body language, social status, gender, emotional stability, etc. A person's traits can be used to decode the strength of their defenses. All this time, the manipulator will be asking themselves questions like, "Are you introvert or extrovert?" "Are you weakly?" "Are you emotional?" "Are you self-confident?" Humans give a lot of information about themselves when interacting with each other. This is something that the controller knows all too well. From these signs, they can quickly tell if the person is cooperating. They will look at body posture and immediately analyze the victim. Excess blinking might insinuate that a person is lying. Arms folded across the chest might show a lack of interest or insecurity. Taking enormous strides while walking might portray fear. As you can see, the body releases so much data at any given time that it is essential to be aware of the signs that you are giving out

When the attacker has collected enough data from the target, they now understand their interests, strengths, weaknesses, routines, and so on. Using this information, they can decide on an entry point, which will allow for easy and accurate manipulation. They also determine whether the target is worth the effort. If they see one as a favorable target, they move to the other step in the mind control process- unfreezing factual beliefs and values.

Step 2: Unfreezing Solid Beliefs and Values

All of us have some beliefs and values engraved deep within. Most of them are the principles that were instilled in us since childhood, and others have been acquired from experiences are we grow older. We rarely let go of them, but revise them as we proceed. Most of them make up our identities, so we do not like them being interfered with. If these principles are threatened, contradicted, or questioned at any point in time, our natural reaction is to defend them through all means possible. However, if a good-enough reason is given to us, so we voluntarily question them ourselves; we undergo a process known as "unfreezing."

Tons of reasons can lead us to unfreeze: a breakup, the death of a loved one, religious interference, getting evicted from our houses, to mention but a few. These situations force us to seek answers to complex cases, which goes as deep as questioning our sole beliefs and values. Take this, for example:

Way back when I am a teenager, we had some family friends who were solid Christians. It happens that my best friend, who was my exact age, came from this family. His name was Sam. Sam used to tell me about the Bible and its teachings, trying to convince me to accept salvation and live according to its instructions. I remember asking him why he was so insistent on this issue. He would respond that all problems were solvable with saving and that life was much more comfortable and happier. Fast-forward about fifteen years, Sam's mother was diagnosed with breast cancer. They tried all forms of treatment available at the time, but the cancer would grow back. One day, while talking to him about the issue, he looked at me with a pale face and said, "I think what they say about Christianity is not real!" Unsure about what he had just said, I asked him why he thought so. He responded that they had met tens of spiritual leaders for prayers, but his mother's cancer was only getting worse. What's worse, she would not live for more than a year.

Sad as Sam's story is, it makes us realize that some situations in life might force us to question the vital principles that we grow up with. In this case, my best friend had come to doubt the very same religion that he once felt had automatic solutions to all of life's problems. In the very same manner, a manipulator will dig deep into their victim's life to understand their vulnerabilities and exploit them fully. These people will say anything they think their targets would love to hear. Once the victim swallows the manipulator's comfort, there is a shift in power dynamics, and the target is now ready for the manipulation.

Step 3: Reprogramming the Mind

The mind control process seeks to separate the target from their initial beliefs and begin reprogramming their mind. The reprogramming is meant to install the manipulator's beliefs and values into the victim's mind. Apart from distancing the initial principles, the controller also tries their best to make them look wrong or harmful, or the cause of past mishaps in the victim's life. If the victim absorbs this reprogramming, their defense is lowered to zero, and they now become a robot that is ready to accept any operating system that is offered.

During the reprogramming phase, the attacker will ensure the victim has minimal contact with the outside world. They make everyone else appear insignificant to the victim because this raises their opportunity to deposit their malicious principles. This behavior is typical in cults, mostly crafted to sway their followers from mainstream human life. Some cults go as far as controlling their followers' food intake as a way of weakening them. The psychology behind this idea is that a weak person will always turn to the person they feel has the power to protect them or alleviate their suffering. The same happens in relationships, where one partner plays the controlling role. The victimized one has no choice but to adhere to the other. You might wonder why some people put up with violent partners. Still, so far, you must already understand that the problem is more profound than it appears. If you control a person's mind, you can control their lives.

Once the victim has been reprogrammed, the manipulator moves into the final phase of the mind control process known as "freezing."

Step 4: Freezing the New Beliefs and Values

Once the victim has been fed with contrasting principles by the offender, the offender applies tactics to cement the new beliefs into their brains. This is what psychologists call "freezing." The freezing bit is necessary because the controller is aware of the person's original ideas that might clash with their initial ones. As such, they need to force the victim to choose their malicious principles over their old ones. To do this, they might apply any of the following methods.

One of the methods is using the reward/punishment approach. When the victim acts according to the manipulator's demands, they are rewarded. Hopefully, you see the similarity between the freezing process and dog training. The dog is given treats when it follows the trainer's instructions. The trainer aims at solidifying the new skill in the dog by rewarding it. In the future, if the dog is instructed to do the same thing, it will not hesitate since it has been made to think that obeying the command is useful and attracts a reward. The same applies to mind control; when the victim follows, they are made to feel that what they did was right and deserves a reward.

Punishments are the second most-applied approach in the freezing process. If the victim deviates from the controller's commands, they are punished. If we go back to a cult scenario, they usually have defined punishments for violations of terms. During the Holocaust, for instance, any Germans who failed to hail Hitler were punished through imprisonment or death. In the same way, any German who was suspected of protecting the Jews was shot. Hitler understood that by punishing anyone who went against his rules, he would force every German to help him attain his ethnic cleansing objective. The psychological trick used in these situations is that the victim is made to see punishment as justice being served for breaking the rules.

Mind controllers' final method to solidify their manipulation is to transform their victims into their agents. Better put, once the controller feels that the victim's pseudo personality has materialized, they use them to distribute their worldviews. We said that the mind controller's list is to create a replica of themselves in the other person. Therefore, once the controlling process is complete, the victim starts living like the attacker without realizing it. Depending on the manipulation's nature, the victim might also be used to recruit more victims into the oppressor's way of thinking and living. This is especially true in the context of marketing and networking. From this explanation, we can readily tell why a wife is likely to be violent towards the kids if the husband is violent. The kids are also expected to be violent towards each other or their friends. The process of mind control is slow, but once it solidifies, it can result in devastating effects.

Chapter 38. Dark Persuasion

Whenever folks try to provide meaning to the notion of demeanor, their responses always come in various forms. Even though some could put their thoughts on the ads and advertisements which are everywhere in contemporary society, advocating you to patronize a specific product or service over the other others' heads fall back into the politicians who attempt to modify the minds of Republicans simply to get yet another vote in the polls. Both instances are right since they are messages targeted at altering the understanding of this topic. The purpose of diversion between ordinary persuasion and dim persuasion is the dark persuasion doesn't necessarily have a moral rationale.

Even though a standard persuader might attempt to convince someone for this individual's own great, a dim persuader does so together with motives that are not always great for another individual. They try to obtain a total grasp of the individual they would like to convince and take pains to do this since they understand the greatest motivation.

While persuasion consistently has ethical consequences, a dim persuader doesn't concern themselves with those consequences. In reality, they are mindful of these, but decide to put their eyes on their goal (s) rather than persuasion as a mental phenomenon in an individual's regular life. It's either that you're the person attempting to convince someone else or you're being persuaded. What makes the distinction between dark and ordinary is that the motivation for this. In mass media, politics, legal and advertising conclusions, persuasion comes to play all of the time. The results of instructing it in such areas are set utilizing persuasion to determine the topic of influence.

There are a few clear and crucial differences between behavioral and other brain control varieties, like brainwashing and hypnosis. Even though these two demands that the topic should be isolated from modifying their thoughts and individuality, persuasion doesn't require isolation. To be able to reach the target, manipulation is utilized on a single individual. Although persuasion may also be performed on a single topic to make them change their thoughts, there's also a chance of using it on a vast scale to alter the heads of an entire group or a whole society.

Because of this, persuasion is a much better mind control procedure and maybe more harmful since it can alter the minds of lots of people at precisely the same time rather than the head of only one individual at one time. Many people produce the error of believing that they have immunity to the consequences of persuasion because they think that they will always have the ability to observe every sales pitch that comes in their way.

They think they'll always have the ability to use logic to grasp what's happening and find a logical decision for this. As a result of how people aren't ever likely to fall for whatever they hear, this might be accurate if they utilize logic. It's likewise feasible to steer clear of persuasion since the debate doesn't augur nicely with the individual's beliefs, whatever the strength of this debate. Some individuals understand how to use clear messages to inspire people to market the industry's newest gadgets or goods. This information action is quite delicate, so the topic won't always recognize it; therefore, it's going to be rather difficult for them to continually have the ability to decide the information they will get.

Every time is said, it's extremely probable that you think about it in a terrible light. That is because it is inclined to automatically consider a conman or salesman who's always attempting to make them modify their view, and that will finally push them till this shift is reached. While black persuasion is notable in earnings and conning clinics, also, there are ways that persuasion may be used permanently, such as in diplomatic relationships between global bodies or at public service attempts. The difference only lies in the method by which in which the practice of persuasion is attracted to perform.

Dark Persuasion Methods

When an individual is prepared to modify the head of the topic by devoting them to do anything against their first frame of mind, the persuader will get some nicely laid out methods to help them reach their targets. Every day that passes, the goal will face various kinds of persuasion. Food manufacturers aim to receive their goal to test the recipes that are new or have them adhere to the earlier ones, even while studios may flaunt their most recent blockbuster films about the faces of the aims. In any situation may be whatever merchandise they're promoting, their principal intent is to generate more revenue, and that's the reason they're attempting to convince you. They couldn't care less about how this may affect you, and that is why they need to be quite careful and proficient in the art of subtle persuasion to make sure they don't deceive you off or make you plump.

As there are also lots of different brands attempting to convince you, they need to locate an exceptional approach to impress their perspectives on you. As a result of the effect of info on a vast selection of individuals, the methods used in it's been a topic of research for several decades, dating back to early times. That is because the influence is a really helpful instrument in controlling a large assortment of individuals. Beginning in the early 20th century, the proper analysis of those techniques started to grow. Bear in mind that the objective of attempting to convince people would be to push a compelling debate in an audience and have the positive.

They'll then internalize this information and embrace it as their fresh mindset or even means of life. Because of this, there's a great need to find very prosperous persuasion methods. Three dark persuasion methods are of fantastic value through recent years. We will go over those three:

Create a Need

This is only one of the most profitable methods of obtaining an individual to change their perspective or lifestyle. The individual hoping to convince a goal will create demand or concentrate on a demand that the topic already has. If that is achieved suitably, it's the capacity of enticing a fantastic deal to your goal. This signifies that to become prosperous, the persuader should interest in the demands that are far more significant to the goal.

This could be their requirement to fulfill their fantasies of fostering their self-esteem. It might also function as a desire for love, food, or shelter. This method will work out nicely since there's not anyway the topic isn't likely to require one or more of these items or need of anything at all for that matter. As there's not always, the goal is not likely to get dreams and ambitions. The persuader will probably simply find strategies to produce the sufferer understand how they can easily help the sufferer attain those dreams. The persuader can also tell their goal the goal will probably recognize their visions if they make certain adjustments to their faith or outlook.

As stated by the persuader, doing this will provide the target with a greater prospect of attaining success. For example, a young guy who wishes to get romantic with a woman may inform her that he'll help her boost her grades and eventually make her parents happy by obtaining a. Still, only when she's friends with his or her although this woman may believe she has finally discovered the salvation she desires, the simple truth is that the young guy is not very curious about how she plays in college. Her teenagers are just a lure for obtaining access to sexual activity.

Appealing to Social Needs

Another technique the persuader may utilize is identifying the goal of social demands. Even though this might not yield as many outcomes and the goal's main requirements will, it's still a powerful instrument in the hands of the persuader. Some are naturally attracted to audiences and want to be desired. They always wish for certain things, not because they want them, but because it includes certain prestige, making them feel like they belong to a bigger course. The idea of appealing to your target's societal needs is what's accessible through several TV advertisements where audiences are invited to purchase a product so they won't be "left behind." When they could recognize and allure to the societal needs of their goal, the outcome is that they can achieve a new field of the goal's interest.

Making Use of Loaded Words and Images

When an individual is hoping to convince someone else, they need to be cautious with their selection of words because words could make all of the difference. When there are many means to say something, one way of stating it might be more potent than another. When it's related to persuasion, among the essential things is understanding how to say the ideal thing at the ideal moment. Words are the most effective tools in communicating and understanding the perfect call-to-action phrases.

Dark persuasion is just one of the most effective dim psychology theories, but regrettably, it's always overlooked and suppressed. This might be because, unlike many different head control procedures, persuasion renders the goal using a selection. At another mind control procedure, the aim is forced to enter. Occasionally, this is achieved by placing them into isolation to ensure, in conclusion, they don't have any say in the procedure results. Regarding persuasion, the chips have been laid bare (though with the ulterior purpose in dim persuasion), so the goal is made to make the choice they think will fit them best.

Chapter 39. Dark Persuasion To Lookout For

After looking at the different types of persuasion and what they all mean, you may see why dark persuasion is such a bad thing and can be harmful to the victim. Recognizing the different techniques that the manipulator may use can make it easier to understand when used on you.

So, how exactly is a dark persuader able to use this idea to carry out their wishes? There are a few different types of tactics that a dark manipulator is going to use. Still, some of the most common options include:

The Long Con

The first method that we are going to look at is the Long Con. This method is kind of slow and drawn out, but it can be effective because it takes so long, and it is hard to recognize or pinpoint when something went wrong. One of the main reasons that some people can resist persuasion is that they feel that they are being pressured by the other person, making them back off. If they feel that there is a lack of rapport or trust with the person trying to persuade them, they will steer clear. The Long Con is effective because they can overcome these main problems and give the persuader precisely what they want.

The Long Con will involve the dark persuader to take their time, working to earn their victim's trust. They will take some time to befriend the victim and make sure that their victims trust and like them. The persuader will achieve this with artificial rapport building, which sometimes seems excessive, and other techniques will help increase the comfort levels between the persuader and their victim.

As soon as the persuader sees that the victim is adequately readied psychologically, the persuader will begin their attempts. They may start with some insincere positive persuasion. The persuader will lead their victim to choose or do some activities that will benefit the persuader. This is going to serve the persuader in two ways. First, the victim starts to become used to persuasion by that persuader. The second is that the victim will start making that mental association between a positive outcome and the persuasion.

The Long Con will take a long period to complete because the persuader doesn't want to make it too obvious what they are doing. An example of this is a victim who is a recently widowed lady who is vulnerable because of her age and from their grief. After her loss, a man starts to befriend her. This man may be someone she knows from church or even a relative. He starts to spend more time with her, showing immense kindness and patience, and it doesn't take too long for her guard to drop when he comes around.

Then this man starts to carry out some smaller acts of positive persuasion that we talked about before. He may advise her of a better bank account to use or a better way to reduce any monthly bills. The victim will appreciate these efforts and the fact that the man is trying to help her, and she takes the advice.

Over some time, the man then tries to use some dark persuasion. He may try to persuade her to let him invest some of her money. She obliges because of the positive persuasion that was used in the past. Of course, the man is going to work to take everything he can get from her. If the manipulator is skilled enough, she may feel that he actually tried to help her, but the money is lost because he just ran into some bad luck with the investment. This is how far dark persuasion can go.

Graduality

Often when we hear about acts of dark persuasion, it seems impossible and unbelievable. They fail to realize that this dark persuasion isn't ever going to be a big or a sudden request that comes out of nowhere. Dark persuasion is more like a staircase. The dark persuader will never ask the victim to do something big and dramatic the first time they meet. Instead, they will have the victim take one step at a time.

When the manipulator has the target only go one step at a time, the whole process seems like less of a big deal. Before the victim knows it, they have already gone a long way down, and the persuader isn't likely to let them leave or come back up again.

Let's take an example of how this process is going to look in real life. Let's say that there is a criminal who wanted to make it so that someone else committed the crimes for them. Gang bosses, cult leaders, and even Charles Manson did this same thing.

This criminal wouldn't dream of beginning the process by asking their victim to murder for them. This would send out a red flag, and no one in their right minds would willingly go out and kill for someone they barely know. Instead, the criminal would start by having the victim do something small, like a petty crime, or simply hiding a weapon for them. Something that isn't that big of a deal for the victim, at least in comparison.

Over time, the acts that the manipulator can persuade their victim to do will become more severe. And since they did the smaller crimes, the persuader now has the unseen leverage of holding some of those smaller misdeeds over the victim, kind of like for blackmail. Before the victim knows it, they are going to feel like they are in too deep. They will then be persuaded to carry out some of the most shocking crimes. And often, by this point, they will do it because they feel like they have no other choice.

Dark persuaders will be experts at using this graduality to help increase the severity of their persuasion over time. They know that no victim would be willing to jump the canyon or do the big crime or misdeed right away. So, the persuader works to build a bridge to get there. By the time the victim sees how far they are, it is too late to turn back.

Masking the True Intentions

There are different methods that a persuader can use dark psychology to get the things that they want. Disguising their true desires is very important for them to be successful. The best persuaders can use this approach in various ways. Still, the method they choose is often going to depend on the victim and the situation.

One principle used by a persuader is that many people will have a difficult time refusing two requests when they happen in a row. Let's say that the persuader wants to get $200 from the victim, but they do not intend to repay the money. The persuader may begin by saying that they need a loan for the amount of $1000. They may go into some details about the consequences to themselves if the persuader doesn't come up with that kind of money sometime soon.

The victim may feel guilt or compassion for the persuader, and they want to help. But $1000 is a lot of money, more than the victim can lend. From here, the persuader is going to lessen their request from $1000 down to $200, the amount that they wanted from the beginning. Of course, there is some emotional reason for needing the money. The victim feels like it is impossible to refuse this second request. They want to help out the persuader, and they feel bad for not giving in to the initial request when they were asked. In the end, the persuader gets the $200 they originally wanted, and the victim is not going to know what has taken place.

Another type of technique that the persuader can use is known as reverse psychology. This can also help to mask true intentions during the persuasion. Some people have a personality that is known as a boomerang. This means that they will refuse to go in the direction they are thrown away and instead will veer off into different directions.

If the persuader knows someone more of a boomerang type, they can identify a key weakness. For example, let's say that a persuader has a friend attempting to win over some girl they like. The persuader knows that the friend will use and then hurt that girl. The girl is currently torn between a malicious friend and an innocent third party. The persuader may try to steer the girl in the direction of the guy who is a good choice, knowing that she will go against this and end up going with the harmful friend.

Leading Questions

Another method of dark persuasion that can be used is known as leading questions. If you have ever had an encounter with a skilled salesman, verbal persuasion can be really impactful when deployed in careful and calibrated ways. One of the most powerful techniques that can be used verbally is leading questions.

These leading questions will be any questions intended to trigger a specific response out of the victim. The persuader may ask the target something like, "how bad do you think those people are?" This question will imply that the people the persuader is asking about are bad to some extent. They could have chosen to ask a non-leading question, such as "how do you feel about those people?"

Dark persuaders are masters at using leading questions in a way that is hard to catch. If the victim ever begins to feel that they are being led, they will resist, and it is hard to lead them or persuade them. If a persuader ever senses that their victim starts to catch what is happening, they will quit using that one and switch over to another. They may come back to that tactic, but only when the victim has quieted down a bit and is more influenceable again.

The Law of State Transference

The state is a concept that will take a look at the general mood someone is in. If someone is aligned with their deeds, words, and thoughts, this is an example of a healthy and harmonious state. The law of state transference will involve the concept of someone who holds the balance of power in a situation and can then transfer their emotional state onto the other person they interact with. This can be a potent tool for the dark persuader to use against their victim.

Initially, the influencer will force their state to match the state that their target naturally has. If the target is sad and talks slowly, the influencer will make their state follow this format. The point of this is to create a deep rapport with the target.

After we get to this state match, the influencer will alter their state subtly and see if they have some compliance for the victim. Perhaps they will choose to speed up their voice to see if the victim will speed up as well. Once the victim starts to show these signs of compliance, the influencer is at the hook point.

Chapter 40. Subliminal Persuasion

Subliminal persuasion means an advertising message displayed below the threshold of awareness or consumer awareness to persuade or help people change their minds without making them aware of what is going on. This is about affecting individuals with more than words. Some subliminal persuasion methods impact our stimuli with smell, eyesight, sound, touch, and taste.

There are 3 subliminal methods of persuasion that affect everyone. They are:

Building a Relationship

Building a relationship makes the other person feel comfortable. This will open up the individual even more. This can be accomplished through a healthy observation that matches their mood or state. This helps create confidence.

Power of Discussion

The power of discussion and convincing a person is connected to an advertiser's conversion. The correct words and inflections help you to be openly straightforward.

Suggestive Power

Associating useful and desirable stuff in a discussion or interaction enables an individual to become more open to fresh thoughts.

Suggestion and Emotional Intelligence

This stage may be described as having one central and dominant idea focused on the participant's conscious mind, which was to stimulate or decrease the various regions' physiological performance within the participant's body. Using different nonverbal and verbal suggestions was increasingly emphasized to convince the participant easily.

Achieve Optimal Persuasion With Subliminal Psychology

When you can expertly utilize a person's subconscious depths, your control over them is easy and vast. Subliminal psychology is one of the most effective ways to do this. This is an advanced technique, so do not expect to become effective overnight, but know that with time and dedication, you will be able to start putting subliminal messages into the minds of those around you. Once you can do this, you will control what they think and the actions they take. Essentially, you become almost like a puppet master for those around you.

Subliminal Message Techniques

This type of message or affirmation presented either visually or auditory sent in a way below what is considered normal for human visual or auditory perception. For example, a record might be playing on repeat, but you cannot hear it with your conscious mind. However, deep in your subconscious, you hear it and fully register everything that it is saying. In most cases, the messages used are meant to control you in some way or suggest that you do something.

For example, subliminal messages are commonly used in today's world to promote smoking cessation or weight loss. In general, you listen to recorded tapes with a specific message when you are sleeping. Your unconscious mind gets the message, but you never really hear it as your conscious self. Either way, research shows that it can be an effective tool to change your smoking or eating behaviors. You can use a similar technique to help change how people think to make them more vulnerable to the types of persuasion you prefer to use.

This is an effective way to control both your mind and others' minds, but it can be obvious when you do not use the techniques properly. As you read into the primary techniques, pay close attention to how you might introduce a person to them. This is important. Ultimately, your relationship with the person you are seeking to control will determine which of these techniques works the best.

Subliminal Messages During Sleep

This is one of the most common ways to use these types of messages. Most people will use them for themselves in this manner, but you can also use them with people you live with. For example, once you know your spouse is asleep, play a subliminal recording for about one hour. This is all it takes to get your message across.

Now, you must know for sure that they are sleeping, or else you could do more harm than good to your persuasion efforts. When you create your recording, use a calm and steady voice. State precisely what you want the person to do. Use no filler words. Use a maximum of 10 words and simply repeat it for an hour. Then, once the person is sleeping, play the recording at a very low volume close to their head so that their unconscious mind hears it.

Subliminal Flashes

These do not take as long as they are not as risky as the above method. These are a type of visual subliminal message. You can create the flashes to say what you want. What is nice about this technique is that the messages flash so quickly that the conscious mind often does not see what it says. Only the subconscious can understand and record it. So, you can get some control over a person's mind without them knowing what you are attempting to control.

Unless the person you want to do this with knows about subliminal psychology, you can just tell them you want to show them something you created. It is best to do this on a computer so that the screen is large enough to read and keep their full attention during the flashes.

Mixed Subliminal Messages

You can insert subliminal messages into the music or audiobooks that someone listens to regularly. Some programs can do this, so you do not have to be a tech expert to take advantage of this method. Just like with the subliminal messages during sleep, you will use a calm and steady voice. You want the messages to mix into the audiobook or music without being detected. Remember, the subconscious mind will pick up on it even when they cannot hear it when they are awake.

Just make sure to use these messages in something they listen to daily, or almost daily. They must hear it regularly to gain the most control.

Subliminal Notes

This is the easiest method, but it is also the simplest to figure out if you are not careful. You can put messages inside messages throughout your home. For example, when you create the grocery list, add something else you want but do not usually shop for. This puts the thought in the person's head when they are reading the list. This is ideal for smaller things that you want to persuade someone to think or do. So, keep it simple and use this method periodically. Unlike the above methods, it is not a good idea to use it every day.

Chapter 41. Psychological Manipulation

Today, the greatest battles are not fought on battlefields but in our minds and hearts!

And one of the biggest and strongest reasons for an inner battle is psychological manipulation. The biggest problem with psychological manipulation is not only the fact that we are often not prepared to deal with it but also the way we respond to it. And then, our greatest enemy, beyond the manipulator/oppressor, will become ourselves!

One of the main characteristics of psychological manipulation is that the manipulator (who can be a father, a mother, a brother or sister, a romantic partner, or a friend) exercises great control and power over us. And in that instant, our life becomes a real hell, and we live in tremendous anguish.

However, it is crucial to know that we are not, and should not be, impotent in this situation. There are various ways of combating these techniques of psychological manipulation.

The first step is to achieve consciousness, that is, to become aware of these techniques. Take a closer look and learn more objectively how your handlers "work" so you can protect yourself in the future. There are several Manipulation Techniques. See some of them below:

Psychological Manipulation Technique 1: Emotional Blackmail

Emotional blackmail is one of the oldest and most used manipulation techniques employed by human beings. But how does this work exactly?

Many people succumb to this trick because they feel they have no choice. At this point, phrases such as "If you cared about me, you would do this for me" are very common and make the manipulated person feel "forced" to make decisions they do not want. The target will make them anyway just to please the person who manipulates.

To avoid this manipulation technique, you will have to develop a strong sense of yourself, which involves knowing who you are, what your responsibilities are towards others, and who your true friends are. Usually, manipulative and blackmailing people tend to stay away from people with strong and solid personalities. Always remember: you always have a choice, and it is you who decides what you do with your life and how you want to react to the world.

Psychological Manipulation Technique 2: Focus on Negative Aspects

Some people like to put a "brake" on another's ideas and brilliant projects by emphasizing everything that could go wrong with them. These people often push him to doubt his projects and all the good things they would bring if they were put into practice. And at these times, the manipulators offer an endless list of questions that will only serve to create and raise doubts in their target's mind and heart.

For example, if you tell someone, you are thinking of traveling somewhere for a month to relax or go on vacation. If that person does not feel comfortable with the idea for some reason, they will probably react to your news by talking about the big travel hazards and the endless number of negative things that can be expected at the airport, etc.

At such times, if there is no apparent reason for such a reaction from the other person. If you are comfortable with your decision, bearing in mind that it will not harm you or others, choose not to listen to them and follow through with what you have decided.

Do not be overly swayed by this negative thinking pattern. If we think about something a lot, we attract it. If you put it in your head that something bad will happen and focus on it excessively, it is very likely to happen because the thought has life and is a great magnet.

Psychological Manipulation Technique 3: Teenage Rebellion

Unfortunately, sometimes the manipulative person adopts a childlike attitude to respond to his decision or something you have said to him.

For example, you want to leave your home and live independently. At first, it may even seem like everyone is happy and comfortable with your decision. But with time, as soon as you start looking for the perfect apartment, things start happening one after another. Some personal crisis occurs in the family, your mother or father suddenly (re)starts smoking, etc. These are adult people, but they adopt the behavior of a teenager and rebel against the idea.

The easiest way to deal with this is to make them see that their efforts to make you give up are worthless and that you will go ahead with your decision.

At first, it can be challenging and hard for you, especially if you have been exposed to this type of psychological manipulation for a long time. But as time goes by, it will become much easier, and you will see that even the people who manipulate you will come to respect you much more.

Psychological manipulation can be done throughout life, but always remember that you have the power to break this vicious cycle, and above all, remember that only one person can change your life: You!

Love and life together can be sources of well-being, pleasure, and support or a dead-end in which you feel suffocated and as if you are in the dark. The worst is that in many cases, these can be combined in a single day. Both feelings and problems begin when the relationship shifts rapidly. You find yourself immersed in a constant storm of feelings. This mainly happens to those who do not know how to escape such situations.

Many people are immersed in insane and toxic relationships in which they suffer psychological abuse of various kinds. They receive continuous damage to their integrity and honor and levels of disrespect that seem crazy when seen or heard from outside. Still, to the person who is now accustomed to suffering, they do not even produce a minimal reaction in their daily lives.

Love is not an excuse to hide the emotional pain that another person can cause us. It is our responsibility to ourselves to learn how to defend our rights and enforce them. Beyond your insecurity, the parental patterns that you picked up in your childhood, and all the mechanisms of self-deception that you can activate so as not to see reality, at the bottom of your being, you know how to differentiate what is right and what hurts you. That said, sometimes we need someone to tell us in a neutral and unbiased way that we have the right not to put up with what we know we do not deserve. Present a list of the main techniques of manipulation in unhealthy couples.

Manipulation to maintain social control: This technique usually begins in a very subtle way. The couple criticizes friends, family, work colleagues, and anyone in your social circle until they can completely annul the other's social network in such a way that the only source of effort and social support is the couple. This is manifested through jealousy: "If you love me, you would prefer me over your friends," etc. Emotional blackmail: This mechanism is famous for being used between pairs of individuals. It is also widely used by almost everyone, and you likely know it very well. It is about using phrases to handle guilt and repentance as a tactic to get something or as an impediment so that the other does not do something or does not abandon the manipulator. The manipulative person usually uses phrases like: "If you do that, it means you don't love me," "I do not want you to suffer, I would never do that to you," "I want the best for you, even if you let me destroy my life," "If you let me die," etc.

Chapter 42. Psychological Manipulation Technique

What Are Manipulators Looking For

Deceptive people in general: sociopaths, narcissists, liars, and so-called emotional vampires, and it is more a practical question to consider them than a theoretical one. For this purpose, if you've been victims of them at times, it's easier for you to identify and precede them now.

However, it can be said that deceptive people's aims are very straightforward, instrumental and that they follow a specific pattern. Most of them include:

- **Cancel your willpower**: they're trying to sow suspicions and want to bind you to their safety.

- Destroying your self-esteem: bringing a spoken word into the wheel of all you do or have done. We are not helpful and just want to point out the shortcomings.

- Passive-aggressive revenge: By avoiding you, they threaten you. They neglect you when you need them; it's enough to ask something, to get to stand up and not even speak to you.

- Prevent reality: they enjoy confounding people and creating misunderstandings and discussions. We step back after provoking a debate, loving the rants of others.

What Are the Psychological Manipulation Techniques?

Gaslighting

Gaslighting is one of the most subtle methods of deception. "It's never happened," "Imagine you" or " You're kidding?" These are some of the words that they use to manipulate and confuse our perception of reality, making us believe things have changed.

This instills an intense sense of anxiety and uncertainty in the victims, to the point of causing them not to trust in themselves, their memory, their understanding, or their judgment.

Projection

The manipulator transfers the negative characteristics to another person or shifts blame for his actions. This is being used heavily by narcissists and psychopaths, saying that the wickedness surrounding them is not their fault but anyone else's.

Meaningless Conversations

The conversation lasts ten minutes. Now is the time for you to leave the conversation. Manipulators say ridiculous things, offer illogical excuses, refer to past events, and throw smoke in the eyes…

We generate discord and misunderstanding. We are doing monologues, and they are trying to confuse you with their gab. Some advice? Get straight to the point and then better if you can leave after 5 minutes. Your feelings would be thankful.

Generalizations and Denigrations

They make generic, vague, and abstract statements. They may seem intellectual. In reality, they are just elusive. Their conclusions are too general; their goal is to demean your e debilitate your opinions.

For example, "you always want to be right," "anything annoys you," "never once you agree." Keep calm. You can opt for irony, with a simple "thank you," or you can ignore them with a curt, "I think you're a little upset. We'll talk later."

Absurdity

Remember that they try to undermine your morals and cause you to question what you believe. They can put words you have never said in your mouth; they will make you think you have the superpower to "read your mind." But that's not the case, and they are just tricks and deceptions. You can help yourself with simulated defeat. Tell them they are right for them to believe it, but stick to your position. You can also respond to their blackmail with an "okay" or with harsh sentences.

The important thing is that you take your self-esteem out of their hands. Remember that they want to demoralize you so that they can control you. After making you weak, the task will be much easier.

Good Mask

"Yes, but..." If you manage to buy a house, they will tell you that it is a pity that you do not yet have a place by the sea; if you are dressed more elegant than ever, they will tell you that another pair of earrings would have been better for you. If you have written an impeccable report, they will tell you that the staple is not well fixed.

But don't let yourselves be influenced: you know what you are worth! Your successes and virtues are worth more than their manipulation techniques. Don't give them any credibility and hang out with people who spend more time pointing out the positives and encouraging you; those who compliment you when you deserve them and who make constructive, non-destructive criticisms.

Positive Reinforcement

Through positive reinforcement learning, behavioral performance is linked to achieving a good outcome. This does not have to be an entity, not even tangible; in many cases, food, liquids, a smile, a verbal message, or the presence of a friendly emotion are likely to be seen as favorable reinforcement.

A father who congratulates his young daughter if she uses the toilet correctly promotes positive reinforcement learning; the same thing happens when a business offers cash incentives to its most successful workers. When we get a bag of potato chips after placing a coin into a retailer.

The definition of "positive reinforcement" refers to the reward that accompanies the action. In contrast, positive reinforcement is the process that creates the connection the learner produces. Nevertheless, the words "reinforcement" and "reinforcement" are frequently used interchangeably, possibly because such a distinction does not exist in English.

From a technical point of view, we can conclude a favorable variance between a particular response and an appetizing stimulus in positive reinforcement. The knowledge of this risk motivates the subject to act to get the reward (or strengthening).

Negative Reinforcement

In comparison to what occurs in the positive, the instrumental response in the negative reinforcement includes the absence of an aversive stimulus, i.e., an event or condition that motivates the subject to avoid or attempt not to come into contact with it.

In behavioral terms, the reinforcement of this technique is the absence or non-appearance of the aversive stimulus. As we stated earlier, the word "negative" refers to the fact that the reward does not consist of obtaining inspiration but in the absence thereof.

This type of learning is divided into two processes: training to escape and train to prevent it. The conduct precludes the presence of the aversive stimulus in the negative reinforcement of avoidance. For example, when an agoraphobic individual avoids using public transport to escape the fear this presupposes, it is reinforced negatively.

On the contrary, the escape is the disappearance of an aversive stimulus present before the subject executes the behavior. Some examples of negative escape reinforcement include an alarm clock that stops by pressing a button, a mother buying a request for her child to stop weeping, or taking a pain reliever to relieve pain.

Brainwashing

The concept of brainwashing is very close to that of 'mind control.' It is an idea without a strictly scientific basis that suggests that the will, thoughts, and other mental facts of individuals can be modified through techniques of persuasion that would introduce unwanted ideas into the psyche of the 'victim.' If we define the concept in this way, we see that it has a marked similarity. However, the term "suggest" is less ambitious.

Although the idea of brainwashing is not entirely wrong, this popular concept has some scientific connotations which have led many experts to reject it in favor of more modest ones. The instrumental use of the term in legal proceedings has contributed to this, particularly in child custody disputes.

Mind control is also known as brainwashing, coercive persuasion, mind control, and mental manipulation. All these terms mean a process that a group or individual systematically uses to force someone to do what they want through thinking of that person. In the majority of cases, these systematic processes are realized without the conscious knowledge of the person.

There are times when we can use mind control over ourselves for a variety of reasons. Self-hypnosis is in this category. We use this kind of mind control, which is voluntary on our part, with our conscious consent, to reinforce a positive idea or to change our minds.

However, this is not the same as the "mind control" phase, or it involves brainwashing. These phrases mean that a person's mind is systematically changed without knowing it, either in the agreement or against his will.

They are carried out through unethical, manipulative tactics, and other means, all designed to control someone's mind. In such cases, they are realized so that one person or group can take full control of others' thoughts and actions. So, when the terms "mind control" and "brainwashing" are used, it is said that specific tactics are used to take control of another at the expense of the manipulated person.

This is interesting because the idea of brainwashing falls under the category of social influence. This is because the concept of brainwashing is used to induce a victim's mental manipulation. This means that brainwashing and mind control are used to completely change how someone thinks and perceives things concerning their beliefs in a particular social device. This is achieved by using various means to change a person's attitudes, behaviors, and thoughts. The person is like a puppet who does everything the manipulator wants.

Chapter 43. Covert Emotional Manipulation

Covert emotional manipulation is used by people who want to gain power or control over you by deploying deceptive and underhanded tactics. Such people want to change the way you think and behave without realizing what they are doing. In other words, they use techniques that can alter your perceptions in such a way that you think that you are doing it out of your own free will. Covert emotional manipulation is "covert" because it works without you being consciously aware of that fact. People who are good at deploying such techniques can get you to do their bidding without your knowledge; they can hold you "psychologically captive."

When skilled manipulators set their sights on you, they can get you to grant them power over your emotional well-being and even your self-worth. They will put you under their spell without you even realizing it. They will win your trust, and you will start attaching value to what they think of you. Once you have let them into your life, they will then begin to chipping away at your very identity in a systematic way. As time goes by, you will lose your self-esteem and turn into whatever they want you to be.

Covert emotional manipulation is more common than you might think. Since it's subtle, people are rarely aware that it's happening to them, and in some cases, they may never even notice. Only keen outside observers may be able to tell when this form of manipulation is going on.

You might know someone who used to be fun and festive. She got into a relationship with someone else, and a few years down the line, she seems to have a completely different personality. If it's an old friend, you might not even recognize the person she has become.

That is how powerful covert emotional manipulation can be. It can completely overhaul someone's personality without them even realizing it. The manipulator will chip away at you little by little. You will accept minute changes that fly under the radar until the old a different version of you replaces you, build to be subservient to the manipulator.

Covert emotional manipulation works like a slow-moving coup. It requires you to make small progressive concessions to the person that is trying to manipulate you. In other words, you let go of tiny aspects of your identity to accommodate the manipulative person, so it never registers in your mind that there is something bigger at play.

When the manipulative person pushes you to change in small ways, you will comply because you don't want to "sweat the small stuff." However, there is a domino effect that occurs as you start conceding to the manipulative person. You will be more comfortable making subsequent concessions, and your personality will be erased and replaced in a cumulative progression.

Covert emotional manipulation occurs to some extent in all social dynamics. Let's look at how it plays out in romantic relationships, in friendships, and at work.

Emotional Manipulation in Relationships

There is a lot of emotional manipulation in romantic relationships, and it's not always malicious. For example, women try to modify men's behavior to make them more "housebroken"; that is just normal. However, certain instances of manipulation where the person's intention is malicious, and he/she is motivated by a need to control or dominate over the other person.

Positive reinforcement is perhaps the most used covert manipulation technique in romantic relationships. Your partner can get you to do what he wants by praising you, flattering you, giving you attention, offering your gifts, and acting affectionately.

Even the seemingly nice things in relationships can turn out to be covert manipulation tools and props. For instance, your girlfriend could use intense sex as a weapon to reinforce a certain kind of behavior in you. Similarly, men can use charm, appreciation, or gifts to reinforce certain behaviors in the women they are dating.

Some sophisticated manipulators use what psychologists call "intermittent positive reinforcement" to gain control over their partners. The way it works is that the perpetrator will shower the victim with intense positive reinforcement for a certain period, then switch to just giving her normal levels of attention and appreciations. After a random interval of time, he will again go back to the intense positive reinforcement. When the victim gets used to the special treatment, it's taken away. When she gets used to standard therapy, the special treatment is brought back, and it all seems arbitrary. Now, the victim will get to a place where she becomes "addicted" to the special treatment. Still, she has no idea how to get it. Hence, she starts doing whatever the perpetrator wants, hoping that one of the things she does will bring back the intense positive reinforcement. In other words, she effectively becomes subservient to the perpetrator.

Negative reinforcement techniques are also used in relationships to manipulate others covertly. For example, partners can withhold sex to compelling the other person to modify their behavior in a specific way. People also use techniques such as the silent treatment and withholding of love and affection.

Some malicious people can create a false sense of intimacy by pretending to open up to you. They could share personal stories and talk about their hopes and fears. When they do this, they create the impression that they trust you, but their intention may be to get you to feel a sense of obligation towards them.

Manipulators also use well-calculated insinuations to get you to react in a certain way at the moment to modify your behavior in the long run. Such insinuations can be made through words or even actions. In colloquial terms, we call this "dropping a hint." People in relationships are always trying to figure out what the other person wants out of that relationship, so a manipulative person can drop hints to get you to do what they want without ever having to take responsibility for the actions that you take because they can always argue that you misinterpreted what they meant.

Dropping hints isn't always malicious (for example, if your girlfriend wants you to propose, she may leave bridal magazines out on the table). However, malicious insinuations can be very hurtful, and they can chip away at your self-esteem. Your partner can make insinuations to suggest you are gaining weight. You aren't making enough money or implying that your cooking skills aren't any good. People use hints to get away with "saying without saying," any number of hurtful things that could affect your self-esteem.

Emotional Manipulations in Friendships

Covert emotional manipulation is quite common in friendships and casual relationships. Companies tend to progress slower than romantic relationships, but that just means that it can take a lot more time for you to figure out if your friends are manipulative. Manipulation in friendships can be confusing because even well-meaning friends can come across as malicious. That's because there is a certain social rivalry between even the closest friends, which explains the concept of "frenemies."

Manipulative friends tend to be passive-aggressive. This is where they manipulate you into doing what they want by involving mutual friends rather than directly coming to you. Passive aggression works as a manipulation technique because it denies you a chance of directly addressing whatever issue your friend is raising. So in a manner of speaking, you lose by default.

For example, if a friend wants you to do her a favor, instead of coming out and asking you, she goes to a mutual friend and suggests that she asks you on her behalf. When a mutual friend approaches you, it becomes very difficult for you to turn down the request because of added social pressure. When you say no, your whole social circle now perceives you as selfish.

Passive aggression can also involve the use of silent treatment to get you to comply with a request. Imagine a situation where one of your friends talks to everyone else but you. It's going to be incredibly awkward for you, and everyone will start prying, wondering what the issue is between the two of you, and taking sides on the matter.

Friends can also covertly manipulate you by using subtle insults. They can give you back-handed compliments that have hidden meanings. When you take the time to think about what they meant by the compliment, you will realize that it's an insult in disguise, which will bruise your self-esteem and possibly modify your behavior.

Some friends can manipulate you by going on a "power trip" and controlling your social interactions. For example, there are those friends who insist that every time you hang out, it should be in their apartment or at a social venue of their choosing. Such friends often intend to dominate your friendship, so they are keen to always have the "home ground advantage" over you. They'll try to push you out of your comfort zone just so that you can reveal your weaknesses, and you can then become more emotionally reliant on them.

Manipulative friends tend to excessively capitalize on your friendship, and to a disproportionate degree. They will ask you for lots of favors with no regard for your time or your effort. They are the kinds of friends who will leverage your friendship every time they need something but then make excuses when it's their turn to reciprocate.

Emotional Manipulation at Work

There are many reasons why your colleague may want to manipulate you. It could be you are on the same career path, so he wants to make you look bad. It could be that he is lazy, and he wants to stick you with his responsibilities. It could also be that he is a sadist, and he just wants to see you suffer.

One-way people at work exert their dominance over others is by stressing them out and then, almost immediately, relieving the stress. Say, for example, you make a minor error on a report, and your boss calls you into his office. He makes a big fuss and threatens to fire you, but then towards the end, he switches gears and reassures you that your job is secure as long as you do what he wants. That kind of manipulation works on people because it makes them afraid and gives them a sense of obligation at the same time.

Some colleagues can manipulate you by doing you small favors and then reminding you of those favors every time they want something from you. For instance, if you made an error at work and a colleague covered for you, he may hold it over your head for months or even years to come. He is going to guilt you into feeling indebted to him.

Chapter 44. Covert Emotional Manipulation Tactics

Dark Psychology also spends time looking at Covert Emotional Manipulation. It is more commonly referred to as CEM. CEM is a way to gain real power over someone without them, even realizing it is happening. You will be so enthralled that these sneaky tactics will have you doing things you would not usually agree to.

We have already talked about manipulation, but there are so many different forms of it, which is pretty important. It allows criminals and people with mal intent into your life and breaks you down mentally. The effects of this type of manipulation can last forever if you are not careful. As noted, it is insanely subtle, which means looking for the red flags are very important.

Covert Emotional Manipulation looks different depending on the people involved. Often, the victim will be slowly made to feel like they can't do anything without the other. It is a strange sort of codependency that happens over time. This happens without manipulation on occasion; the difference is when your partner intentionally gets you to behave or think differently.

It may start with offers of help for simple tasks that you usually do on your own. They may follow it up with a critique to make you question your ability to do it. It starts small, but they will continue to poke at it until you start to believe you can't do it on your own truth. You can see it worked into all kinds of things and a ton of relationships.

Depending on who you have allowed doing this to you, it could be mostly harmless. On the other hand, many people with less than genuine intentions could take this to an extreme.

This type of manipulation can turn it to flat out brainwashing. In that case, you may lose your free will forever.

People that use CEM against other people pay great attention to detail. This can be endearing as it appears as if they are learning about you. In reality, they are observing your behavior, understanding what makes you tick. This will grant them access to how to manipulate your emotions subtly to get what they want. They are truly hunting for your weaknesses.

The heinous people and criminals that do this in life are calculating. They tend to have bigger plans, and you are simply playing a role. They have no care or regard for how you feel or for the damage they are causing you. All they can see is the outcome that they are striving for. Finding that they are unable ever to sustain relationships is not surprising because of the selfish nature of how they are wired.

As time goes on, CEM turns into something else. What started as little jabs that looked like they were made from love become something much darker. As you start to lose control and bend your will, the aggressor will pounce. They can become domineering. Also, they will begin to tear you down piece by piece to gain complete control.

Playing with someone's emotions is a great way to gain control over them. Some people would rather bombard someone with love to get them to do what they want, rather than being crasser or crude about it. Love bombarding is very typical of the narcissist. It is its form of manipulation, and it can be downright cruel in reality.

You will feel like the most important person in someone's world. You will go along with what they say hook, line, and sinker because you truly trust in what they say. Once this person has you there, they can easily force their will and beliefs onto you. Fighting against this is extremely difficult for some people.

Becoming solid in your belief system will make it more difficult for someone to pray on your emotions. Another way to combat this dark tendency is to work on really knowing yourself.

When you spend the time meditating, self-actualizing, and maintaining control of yourself, it is much easier to fend off attacks on your emotions.

When someone manipulates your emotions, it can have a detrimental impact on the rest of your life. Narcissists and Psychopaths cannot often have true feelings. They are shut off, in a way. So, them playing with yours is a simple way to gain control of you and the situation they are in. Practicing NLP's art can also give you signs of when these types of people are trying to harm you.

Gut feelings and red flags should be paid attention to. Naturally, we have instincts, and sometimes something just feels off from the beginning. Maybe you meet someone, and they seem just a little too perfect, or you just feel a bit uncomfortable around them, don't disregard these thoughts and feelings. We are wired to sense danger. This is not just the physical danger that we sense but also an emotional and mental danger. The phrase "go with your gut" is a good one that can help you avoid unpleasant situations.

Chapter 45. Brainwashing

Brainwashing is a particular form of manipulation or control over someone else used through very specific means. Usually, when you use brainwashing, you refer to a particular pattern typically used in hostage situations to try to get the other person to give in to control. Brainwashing most often occurs in the context of trying to get someone else to conform to something new. The purpose of brainwashing comes right down to thought reform—when it is used, the entire purpose is to get compliance and reeducation to encourage someone to become someone they are not. We will also take a look at the most common steps to going through the process.

Defining Brainwashing

Perhaps the first reported source of brainwashing was recorded during the Korean War. During this time, it is said that several American prisoners of war were held in prison camps and were brainwashed into believing that they had engaged in germ warfare and pledged allegiance to communism. When this happened, they were effectively stripped of their identities, forced to comply, and denounced everything that they had known of their past lives. They had their thoughts rewritten through coercion and threat.

Brainwashing is a form of influence designed to be invasive and forceful to break down others' minds. They eventually comply in hopes of protecting themselves from being hurt worse. It becomes self-preservation to do whatever they are told to do to protect themselves. As a result, they are willing to take on complex personas that are entirely dictated by the captors.

The Science of Brainwashing

Brainwashing is believed to work because the agent, that is to say, the person doing the brainwashing, is gaining complete and utter control over the target. This person is being brainwashed in the first place. This makes it so that the agent has complete power over everything and anything related to the individual. The agent gets to determine when needs can be met and how they are. Over time, the result is a systematic destruction of everything that goes into making that person who they are. Over time, because they can't meet their needs, they feel like their identities are destroyed to the point of no longer being viable. Over time, through torture, coercion, and control, brainwashing can occur. Typically, however, it should be noted that the individual's old identity can be returned over time. After leaving the dangerous situation, it is possible, with therapy, for the old identity to be returned.

Using Brainwashing

When brainwashing happens, it is usually done through several steps designed to be as effective as possible. These steps are brutal, but that is the entire purpose of it all. It is designed to be brutal so that it can have its intended effect. Let's go over the steps that go into this method now.

1. Assault on identity: The first step is designed to help to break down the self. It is an assault on your direct identification. It is designed to make you feel like you are not who you are. Typically, in the actual context, the agent will deny everything. They will directly contradict anything that the individual may say is true. As this happens, the individual is repeatedly attacked to the point of exhaustion and eventually even giving in to what the other person said.

2. Guilt: The individual has to be made to feel guilty. This is done so that the individual is more likely to give up his or her identity. When that entire identity is wrapped up in guilt, it is easier to get rid of it and pretend that it is not there than it is to do anything else. By rejecting the identity entirely, the individual is even closer to being brainwashed.

3. Self-betrayal: The stage in which the agent gets the target to agree with what has been said. The agent wants the target to recognize that he or she is bad and that it is time to denounce who they once were. They need to feel like they were wrong to have the opinions that they can do better.

4. Breaking point: That betrayal culminates in what is known as the breaking point—the point at which the individual just cannot cope any longer. At this point, the target goes through what is commonly referred to as a nervous breakdown—sobbing, depression, and generally just not coping well. They may be in the middle of a psychotic episode or may have other problems going on as well. They believe that all hope is lost, and that is the key to the whole process.

5. Leniency: When all seems beyond help, that is when the agent can get in and take control. Usually, with a small kindness—offering a bit of leniency or otherwise offering a drink of water, and that small kindness is enough to make the individual feel indebted.

6. The compulsion to confess: At this point, the target realizes that they have hope. All is not lost, and they can do what it will take to protect themselves. So, what they do is they confess. They want to try to channel and relieve their stress and guilt, so they confess.

7. Channeling the guilt: At this point, the target assumes that they are just wrong. The target assumes that they are wrong for some reason, and want to get rid of that sense— which gets connected to their guilt. They wrap all of their guilt about identity together to release it.

8. Releasing the guilt: The target realizes the problem is not with him or her, but rather with the guilt and beliefs. They do not have to be permanently bad or problematic—they can get better and do better to release the pain and escape. So, they do this through confessions.

9. Progress toward harmony: At this point, the target can begin making a move toward what they perceive as salvation or goodness—they can rebuild themselves to be good. In doing so, in deciding to assimilate and comply, they can make the abuse stop. In denouncing the past, the target can begin choosing the new belief system, making a conscious choice to assimilate and comply. As a result, they conclude that this new identity is reliable and safe, and they follow it.

10. Final confession: Finally, the new life is clung to. All old beliefs are rejected, and the individual pledges allegiance to the new life instead.

Chapter 46. Brainwashing Technique

While we are focusing more on the dark psychology that comes with manipulation, you will find examples of manipulation that can occur in our daily lives. Often we don't think that we are doing it at all. We think of manipulation to get what we want from other people, but sometimes we do it to save others' feelings. For instance, how many times have you lied to someone to let them know they looked good in something, even though you didn't think so. You did this to spare their feelings, whether they are a family member or a close friend!

Even though the point of doing this was good, you still were looking to save yourself. You didn't need to be the one who said something means about the other person and how they looked. This kind of manipulation can be seen as a good thing, though, because it was done to spare the other person's feelings in the process.

With that in mind, we will take a brief look at some of the most common manipulation techniques available to us to get what we want. You are sure to recognize at least a few of these as ones that you have used at some point or another in your life, even if you did not think of it as manipulation at the time. Some of the most common manipulation techniques that you can use includes:

Lying is something that we have all done at one point or another. We do this to confuse the other person, make sure that others believe something we want, or even get ourselves out of trouble. You may decide not to go to a party one night because you don't want to go, so you say you had something with family come up. You don't like the gift, but you smile and tell the giver that you love it. We have all used lying at one point or another, and it is considered a type of manipulation. When it comes to a dark manipulator, though, lying will be done in a deliberate way that helps them succeed while ensuring that the other person gets harmed.

Another method that you can use is going to include not telling the whole story. You can imagine yourself as a teenager with this one. Your parents asked you where you were, and you say at the mall with Susan and Sally. But you leave out the fact that the boy they don't like, John, was there as well. You technically were at the mall with your friends, but you leave out the part of the story that will get you in trouble or make someone else mad.

Punishment. This is often reserved for the dark forms of manipulation, but it will still be used on occasion. Without thinking of it as manipulation, we may punish someone else when they don't do what we want. How often have we used the silent treatment against a friend or a spouse who didn't do something that we wanted?

None of us want to end up being the one to blame for something even if we were the ones who did it. We will try to get out of it by denying that anything happened at all. With another tactic known as minimizing, we may admit that something did happen. Still, we will downplay the actions and make it feel like the other person was overreacting and misreading the situation. How many occurrences have we said something we didn't mean. When the person came back to get mad at us about it, we turn it around and minimize it by saying they didn't hear the words the right way. These are probably the two methods of manipulation that we use the most to help keep us out of trouble as much as possible.

Another option that you can work with is going to be known as spinning the truth. This is something that we see all of the time with politicians. It is done so often we can usually see it happening ahead of time. The spinning of the truth will be done to turn some lousy behavior into something that doesn't seem as bad to others. This takes a bit more work to accomplish because you have to think on your feet and develop something plausible. Still, the point is to change up the story to change your perception from other people.

Even though we are not fond of it when other people do this to us, we can all admit that we have played the victim at one point or another. We know that people are more likely to feel bad when we can come up with a sob story. Maybe we try to make one particular person feel bad about how they treated us, and we will do it in front of others so that we can get what we want. Other times we may come up with a big sob story to get out of a group thing, out of late work, and more. The point here is to turn ourselves into a big victim, even though we don't deserve to have that kind of attention or that title.

Positive reinforcement is something that every parent who has wanted to keep their sanity and who has wanted to make sure that their children will follow the rules and behave will use at one point or another. This is where you will reward the behaviors you really like, the behavior you want to make sure sticks around. This can include paying a lot of attention to the target, excessive charm, and expensive presents.

Think of it this way. When your toddler is learning the rules, it is often more efficient to convince them to listen and do what they should when they get a reward. Whether it is a sticker chart, a reward of a toy or some candy or lots of praise, you will find that the more consistent you are with these, the more the toddler will continue to follow the rules. This is precisely how the idea of positive reinforcement is going to work whether you use it on a child or an adult with manipulation.

Diversion can be another way to focus on yourself and work to make sure that the other person doesn't catch on to your true meaning. How many times have you felt that someone was trying to get at your lie or coming close to figuring something you had hidden? Then you would divert the conversation away? No matter how firm they tried to get back to it, you would just push it all back at them or turn the conversation over to a new topic to get the results you wanted and keep the target away from guessing your true intentions.

Sarcasm is a technique that we have all used at one point or another, especially when we want to feel frustrated about something. We may not be able to explain things to someone else. This is going to be done in a way to make us feel more superior to other people and to lower the self-esteem of the victim. Whether we are doing it with friends as a joke or using it against someone else we want to belittle to make ourselves feel better, sarcasm is something that we are all going to be pretty familiar with.

Guilt-tripping is an excellent way for us to make sure that we can get what we want from other people. We will say things like the other person have life easy, really selfish, or don't care about us. This will make the other person feel bad and like something they did was wrong, even if they were trying to help you out with something, and they are more likely to want to try and help you some more.

How many occurrences have we all tried to use some form of flattery to get what we want from other people? This helps us get on the other person's right side, and all it takes is flattering the target praising them and using all our charm. No matter who they are, the target will be happy to get all of this praise and compliments, and it will help lower their guard a little bit in the process. This is a great one that can be used when we want to get a new job or gain up in our position when an opening happens.

As you will notice, there are many different methods of manipulation that we can use in our daily lives. It doesn't seem to matter whether we are using them just to help us get by or if we are trying to use them to help us be dark manipulators and always get what we want, no matter the consequences. How many of the methods on the list have you used at one point or another in your own life to get what you wanted?

Chapter 47. Hypnosis

What is Hypnosis

There have been many definitions of what hypnosis is. The American Psychological Association has defined hypnosis as a cooperative interaction where the hypnotist will give suggestions to the person; he picks which he or she will respond to. Edmonton said that a person is simply but in a deep state of mind when undergoing hypnosis. Hypnosis is, therefore, when a person enters a state of mind in which a person finds himself or herself vulnerable to a hypnotist's suggestions. Hypnosis is not new to us because many people have seen it in movies, cartoons, or been to magic shows or performances where participants are told to do usual acts, and they do it. For sure, some people believe that hypnosis exists and would do anything to avoid being a victim, while others believe that its fiction.

Induction

Induction is considered as stage one of hypnosis. There are three stages in total. Induction aims to intensify the partaker's expectations of what follows after, explaining the role they will be playing, seeking their attention, and any other steps needed during this stage. There are many methods used by hypnotists to induce a participant to hypnosis. One of them is the "Braidism" technique, which requires a hypnotist to follow a few steps. This technique is named after James Braid. The first step would be to find a bright object and hold it in your left hand and specifically between the middle, fore, and thumb fingers.

The object should be placed where the participant will fix their stare and maintain the stare. This position would be above the forehead. It is always crucial that the hypnotist remind the partaker to keep their eyes on the object. If the participant wonders away from the object, the process will not work. The participant should be focused entirely on the item. The participant's eyes will begin to dilate, and the participant will start to have a wavy motion. A hypnotist will know that his participant is in a trance when the participant involuntarily closes his or her eyelids when the middle and forefingers of the right hand are carried from the eyes to the object. When this does not happen, the participant begins again, guiding that their eyes are close when the fingers are used in a similar motion. Therefore, this puts the participant in an altered state of mind. He or she is said to be hypnotized. The induction technique has been considered not to be necessary for every case. Research had shown that this stage is not as important as already known when it came to the induction technique's effects. Over the years, there have been variations in the once original hypnotic induction technique, while others have preferred to use other alternatives. James Braid's innovation of this technique still stands out.

Suggestion

After Induction, this follows the suggestion stage. James Braid left out the word suggestion when he first defined hypnosis. However, he described this stage as attempting to draw the partaker's conscious mind to focus on one central idea. James Braid would start by minimizing the functions of different parts of the partaker's body. He would then emphasize using verbal and non-verbal suggestions to get the partaker into a hypnotic state. Hippolyte Bernheim also shifted from the physical form of the partaker. This well-known hypnotist described hypnosis as the Induction of a particular physical condition, which increases one's susceptibility to the participant's suggestions. Suggestions can be verbal or one that doesn't involve speech. Modern hypnotist uses a different form of suggestions that include non-verbal cues, direct verbal suggestions, metaphors, and insinuations. Non-verbal suggestions that may be used include changing the tone, mental imagery, and physical manipulation. Mental imagery can take two forms. One consists of those that are delivered with permission and those that are done none the less and are more authoritarian.

When discussing hypnosis, it would be wise if one would be able to distinguish between the conscious mind and the unconscious mind. While using suggestions, most hypnosis will try and trigger the conscious mind other than the unconscious mind. In contrast, other hypnotists will view it as a way of communicating with the unconscious mind. Hypnotists such as Hippolyte Bernheim and James Braid, together with other great hypnotists, see it as trying to communicate with the conscious mind. This is what they believed. James Braid even defines hypnosis as the attention that is focused upon the suggestion. The idea that a hypnotist will be able to creep into your unconscious mind and order you around is next to impossible as according to those who belong to Braids school of thought. The determinant of the different conceptions about suggestions has also been the nature of the mind. Hypnotists such as Milton Erickson believe that responses given are normally through the unconscious mind. They used the case of indirect suggestions as an example. Many of the nonverbal suggestions, such as metaphors, will mask the hypnotist's true intentions from the victim's conscious mind. A form of hypnosis that is completely reliant upon the unconscious theory is a subliminal suggestion. Where the unconscious mind is left out in the hypnosis process, then this form of hypnosis would be impossible. The distinction between the two schools of thought is quite easy to decipher. The first school of thought believes that suggestions are directed at the conscious mind will use verbal suggestions.

In contrast, the second school of thought who believe that suggestions are directed at the unconscious mind will use metaphors and stories that mask their true intentions. In general, the participant will still need to draw their attention to an object or idea. This enables the hypnotist to lead the participant in the direction that the hypnotist will need to go into the hypnotic state. Once this stage of suggestion is completed and is successful, the participant will move onto the next stage.

Susceptibility

It has been shown that people are more likely to fall prey to the hypnotist tactics than others will. Therefore, it will be noted that some people can fall into hypnosis easily, and the hypnotist does not have to put so much effort. At the same time, for some, getting into the hypnotic stage may take longer and require the hypnotist to put quite the effort. While for some, even after the continued efforts of the hypnotist, they will not get into the hypnotic state. Research has shown where a person has reached the hypnotic state at some point in their lives. They will likely be susceptible to the hypnotist's suggestions, and those who have not been hypnotized, or it has always been difficult for them to reach that state. It will be likely that they may never be able to get that hypnotic state.

Different models have been established to determine the susceptibility of partakers to hypnosis. Research done by Deirdre Barrett showed that there are two types of subjects that considered being more susceptible to hypnosis and its effects. The two subjects consist of the group of dissociates and fantasizers. Fantasizers can easily block out the stimuli from reality without the specific use of hypnosis. They daydream a lot and also spent their childhood believing in the existence of imaginary friends. Dissociates are persons who have scarred childhoods. They have experienced trauma or child abuse and found ways to put away the past and become numb. If a person belongs to this group finds him or herself daydreaming, it will be associated in terms of being blank and fantasizing. These two groups will have the highest rates of being hypnotized.

Types of Hypnosis

A hypnotist can use different types of hypnosis as a participant. Each of them will use different ways and will help with certain issues. Some types of hypnosis will assist in weight loss, while others will help a participant relax.

Traditional hypnosis

This type of hypnosis is very popular and used by hypnotists. It works by the hypnotist, making suggestions to the participant's unconscious mind. The participant who is likely to be hypnotized by this does what he is told and does not ask many or frequent questions. If one was to self-hypnotize themselves, they would do this by using traditional hypnosis. As we have said, this type of hypnosis is very popular, and this could be attributed to it not requiring much skill, and it is not technical. The hypnotist will just have the right words and just tell the participant what to do. This might pose a problem to the hypnotist where the participant is a critical thinker and can analyze a given situation.

Neuro-Linguistic Programming (NLP)

This type of hypnosis gives the hypnotist wide criteria for the methods they can use in hypnosis. The hypnotist can save time during the process as the hypnotist will just use the same thought patterns to create the problem in the participant. For example, if it is stress, the same thought pattern causing this stress will be used to counter the stress.

NLP Anchoring

To understand how anchoring works, think of a particular scent. The first time you had that scent, you were going through some feeling in which the unconscious mind attached these feelings to that scent. Through this, the scent will become the anchor for those particular feelings. Every time you heard the scent, those feelings come rushing back, triggered by the unconscious mind. This type of NLP has been useful to hypnotists in the process of hypnosis. If you won a prize or some money, for example, the hypnotist will try and recreate those feelings you had when you won the prize. While recreating these feelings, the hypnotist will ensure the participant does an action during this process. Each time the subject does the said action, they will be reminded of those feelings.

This type of NLP can motivate a person to accomplish their goals, for example, if they are trying to be healthier or lose weight. The hypnotist will create a positive anchor that is in line with the mental image of the participant. The mental picture will be that of a sexy slim body. This image will be used as the motivator to start losing weight.

NLP Flash

This technique should only be done by a certified professional because it is considered very powerful and used to alter thoughts and emotions around the participant's unconscious mind. It is deemed to be helpful to persons who experience chronic stress or are addicted to a substance. Here is what the hypnotist will do; he or she is addicted to a substance instead of it, causing some feelings of happiness the act will now cause feelings of pain. Where the person had chronic stress, the cat will bring a sense of relaxation. Those addicted to substances such as cigarettes and alcohol will now feel pain when they take these substances, which can effectively help them get over their addiction.

Chapter 48. Hypnosis Techniques

Once you have mastered the process of hypnosis that can often be called the long process, you can begin to use another powerful form of hypnosis to your advantage, instant hypnosis. These techniques play with the basics of the mind and what can happen to everyone from time to time daily. Have you ever gazed out of the window and simply watched the rain come down? What about listening to music that makes you feel soothed and relaxed? Maybe watching a favorite movie or television show, and you just feel yourself tune out. Often when this happens, you may not even notice that your brain has checked out. You're comfortable, relaxed, and completely absorbed in what you are doing. It happens every day and has three characteristics that are telltale signs.

1. Increased focus and concentration.

2. Increased relaxation of the body.

3. Increased access to the subconscious mind.

Hypnosis simply uses this natural state of things to put your subject into that state of mind as quickly as possible.

The Handshake Technique

This technique requires that you and the subject have some trust between you. As you will reach out your hand to shake with and then pull sharply towards yourself, you will forcefully, but calming say the word sleep as you do this. If you don't have a little trust built between you, this could just as easily backfire and make the subject tense when you pull them in. How does this technique work so easily? It works by using two different methods of inducing hypnosis: moving the subject off balance, so the brain does not have time to compute a response and giving the forceful suggestion of sleep, which seems like a good idea to the brain. People are far more suggestive than they think, and that is how this simple but powerful instant technique can work.

Falling Backward Method Technique

This form of instant hypnosis again works in the process of putting someone off balance and giving them a suggestion to follow. Instead of pulling them forward towards you, however, the subject will tip slightly backward. By following simple steps, this process can put your subject under in less than a minute:

Step 1: Ask your subject to stand with their feet together and their arms hanging loosely at the side. As they get into a position to explain what you will be doing with them step by step to know what is coming next, you will let them also know this will test their relaxation reflexes.

Step 2: Move to stand directly behind your subject and place both hands on their shoulders.

Stand close enough to control them as they fall, but not close enough so that they will fall directly on you. Control the fall but don't take too much weight.

Place one foot in front of the other, and you will be able to keep the right balance to hold their weight as they fall back. Tell the subject this is just a trial run.

Step 3: Ask your subject to relax and explain that you will pull them a few inches back but that you will not let them fall. Place a strong emphasis on this fact that you will not let them fall and ask them to stay relaxed and bend their body at the ankles only, not at the waist, knees, or anywhere else.

Step 4: With your hands still on the subject's shoulders, ask them to close their eyes and pull them back only a few inches. A space of two or three inches is sufficient. Remember not to jar of force them, but allow them to gently tip backward and then rock them forward again. Keep your hands firmly on their shoulders and stand the client upright again, ensuring they regained their balance.

Step 5: If your subject seems relaxed, move on to the next step. If not, assure the subject that they have done well, and repeat the earlier step again to make certain the subject knows what to expect. You may find that certain nervous subjects might require several attempts before they're fully comfortable.

Step 6: After having them fall back, you can sit them down and use a short and brief deepening technique to make sure they are deep in hypnosis. This is usually done simply using phrases such as "move deeper and deeper into hypnosis, relax" repeat this as needed to make sure that your subject is deep into hypnosis.

The Eye Test

To confirm for both you and the subject that a state of hypnosis has been reached with an instant technique, you want to use this simple process. With your subject comfortable and sitting, follow this process:

Step 1: "You feel your eyes are very heavy and completely relaxed. Each muscle around them is now relaxed. This makes your eyelids very heavy."

Step 2: "On the count of three and not before, I will ask you to open your eyes. When I ask this, you will not be able to. You are so completely relaxed that your eyelids are too heavy. You will not be able to open your eyes because your eyelids are so heavy, and you are so relaxed that you will not even try to open them."

Step 3: "Your eyelids are closed. Heavy. Sealed shut, and you can't open them."

Step 4: "One. Your eyes are closed; your eyelids are heavy. You can't open them, not even if you try. You simply can't open them. They are too heavy, so very heavy."

Step 5: "Two. You cannot open your eyes."

Step 6: "Three. Your eyes are tightly closed. Try opening them. You cannot open them, right? Your eyelids are too heavy. Stop trying, just simply relax your eyes again, no more trying to open them. As go your eyes, so you should go your body. Relax."

When you are doing this process, you do not allow your subject to try opening their eyes for more than a second or two. If you give them too much time, they will eventually be able to force their eyes open, and once they have done that, they will come out of hypnosis. If they can open their eyes right away without any effort, they have not been put under, and you will have to start again. If this does occur and open their eyes, simply tell them it's okay and that their eyes were not relaxed enough, so you will begin again. Remember to keep a festive air.

Relaxation Technique

Therapists usually ask you to make yourself feel at home and be comfy during an introduction meeting. They may even provide you with a soft couch to lay on. Why? Are they just being courteous? The truth is, it's more than that. Therapists use relaxation as a common method to induce hypnosis. If you are relaxed, you will likely fall into a trance quicker, and your mind becomes more open to accepting suggestions. Listed are some of the usual methods to promote relaxation:

- Be comfortable.

- Lay down.

- In your head, start to count down.

- Control your breathing.

- Tense your muscles and then relax.

- Speak in a calm, soft tone.

Handshake Technique

The father of hypnotherapy, Milton Erickson, became famous for using a handshake technique to get a person into a hypnotic trance. Handshake is a common greeting, but in hypnosis, it can be more than just a gesture. Hypnotists do not just shake hands in a normal way. They interrupt the subject's mind by grabbing his wrist or pulling him forward to break the balance. Because the pattern established by the subject's mind was interrupted, the client's subconscious mind will suddenly be open to suggestions.

Eyes Cues Technique

The brain has two spheres – the conscious and creative side (right) and the practical and subconscious side (left). When we are in a conversation with someone, we look for feedback to know how they feel or react to what we say. Watch your subject's eyes. Are they looking to the right? Or are they looking to the left? Remember, when they're looking to the right, that suggests that they are conscious of the current situation. If they are looking to the left, that means they are in subconscious thought.

Visualization Technique

You can use visualization to induce your subject into a hypnotic trance and make suggestions. For instance, ask your subject to visualize a room that they know very well. Instruct them to visualize each detail in that room: the windows, the smell, the lighting, the color of the wall, the texture of the floor. Then, ask them to visualize a room they do not know, such as your office. As they struggle to remember the exact details of the room they are less familiar with, they open their minds to suggestions.

Arm Levitation Technique

You can perform this by asking your subject to close their eyes. Then, ask them to notice the difference between their arms. They might say their arms are heavy or light. Subconsciously, they will enter a trance and lift their arms or make their mind believe they have lifted their arms. Either way, induction is a success.

Sudden Shock/Falling Backwards Technique

As with the handshake technique, a subject in shock can enter into a trance. You might have heard about "trust falls." The feeling of falling backward can put the body into shock. Thus, it opens the mind to accept suggestions. Of course, you must catch your subject and be very careful not to drop him/her.

Hypnotic Trigger Technique

There are several forms of hypnotic triggers. A trigger lets the subconscious remember a desired feeling or action that is suggested while under hypnosis. Here are some examples:

- Finger snap
- Clap
- Sound of ball
- Opening eyes
- Standing or sitting

Touch Technique

In this technique, the hypnotist or psychiatrist will put the subject into a relaxed state of mind. Then, gently, the hypnotist will tap the subject's hands with his/her own with slight pressure. With a pen held directly in front of the subject, they will follow it with their eyes while visualizing a perfect place in their mind. This technique needs to be repeated several times during each session. Every after the session I have with this technique, I am always relaxed and feel better.

Chapter 49. Mind Controls Hypnotism

How to Hypnotize People

Talking about any professional hypnosis instructor, they notify their clients that a successful hypnotherapist is usually confidential. Ideally, you motivate confidence in your clients with the method of 'Personality Assurance.' In other words, the clients get to the state, whereby they feel better when you are around. Of course, this is the same when you invent the method of delivering speeches to hypnotize your audience. To start with, you need to cultivate confidence in your ability when with the audience. You portray a nervous mood at the same time.

Ideally, you tend to put your client/audience in the state. They feel like you cannot find them in the room; you portray the narratives in their minds. This could be done with the ideology of focusing your attention so carefully to ensure that your words have a real effect on their perception, consciously, and unconsciously. Changing the functioning of your immune system or blood circulation tends to be done by a competent hypnotist.

A good narrator must understand the idea of you wanting to be sufficiently convincing your listeners to concentrate on what you say. This is necessary because you need them to disassociate themselves from their concerns and situations to travel to different times, places, and opportunities with you. So, at least for a while, you tend to make them understand the benefits of implementing the new ways of seeing reality.

Helping people learn new ways of responding to life, with the aim of not letting low confidence, phobias, and attention mess them up is so useful for 'Therapy hypnosis.' You concentrate your audience's attention so selectively when you speak with power that they become hypnotic rather than purely aware of the essence of their living. Therefore, this kind of education seems more profound for people.

Avoiding the Boredom Trance

However, it appears that various kinds of trances are in the crowd. You tend to hypnotize the audience by making them be in the state of leaving the room psychologically when you aren't inspiring them. Instead, the groups will try not to obey your concept and try to avoid your voice. In most cases, they begin imagining what they will do for the day, what their next social arrangements will be like, or even what they will cook for lunch. The audience/participant tends to be disassociating, but not in the ways we would like. However, it appears that the specific technique to guide your audience in the proper direction seems to be available.

Crowd Hypnosis

Professional public presenters tend to captivate the audience with thoughts and words. Also, what they will use are the anticipation, vocabulary, narrative, and initial pace. This means that implementing the ideas for their audience to act on in the future will be their ideal objective. This method tends to be very useful when it comes to hypnotizing the audience. This means that the hypnotic speakers don't give just facts. Instead, they serve the audience with an experience that will improve how they feel, think, or even behave.

Prepare Your Speech With Words That Appeal to Feelings

'Nominalization' happens to be the term in which the people who have to travel inwards to communicate with personal meanings are called. This idea helps in hypnotizing the audience. These happen to be words like mighty, lovely, devotion, wisdom, power, and so on. What's just needed is that you ensure that you align the terms with what you mean. Ideally, such correctly used terms need to contain more than mere concrete words, but words evoke feelings.

Paint Vision of Hearing Minds Through Combining Senses

We portray a paradise-like experience to someone, the moment we hypnotize them. And indeed, in pictures, words, sounds, feelings, tastes, and as well as emotions, we dream. You need to tell what you've seen, felt, heard, and tasted when you say a story about something that has happened to you when giving speeches.

Ideally, an address becomes more elegant with the implementations of this sensory appeal. For instance, "When I heard a sickening scream, I was carrying a huge bag through the mall, I turned around and saw two giant guys trying to mug an old lady who pushed them into the realm" sounds more appropriate. Compared to this, "I went to the shopping center and witnessed a serious physical conflict."

Tell All Your Stories to Hypnotize

When there are great stories to tell, tell your viewers/audience overwhelmingly, even at the moment when you're giving a talk about molecular biology.

Fascinate With Your Voice

Think about words that have significance and relevance. So, in other words, you need to speed up with your voice at times. Then sometimes slow down a bit. Perhaps, this shouldn't happen every single time to avoid getting upset. You need to reduce the speed you implement in your words when you make an argument of significance. Then, also, you can even talk to a real hypnotist calmly and on slow delivery, periodically.

Use Suddenness

We tend to go into a hypnotic spell when we're shocked or surprised, not only when we loosen up.

Humor, as it is, tends to amuse someone. So, great speakers implement the idea of using humor because it is hypnotic. There tends to be a punch on a punch line in some other perspectives, and that is because it is surprising. Mainly, the shock is often used by the hypnotists from different stages to track subjects quickly into a hypnotic state.

Be Powerful

You can create a hypnotic state for people by merely exerting power over others. Look at how people are likely to follow a person who appears to be powerful blindly. When you do this, you can get a following, and the people following you will do what you say because they want to please you and stay in your presence.

You can use this technique among your friends, family, coworkers, and any person you have a pre-existing relationship with. You want to exert your power over time so that it does not feel too aggressive. Once you notice you have followers, start small with what you are asking. They will do it without even thinking twice about it. Over time, you can ask for larger things, and you will have no trouble getting them.

Mirroring

Now, the powerful approach works for people, you know, but what about strangers? This is where mirroring comes into play. This allows you to quickly develop a rapport with someone once they see you both have someone in common. This can almost put them into a trance because they will naturally like you and want to please you since they will perceive both of you as very similar.

To successfully use this technique, pay attention to the stranger's common phrases and body language. Look at their behaviors. Exhibit these things back at them. As you continue your interaction with them, it will not take long to notice the similarities. You do not even have to lie about things you have in common. Simply mirroring their language and behaviors is enough to get them under your spell.

Use Stories

The good stories can put people into a trance-like state. Think back to when you were a kid, and your parents would read stories to you before bed. This would induce a deep state of relaxation. The same is true when you are an adult.

As you are talking to people each day, add in some anecdotes. This shows you personally and can even give you a sense of power and authority. You want people to visualize what you are saying, so use imagery to tell your story.

For example, you want a person to move something breakable because you just do not want to risk it. Do not just ask them to move it carefully. State that you do not want the vase to be dropped since it can shatter. They will visualize the vase shattering, forcing them to not only be careful when moving it, but they will volunteer to do it. They will almost see completing the task successfully as a type of personal challenge.

Lengthy Speeches

When you want to induce hypnosis on a large group, lengthy speeches are how to do it. Think about the television evangelists you have seen. They essentially use this form of hypnosis to get people to hand over thousands of dollars every time they hold a service.

When they are delivering their speech, they take a few pauses. They use varied voice tones to annunciate points and keep people completely engrossed in what they are saying. They know what their message is, and they repeat it frequently. However, they often use different phrasing, so no one in the audience ever feels like something is being forced on them.

It is not uncommon for them to tell you exactly what to do without directly telling you to do it. When you're in this type of situation, you are so enamored with the speaker that you will do just about anything they ask. They always present their lengthy speech, and then they just pass the collection basket. They do not ask you to donate because they know you will. After all, you feel dedicated to them.

You can use this technique too. You do not need an auditorium for it either. If you need something from a person or a group of people, plan out a speech. Make sure that those you are talking to feel empowered throughout the lesson. By the time you get to the end, you have already subconsciously implanted in their minds what you want. You will not need to ask for it. You will just get it.

For example, you want people to invest in your new business idea. Give them a speech about the business, about how much starting it would mean to you, and then insert a bit of a sob story about how this is your dream. Still, financially, you cannot swing it. After listening to your dramatic speech, they will feel compelled to invest.

Stacking

This is a hypnotic technique that works because you nearly overwhelm the people you are talking to. With this technique, you essentially bombard people with information. They are learning so many new things that they do not have time to sort through it. They do not feel they need to check facts because you are speaking with such authority that they automatically believe what you are saying. By the time you end your thoughts, you have essentially put them into a trance.

Cold Reading

This is something that psychics use to convince people that they can read their minds and predict their future. You will start by making a vague statement. For example, if you know a person to be shy, you will state this. You know it is accurate, and they will elaborate, giving you further information. You will use this additional information to make other predictions essentially. Once a person feels that you have this almost clairvoyant ability, they are more prone to believe anything you tell them.

Chapter 50. Dark NLP

Neuro-Linguistic Programming' (NLP) is like a user manual for the brain that helps you communicate the unconscious mind's goals and desires to the conscious self. Imagine you are in a foreign country and craving chicken wings. You go to a restaurant to order the same, but when the food shows up, it ends up being liver stew... because of a failed communication.

Humans often fail to recognize and acknowledge their unconscious thoughts and desires because many get lost in translation to the conscious self. NLP enthusiasts often exclaim, "the conscious mind is the goal setter, and the unconscious mind is the goal-getter."

The idea of being your unconscious mind wants you to achieve everything that you desire. Still, if your conscious mind fails to receive the message, you will never set the goal to achieve those dreams.

NLP was developed using excellent therapists and communicators who had achieved great success as role models. It's a set of tools and techniques to help your master communication, both with yourself and others.

NLP is the study of the human mind combining thoughts and actions with the perception to fulfill their deepest desires. Our mind employs complex neural networks to process information and use language or auditory signals to give it meaning while storing these signals in patterns to generate and store new memories.

We can voluntarily use and apply certain tools and techniques to alter our thoughts and actions in achieving our goals. These techniques can be perceptual, behavioral, and communicative. They can be used to control our minds and those of others.

One of NLP's central ideas is that our conscious mind has a bias towards a specific sensory system called the preferred representational system (PRS). Phrases like "I hear you" or "sounds good" signal an auditory PRS, whereas a phrase like "I see you" may signal a visual PRS.

A certified therapist can identify a person's PRS and model their treatment around it. This therapeutic framework often involves rapport building, goal setting, and information gathering, among other activities.

NLP is increasingly used by individuals to promote self-enhancement, such as self-reflection, confidence, social skill development, but primarily by communication.

NLP therapy or training can be delivered in language and sensory-based interventions, using behavior modification techniques customized for individuals to better their social communication and improved confidence and self-awareness.

NLP therapists or trainers strive to make their clients understand that their view and perception of the world are directly associated with how they operate in it. The first step toward a better future is a keen understanding of their conscious self and contact with their unconscious mind.

It is paramount to first analyze and subsequently change our thoughts and behaviors that are counterproductive and block our success and healing. NLP has been successfully used to treat various mental health conditions like anxiety, phobias, stress, and even post-traumatic stress disorder.

An increasing number of practitioners are commercially applying NLP to promise improved productivity and achievement of work-oriented goals that ultimately lead to job progression.

Here are some prominently used NLP techniques.

Anchoring

Try this yourself! Think of a gesture or sensation on your body (pulling your earlobe, cracking your knuckles, touching your forehead), and associating it with any desired positive emotional response (happiness, confidence, calmness, etc.), recalling and reliving the memory when you experience those emotions.

Content Reframing

This NLP technique is best suited to combat negative thoughts and feelings. With these visualization techniques, you can alter your mind to think differently about situations where you feel threatened or underpowered.

Rapport Building

Rapport is the art of generating empathy in others by pacing and mirroring their verbal and nonverbal behaviors. People like other people who they think are similar to themselves.

When you can subtly mirror the other person, their brain will fire off "mirror neurons" or "pleasure sensors" in their brains, making them feel a sense of liking for you.

Dissociation

The NLP technique of dissociation guides you in severing the link between negative emotions and the associated trigger. For instance, certain words or phrases may instantly bring back bad memories and make you feel stressed or depressed. If you can successfully identify those triggers and make an effort to detach those negative feelings, you are one step closer to healing and empowering yourself.

Future Pacing

The NLP technique of leading the subject to a future state and rehearsing the potential future outcomes to achieve the desired result automatically is called future pacing. It's a type of visualization technique or mental imagery used to anchor a change or resource to future situations by imagining and virtually experiencing those situations.

Influence and Persuasion

This is the most ambivalent NLP technique and houses a gray area between dark psychology and psychotherapy.

NLP is primarily focused on eliminating negative emotions, curbing bad habits, and resolving conflicts. Another aspect of NLP deals with ethically influencing and persuading others. Now pay attention to the word ETHICAL here.

How to Use NLP as a Useful Tool to Manipulate?

Your intentions are the only North Star in a dark and lonely ocean. It is the only thing that sets NLP apart from manipulation by serving as a useful tool to remember the actual purpose of using NLP. Studies show that your brain subtly works towards achieving them when innately aware of your goals, even when you aren't actively thinking about it. It is known as "diffused thinking" when you allow your mind to wander freely, making connections randomly. It's a process that encompasses all parts of the brain and is commonly used to solve problems and difficult concepts. The true motive can sit undisturbed, deep in your subconscious, while your brain works around it, trying to develop ways and plans to achieve it. NLP is a set of skills that allows you as the user to be in control of your own conscious and unconscious mind.

However, that doesn't mean that NLP is unsuccessful if the user's intentions are immoral. It is possible to imbue those habits known to be practiced by historically unsavory characters, such as criminals and terrorists; thus, the patient can be fashioned into the next revolutionary terrorist who ushers in a new era completely reinvents modern violence as we know it. This is an example of the more extreme cases. Subtler manipulation, the kind that may not make headlines and morning news, can be equally deadly.

For example, consider this hypothetical scenario between two rival law firms competing for the same large client. Law firm A plans to manipulate the client's choice by presenting their rival law firm in a bad light. This is done by hiring a programmer to sit in on the regular therapy sessions of law firm B's top attorney and subtly twist the patient's view of his/her relationship with their spouse, thereby planting subconscious suggestions of problems in the relationship that do not exist. This technique would fall under the category of manipulation in court, with or without NLP.

Another instance of manipulation your brain doesn't commonly recognize because humans are sympathetic creatures is the emotional manipulation done by beggars. Though there is a percentage of 'honest' beggars, who are truly homeless and struggling to survive, there is a great majority of those whose trade is begging.

It is quite popular in the South Asian region, and the manipulators often don patchy clothes and have dirty faces. They use words and behaviors to play on the emotions to convince people that they need money. Many even go the extra mile and hire children for the day, just to rub it in. The manipulation is done so well that whether they have trained themselves in NLP techniques or not, they are very good at it.

On the other hand, NLP programmers hired to hold regular workshops in businesses (such as our hypothetical law firms, for instance) use it as a tool to help boost employee motivation, and encourage them to pick up new skill-sets that have been attributed to highly successful individuals, in a bid to improve general worker productivity and employee attitude in the company. It is a technique that has shown positive results.

Similarly, as it is used in business purposes to inspire workers, it is also commonly employed by a door-to-door salesman to sell as many products as possible and earn higher commissions.

Personal programmers work with their clients to help them repair relationships with their friends and family, rectifying and solving conflicts. NLP is also clinically utilized in curing mental illnesses like PTSD, GAD, phobias, anxieties, paranoia, and even substance abuse.

There are many more instances where NLP is employed, for good and bad, but the prevailing truth of the matter is that NLP itself is not guilty. Like any technique or product, there are users and abusers.

The thing being abused is innocent of the crime of the abuser. It's NLP abusers with evil, nefarious motives that have brought a bad name on the personal development and psychotherapy technique so well-intended by Brandler and Grinder.

Chapter 51. The Positive and Negative Aspects of Neuro Linguistic Programming

There are both positive and negative parts of neuro phonetic programming or NLP. Tragically, not many individuals have a complete comprehension of this term, even though they are dependent upon it each and ordinary. More critically, many organizations, associations, and people who realize how to control this idea, regularly do such with exploitative aims.

NLP is the investigation of how verbal correspondence impacts the human cerebrum. The words that you hear are answerable for forming your discernments, thoughts, and even your activities. This is the essential thought behind uplifting feedback. In contemplates, uplifting statements have been appeared to make significant enhancements in mentalities and practices. Neuro etymological programming characterizes why this works.

On the other hand, negative words additionally sway the individuals who hear them. Individuals who are continually encompassed by antagonistic individuals will regularly fall prey to their negative talk. Expressions of demoralization will, as a rule, cause an individual to take on a naysayer mentality. This makes it almost certain that the individual will surrender before attempting. Something else to consider is how your own words may make you stay dormant in certain life territories. You must be cautious about discussing these things on the off chance that you are attempting to create change in specific examples or practices. Your cerebrum will accept a follow up on the very words that you express.

The absolute most noteworthy experts or NLP are significant promoting and publicizing organizations. They realize that their words can shape popular suppositions and free activity. To get mass-market consideration for explicit merchandise, a significant number of these elements will make individuals partner industrialism with satisfaction. Individuals at that point start to accept that they should purchase items to feel glad.

When you have an away from of how verbal correspondence influences your practices, it is critical to be progressively cautious about the words you express and the organization you keep. You can likewise play a progressively active job as an audience. Individuals who listen inactively to verbal messages are unmistakably progressively liable to being influenced by them.

When you realize what neuro phonetic programming or NLP is and how it tends to be utilized, you can become much progressively amazing in your dynamic. You will be able to begin utilizing positive words to fortify yourself and the people around you. You will furthermore turn out to be progressively capable in endeavors to prevent you or to persuade you to burn through cash on superfluous things. This is genuinely one of those occurrences in which information is power.

How Negative Thinking Can Affect Us

Negative reasoning influences us inwardly, however, genuinely. To be sure, negative considerations have genuine implications past simply the idea itself. How might you use neuro etymological programming and entrancing to break liberated from this?

Neuro semantic writing computer programs are methods by which you can truly be instructed to "retrain" how you think. A specialist prepared in NLP can assist you with rethinking and repeat contemplations, and think about them from an alternate perspective, so you truly start to think in various manners that are increasingly adjusted and positive - and without a doubt, progressively practical.

This is an extremely positive advance to take because so regularly, negative considerations are "outside of any relevant connection to the issue at hand" based on what is truly occurring.

Negative Thinking in Every Day Situations

Suppose, for instance, that you've been doled out a venture grinding away, and you're sure you can do it. You complete the activity, and you've done quite well. In any case, you notice one modest mistake. In a split second, you start to converse with yourself adversely, disclosing that you took care of the activity inadequately, even though the one small mistake isn't huge and won't sway on the nature of the undertaking generally. So while your supervisor is stating, "Incredible employment!" you may be stating to yourself, "No, it's most certainly not. I'm so dumb. I will lose my employment on account of that botch."

How Reasonable Is That?

A certified NLP Practitioner may challenge you with this: "All in all, your manager has advised you will lose your employment since you committed one little error?" How will you respond? You'll think, "Obviously not!" and understand that your supervisor is revealing to you that you've worked superbly. Like this, neuro etymological programming truly shows us how to retrain our musings in a progressively adjusted and positive manner, given a target assessment of the natural conditions.

Presently, I don't get this' meaning regarding how you can abstain from following this example by and large? All things considered you make a stride back and take a gander at the task with target eyes. Impartially, without that negative self-talk, you can see that genuinely, you worked superbly and committed one little error. What's more, even though you need to abstain from committing errors, they do occur.

So a good repetition of your underlying response - that you took care of the activity inadequately - may be to state, "I worked admirably and committed one little error. I will focus next time and make an effort not to commit a similar error, yet I can at present be pleased with what I did, all things being equal." You can likewise disclose to yourself that because your supervisor is content with what you did, you ought not exclusively to be glad for what you've done, however. You can be secure that your activity is protected. Truth be told, what is sensible and present and is considerably more precise as self-talk than your past explanation.

Chapter 52. Understanding Body Language

What is Body Language

We sometimes do things unconsciously, much like a nervous habit, such as tapping your foot or rubbing your hands together. Though we may not be aware that we are doing these things, others see these habits and read into them. We may be seen as nervous or agitated by others due to these unconscious behaviors that we are prone to.

At other times, we might engage in an action or pose with a specific intent consciously chosen. We can choose to turn our bodies towards someone we are busy talking to seem more attentive. Imagine your first job interview: you cautiously keep yourself from twitching, rubbing your face, or reclining. You have been made aware by various knowledgeable people such as school counselors and career guides to be aware of these interview bombs. Knowing how bad these make you seem, you learn not to engage in this form of body language.

We can lie with a written and spoken language. Usually, we lie to avoid getting into trouble. Likewise, we can also lie in our bodies. We can project a disingenuous body image and has been carefully polished to accomplish a particular appearance. I imagine that several of us have been caught in a scam at some point in time. This is an ideal example of how intelligent users of body language can manipulate it to convince us of their honesty. We get people to believe us based on what we show and not what we say.

In expressing emotions, the facial expression is essential. It combines the cheeks' movement, nose, lips, eyebrows, and eyes to show a person's various moods. Some researchers showed that body and facial expressions complement each other in interpreting emotions. Some experiments recognized the influence of body expression in identifying facial expression, which means that the brain simultaneously processes body and facial expressions.

Body postures can also detect emotions. If an individual is angry, he will try to dominate another person. His posture will show such approach tendencies. If he is fearful, his approach will be that of avoidance. He will feel submissive and weak.

Even gestures have different interpretations. For instance, if an individual folds his arms during a discussion, it's going to mean that he's unwilling to concentrate on the speaker or features a closed mind. If he crosses his arms over the opposite, it means he lacks confidence and is insecure.

Simple hand gestures show that the individual is self-assured and confident, while clenched hands can mean either angry or stressed. If he wrings his hands, it means he is anxious and nervous.

Finger gestures show the overall well-being of an individual. In some cultures, it is acceptable to point with an index finger. Handshakes also show the levels of emotion and confidence of individuals. They are popular in some cultures. In Muslim cultures, a man cannot shake or touch the hands of a woman. In Hindu cultures, a man greets a woman by keeping his hands together, like praying.

When it comes to learning how to read body language, the main goal is to determine if the person in front of you is genuine. Body language clues are incredibly crucial when deciphering someone's innermost thoughts, personality, and even intentions. In many ways, body language teaches you to become a human lie detector. Humans can be great liars, but while we may have been able to trick our mind into saying words we do not mean, we cannot trick our bodies into executing the lie flawlessly.

BODY LANGUAGE PSYHOLOGY

Reading body language is an excellent skill to have in job interviews when trying to solve a crime or resolve conflict. Being able to see beneath the surface into what is going on inside someone's mind will help you make better, more informed decisions.

What makes body language so tricky to master is deciphering body language cues within the right context. For example, when a person crosses his or her arms in front of the chest, you could construe that as negative body language, perhaps an indicator that the person is not happy to be here. However, depending on the context, it could also mean that the person feels cold, uncomfortable, or frustrated. Not accounting for a situation can lead to misreading of body language cues and a wrong conclusion.

Most people generally display a few categories of body language:

Dominant: Dominant body language comes into play when someone wants to be in command. The most standout cue for this category of body language is standing tall, with chest puffed out.

Attentive: This shows someone's interest and engagement with the conversation or situation.

Bored: A typical representation of this body language is the lack of eye contact and constant yawning.

Aggressive: An aggressive person will display threatening body language cues.

Defensive: A defensive person will look as if he or she is protecting or withholding information.

Closed Off: You can recognize a closed-off person by noticing if he or she is shutting you off by crossing his or her arms and guardedly standing farther away from you.

Open: This body language is friendly and welcoming.

Emotional: We usually display this body language when we feel heavily influenced by current feelings and typically have to change moods.

The Power of Body Language

Body language extends beyond more than just the four types. It can also be divided into positive and negative body language. Positive body language draws people towards you and creates a sense of belonging and accomplishment. This includes encouraging smiles, firm handshakes, making eye contact, facing someone with your body in a neutral position, and using an encouraging tone of voice.

Negative body language is based on avoidance. It includes turning your back on someone, not facing the speaker, looking down, using a soft and insecure tone of voice, and avoiding eye contact. When someone uses this body language tells, we begin to assume the worst about that person. We see them as being dishonest, uninvested, and disinterested.

Knowing these two forms of body language, which would you choose to look at? In all likelihood, you would prefer seeing positive body language. We want to feel acknowledged and valued during our communications with other people. Seeing someone face you, look you in the eye, speak in a clear tone without hiding their mouth, and have a natural appearance due to their open posture is very encouraging and ensures that communication can happen harmoniously and smoothly.

Yet, we often use negative body language when we feel intimidated or unsure of a situation. Being skilled at using your body language would help you achieve more favorable outcomes from your daily interactions and communications.

According to Guilbeault (2018), body language's power lies in that it can help you gain things you want, such as friends or jobs; however, it can also make you lose the things you want negative body language forms. It can cost you your job, friends, and even intimate relationships. Without even opening our mouths, we can attract or repel people.

Body language can build trust, which is the crucial ingredient in all relationships, whether for work, companionship, or intimacy. Using the power of body language, you can lead a more productive and successful life. Hence, it is well worth learning how to recognize body language and its meaning in others and ourselves.

Characteristics of Body Language

In general, body language manifests an individual's emotions, meaning another person can perceive it.

First, it is understood that the signal from the body language to the receiver can be highly complicated. An individual's body language consists of multiple body parts moving or not moving together. All must be taken into account to interpret a specific person's emotion. A specific facial expression taken out of context from the person's other bodily reactions will give an incomplete or otherwise misleading analysis of their emotions.

Another characteristic is that the projected emotion from body language is perceived automatically in a way similar to speech. This characteristic makes nonverbal interaction spontaneous. There is often little need to interpret further what an individual means with their body language.

A third characteristic is that young individuals can acquire and develop body language very easily and rapidly. Children learn what gestures and facial expressions mean from their parents, friends, and even strangers who interact with them. The ease of acquiring knowledge of body language can make children carry on specific body language into their maturity.

Deciphering Body Language

To understand and use body language, you have to learn how to read it in action and view it holistically as an overall picture of what a person is trying to communicate. If you want to begin controlling your body language, you'll have to understand how it all works together in the field as well. Somebody crossing their legs away from you could mean they are shy, it could mean that they are closed off to you, or it could just mean they need to pee desperately. To be able to read what they are feeling, you need to notice how they use the space around them, group behavioral actions into clusters (clusters are multiple body language cues placed together, so if they cross their legs away from you, cross their hands, and face in a direction away from you, it isn't looking good!), and to place them into context.

Actively Listening

Suppose you are looking at somebody's posture or trying to pick up the micro-expressions in their face that occur at one-fifth of a second. In that case, you might be closer to understanding how they feel, but you might also be ignoring something more obvious. The whole point of studying body language is to understand better what people think to build a better connection. The point isn't to make you paranoid that they are continually deceiving you. It's to make you less paranoid about what they are thinking.

Proxemics

Proxemics is a fancy word used in the body language community to mean the study of personal space and proximity. You can't indeed read someone's body language without noticing where they concern you in space.

Someone seems to be paying attention to you. They have open body language. They are even pointing themselves towards you–so they're paying attention to you, right? Well, maybe not if they're on the other side of the room and not moving any closer towards you.

When it comes to reading other people, some aspects of personal space are apparent. If someone is close, it will mean they are or are trying to be more intimate. However, with some people, especially men, there is a tendency to be territorial and to feel they have more access to your personal space than you might feel comfortable with. You can use these cues to determine if someone is aggressive, friendly, or flirtatious. By reading the rest of someone's body language, you can see if they are leaning towards you to be friendly or assertive. It is quite risky to invade other people's personal space to get an advantage over them. In general, try to avoid getting too close to someone unless they invite you to by touching you or speaking at a lower volume that requires you to lean in.

Chapter 53. Deception

What is Deception?

The definition is a theme that usually resonates within the spectrum of dark psychology. Throughout the years, it has been defined as any particular act used by a particular manipulative individual to instill certain beliefs within the victim that are usually false or only those possessing partial truths. It is usually placed in the same category as deceit, mystification, and suffrage. Deception is not usually an easy theme to understand since it involves many different things like, for example, distractions, propaganda camouflage, and concealment. The manipulator is often able to easily control the subject's mind since the victim is often led to placing immense trust in this manipulative individual. The victims often believe in whatever the manipulator will say and might even be basing plans and shaping their world base on the things that the manipulator is feeding their subconscious mind. This strong element of trust towards the manipulator can quickly fade away once the victim realizes what is going on. Because of this very reason, a certain level of skill is needed for deployment of this theme, since only then will a manipulator be able to skillfully change the focus of suspicion towards him and onto the victim's paranoia.

In most cases, deception will often present itself in relationship settings and lead the victim to have dominant feelings of distrust and betrayal between the partners in the relationship. This usually happens because deception is a theme that violates most of the rules of most relationships, together with having a negative influence on the expectations that come with the relationship. When getting into relationships, one of the usually ordinary things is always the ease of having an honest and truthful conversation with their partner. If the then learns that one of them is beginning to show signs of deception, they might have to learn the different ways of using misdirection and distractions to pry out reliable and truthful information that they need from them. The trust would have gone into a permanent rift that will not be easy to come back from since the victim will always be questioning everything that the partner will say and do, wondering whether the story is true of fabricated. Most relationships will end as soon as the deceptive partner is found out.

As we described earlier, this form of communication relies on lies and certain omissions to make the victim believe whatever he is being led to believing by the deceptive individual. This is the case; there are five main types of deceptive tactics that are seen to exist. We shall briefly touch on each one to better understand this theme.

Concealments

Probably taking home the medal of most used type of deception, concealment is basically when the deceptive individual knowingly omits information from his often relevant and important stories to the context. They can also engage in certain behaviors that would signal to hide relevant information to the subject at that particular time. A skilled manipulator is experienced enough to know that he will have to be clever to know that it's safe not to be directly in their approach but rather insinuate the lie leading the victim to their own conclusion, which is predetermined.

Exaggeration

What can be said about this? This is where an individual, in a sense, stretches the truth a bit too much with an intended goal of leading the story towards a direction that best caters to their needs. The manipulator will make a certain scenario appear more severe than it is to avoid lying directly to their victims. This is usually done to let the victim do whatever it is they want.

Lies

This is one tactic that we, as humans, use daily for one reason or another. We are often inclined to lie as a way to avoid some form of penalty. For example, if you work in the bank and you run late because of something minor, you will be inclined to lie to your boss to keep him from cutting you lose. What then can be said to be the meaning of this? This is where an individual gives information that is all south of the actual truth. They will present this completely fabricated truth to the victim, and they will believe it.

Equivocations

This is where an individual will knowingly make a statement of a contra dictionary nature intended to lead the victim to the path of confusion on what is exactly seems to be going on. This clever tactic will allow the manipulator to save his image if he is later discovered.

Understatements

This is where an individual minimizes aspects of the truth in the particular story being told at the time. They will often approach a victim preaching how something isn't that big of a deal when it is of the utmost importance.

What drives a manipulator to the deployment of the theme of dark psychology? According to research done over the years, there are usually 3 main things that motivate an individual to use deception on others. These three motives are under the umbrella of close relationships. They include self-focused motives, relationship-focused motives, and partner-focused motives. Let's look first at the motives focused on the partner. The victim will use deception in this kind of motive to avoid harming the subject or their partner. They may also use front to protect the relationship between the victim and an outside third party, avoid worrying about something about the subject, or keep the subject's self-esteem intact. Such motivation for deception will often be seen as both relationally beneficial and socially polite.

Deception's self-focused motive. This one is not considered noble as the first one and is therefore considered more inferior to the other techniques. Rather than worrying about the victim and how they feel, the manipulator will simply think about how they feel and their self-image. The manipulator uses deception to protect or enhance their self-image in this motive. To shield the victim from criticism, embarrassment, or anger, this form of deception is used.

Finally, we shall look at the relationship-focused motive of deception. The manipulative individual will use this deception to limit any harm that could come to the relationship simply by avoiding the trauma and conflict of relationships. This form of deception sometimes helps the relationship, depending on the situation. It may be the cause of harming the relationship because it will make things more complicated. For example, if you choose to hide how you feel about supper because you don't want to get into a fight, the relationship might be helpful. On the other hand, if you have an affair and choose to keep this information to yourself, it will only complicate things in the end.

Primary Components of Deception

As much as it may be difficult to clarify which factors show clear deployment of deception, some subtle components are immediate identifiers of these themes. The victim will come to be aware of these factors only when the manipulator dispatches a direct lie. Let us now dive deep into the particulars of said components.

Disguise

The first component we shall unravel is that of disguises. What usually goes on here is that the manipulator works tirelessly until he successfully creates the impression of being someone they are not. Manipulators often resort to this tactic if they want to hide something about them so deep that no one ever finds out. This could be a dark secret or just something as harmful as someone's name. This component's popular belief is that it is simply a change of clothes, just like in the moves. However, it goes far beyond this in that it also involves a complete change of one's persona. Having a rough idea of how discuses work, let us look at a few examples of how it can be used in the process of deception.

The first instance is where the manipulator changes himself to another person so as not to be discovered. An individual will do this with a view to maybe be able to get back into a particular crowd of people who are not very fond of him, revamp their whole personality to make someone like them, or further their own goals. In some instances, disguise may be used to refer to the hiding of one's true nature in the hopes of maybe hiding the effect that appears to be unpopular with that proposal. Disguises usually have adverse effects because it is generally hiding one's true intentions for a victim. When information is withheld in this fashion, it often clouds the victim's judgment. The victim ends up having the feeling of being in control of their decisions when they have been swayed towards the directions' manipulator. This is seen mainly in a political setting.

Camouflage

This is where individual works tirelessly to hide the truth in one way or another, leaving his victim clueless as to what exactly is going on. This is characterized by the manipulator's use of half-truths when divulging certain information to his victim. The victim will only be aware that camouflage has taken place when the actual truths are brought to light. A skilled manipulator with a lot of experience using camouflage is more likely to bra undetected in performing certain actions.

Simulation

The third component of deception is what is commonly referred to as simulation. This is simply the process where the victim is shown continuously subject matter that is false in every way. Further on, we get to see that simulation consists of 3 other techniques that can be used. They are mimicry, distraction, and fabrication.

Fabrication is when the manipulator takes something found in actual reality and chafes it to become this completely different thing. The manipulator will seek to either give detailed events that never happened or add some exaggerations that either make it sound better or worse than it sounds. The core of their story, however, is usually true. If the teacher gives them a bad grade, these manipulators may further the story by stating that they were given the bad results on purpose. The reality is that the manipulator did not study for the test hence his bad grade.

Mimicry is another tool that manipulators use when deploying these tactics of deception. The manipulator here usually portrays a persona that is quite close to their own, but not their own. They may present an idea similar to someone else's and give him credit for thinking about it first. This form of stimulation may be able to take pace through visual and auditory stimuli.

The last tool we shall look at is that of distraction as another form of simulation in deception. This is where the manipulator tries to get the victim only to focus their attention on everything else but the truth. How is this usually done? This is generally achieved through baiting or the offering of something more tempting than the reality itself.

Chapter 54. Dark Cognitive Behavioral Therapy

"A small behavioral change can also lead to embracing a wider checklist of healthier choices" - Chuck Norris.

What is Dark CBT?

To understand Dark CBT, we first must realize the necessary cognitive behavioral therapy and its approach to mental health and healing. Dark CBT is founded on the tried and true CBT principles employed by therapists everywhere. That is why it is guaranteed to work. Learning about CBT and then applying them as you see fit to unknowing subjects makes you very powerful. Gain a thorough understanding of how to use CBT and maybe even use it upon yourself for practice. From there, you can begin leveraging Dark CBT as a clandestine healing method or weapon on those around you.

History of CBT

CBT was first developed by a psychologist named Aaron Beck in the 1960s. Beck noticed that his patients had internal monologues, where they spoke to themselves in the privacy of their minds.

Beck began to have his patients analyze their automatic thoughts and report them. As his patients became more conscious of their ideas, they realized how these thoughts could make or break their success. Some thoughts made them make poor decisions or drew them to untrue assumptions that made them feel bad for no reason. Other studies helped them overcome problems and feel better about themselves. By gaining awareness of their thoughts by reporting them verbally to Beck or writing them down throughout the day, his patients were able to gain more control over their thinking.

In time, Beck was able to teach his patients to harness their thoughts and become more self-aware. He taught them to think differently to feel better. He noticed that changes in thinking led to changes in behavior and emotions. Correcting flawed thinking was what helped his patients heal faster.

Since Beck's initial observation, CBT has grown by leaps and bounds. It is now better understood and has become a significant part of psychotherapy. All therapists are aware of CBT, and most therapists employ it to some degree in their practice. There are many forms of CBT, but they all have the same premise and the same goal, putting them under the enormous Cognitive Behavioral Therapy umbrella.

Now we have developed Dark CBT. Dark CBT operates on the same principles as CBT. However, it is more clandestine. Rather than using CBT on yourself or a willing psychotherapy patient, Dark CBT is something you can use on anyone without their awareness. You can apply CBT concepts to change someone's thinking to suit your needs.

You can also use it on yourself, emphasizing becoming successful and achieving what you want in life. Dark CBT goes beyond simple healing and instead gives you the power to shape your life and your relationships as you desire.

Your interest in using Dark CBT may be purely altruistic, as you seek to help others who won't help themselves. Or you may have a more nefarious interest in using it to get your way and to manipulate others. How you use Dark CBT is up to you entirely, but the wealth of opportunity that Dark CBT provides you with is astounding.

Dark CBT is a relatively new method. It has not been applied to many study groups or researched extensively. Therefore, there is room for growth and experimentation in Dark CBT. You may find new applications or new ways of performing Dark CBT that is already unheard of. This is a new field that you can certainly expand and make your own. Supplement your Dark CBT with simple CBT methods and experiment with trial and error. You may just find your type of therapy that works well for you, based on the incredible techniques included and in basic CBT.

Why Use CBT?

There has been much success using CBT to treat difficulties in people's lives, ranging from depression to alcoholism to drug dependency to relationship problems. It can help people quit bad habits and feel better about themselves. It can also help people learn how to cope with their mental ailments to feel better. Even people who are not mentally ill can benefit from using CBT thought processes to tackle challenging problems in their lives, such as marriage difficulties, difficulties with communication, anger management issues, and even financial struggles.

The great thing about CBT is that it is possible to use on yourself. With the help of a CBT journal, you can document your thoughts and emotional reactions to events in your life or emotional wounds you are trying to overcome, or bad habits you are trying to break free of. Then, you ask yourself questions that lead you to change how you look at the situation, wound, or habit. You write down your new mental approach and new emotions now that you are using different thinking. You will notice a drastic improvement in your feelings and outlook on life. Suddenly, you won't have so many difficulties in life, and your problems will become so easy to solve that they will practically disappear before your eyes.

Dark CBT is incredibly useful for two reasons. The first is that Dark CBT is focused on personal gains and success. Rather than just healing your annoying thinking habits, you learn to become a massive success at anything that you wish. You can make yourself invincible if you teach yourself to believe that you are capable of anything. You can also create a monster by teaching someone else to feel the same way.

The second is that Dark CBT is sneaky. So even if someone is not interested in changing his thinking, you can still use Dark CBT on him to achieve the results that you desire. You will enjoy success, and he won't even know what has happened to him. You can fix people who refuse to get help or change people who stand in your way. No one will guess what you are doing. You simply seem to be an interested friend or loved one, trying to help someone think more realistically or positively.

What Separates Dark CBT From Regular CBT?

We already talked about this a little bit. But we want to stress that Dark CBT is the same as regular CBT. Its uses and applications are a bit different, however. That is the only thing that separates the two types of CBT.

Regular CBT is used in therapy or by individuals who are actively interested in changing their thinking. People use CBT knowingly and willingly. Their desire to change can make CBT very useful. You will find that you can use CBT to correct your problems, or you can visit a therapist who will set goals for you and help you adjust your thinking. The entire process is transparent and known to all parties.

Dark CBT is more opaque, hidden by a veil of deception. The subject of Dark CBT most likely is not aware of what is going on. Dark CBT is significant because it is subliminal, and it makes someone think that there is something wrong with him so that he strives to change it. You never reveal that you are the therapist here. You are also never asked to perform Dark CBT on anyone. This can be unethical, but again, you are using Dark CBT at your own risk.

Dark CBT is not evil in and of itself. It can be used for evil, but that is your call. The altruistic and positive applications of Dark CBT can be especially useful if you choose to make someone better through Dark CBT. You can help people who can't help themselves and who are resistant to getting help. You also create your success, furthering your own goals, and getting ahead in life. You don't have to become a monster and use Dark CBT to hurt people to gain from it. Using Dark CBT as a way to help others can improve your own life because it will heal your relationships and make people like you more. People will associate you with feeling better and liking themselves more, so they will want to spend more time around you. And everyone knows that being liked by people gets you what you want.

Even if you do choose to use the darker applications for Dark CBT, you won't ever get caught. People will not be aware of what you are doing. Therefore, you won't hurt your subjects or destroy relationships. You also won't get into trouble because you are not doing anything illegal.

Chapter 55. The Art Of Using Your Mind to Succeed

Many people want to learn about dark psychology because they want to do better in their careers. They aren't content working the job they already have: they want to prove themselves capable of more.

But somewhere along the way, we figure out the truth: that getting ahead in our careers isn't necessarily a matter of skill but manipulation and persuasion. As you know, dark psychology is the best and most legitimate way to learn these skills, and now it's time to learn how to use them specifically in a work setting.

We have to think in a more challenging way about how we interact with our co-workers. For instance, let's say we have a female early 20-something analyst amid a post-graduation down-cycle who has encountered many challenges both professionally and personally since starting work a few years ago.

She frequently finds herself wanting to connect with people who are perceived to be more advanced in their careers or whose interests are different from her own. Identifying why you are attracted to certain people is a valuable skill for early-career practitioners. It likely contributes to her success as an analyst. If she wants to get ahead, she should follow along with all the directions in these pages, where we speak to dark psychology in the workplace directly.

Personality is an incredibly crucial subject for the workplace context because it is an environment where you have to interact with many different kinds of people, many of whom—you will soon find out—you don't know that well as people.

Dark psychology is broader than neurolinguistics programming, but NLP is where all of our tools and techniques of in-depth communication and manipulation come from. NLP is where the three significant steps of manipulation and mind control originate from:

- Establish your state control and perceptual sharpness.

- Imitate the unconscious cues of communication of your subject so that they incorporate you into their mind.

- Use one of the techniques.

People continuously think without even realizing it because most thought is unconscious. NLP is how we take advantage of most studies' cold nature to tell people's minds to change the structure before they even know it.

NLP's topic is vital for discussing workplace personalities because NLP has five main categories for the kinds of characters' people have. In the jargon of NLP, these "personalities" are actually called metaprograms. You would do well to identify the important people at your workplace within these metaprograms. Take advantage of your perceptual sharpness to ascertain this information.

As we have told you before, getting information about the subject is everything. But it is also true that our brains need to sort all the information we get into categories to understand the world better. These metaprograms do that job for you.

Metaprograms are more useful than personalities because they are more objective. They also focus on the motivations people have and how they use logic rather than their mannerisms or less essential behavior patterns. Metaprograms do not merely describe how much you like attention or how nervous or relaxed you are. You may notice some aspects of each metaprogram that overlap with these traits. Still, metaprograms are more specific than these less useful terms.

These NLP-styled personalities are not only a way for you to get more information about your co-workers. Remember the second step of NLP's mind-reading and manipulation: you have to imitate the communications cues the subject shows you. When you do this, you make them unconsciously see you as being like themselves. That means if you take on the traits of your co-worker's metaprogram, you make it easier for you to succeed in this step.

The last thing for you to know about metaprograms, in general, is that they are sorted in dichotomies. A dichotomy is a contrast between two items that are different. But while you should choose just one from each dichotomy in each metaprogram, you must remember that people are not as simple as being A or B. Any time we have a dichotomy—in any situation—picking one of the two is just a category you can use to simplify things and think of them differently. But you should not think of them as being always or exclusively one of the two. People are much more complicated than this.

Our first metaprogram is between the dichotomy of options and procedures. People who are on the options metaprogram don't like being limited or being told what to do. They want as much freedom as possible, and they like to think about things from a general perspective rather than getting in the weeds. On the other hand, people on procedures need to understand every small detail whenever they get into something new. Procedures people hate the feeling that they are missing something. When an element is skipped, they fear they are missing something important.

The second metaprogram is external and internal. This metaprogram is concerned with people's incentives. External people want to be told by others when they do good work, and they want to be notified when they do bad work, too. Internal people don't want to get outside opinions about their work, though. They feel they know when their work is good or not, and hearing what other people think is just a bother.

The third dichotomy in metaprograms is proactive and reactive. These metaprograms describe how someone deals with the future. Reactive people look at a calendar and are always thinking about how the work they are doing. Now fits into the picture of all of their work. This can be a hindrance because they believe so much about planning to lose sight of what they are trying to do right now. Proactive people, on the other hand, hate thinking about the future or planning ahead. They only care about the here and now.

Our second-to-last is toward and away. This metaprogram is about goals and deterrents. All of us have things we look forward to in the future, but toward people are chiefly concerned about their goals, and they don't look behind them at all. Away people are the exact opposite of this. They can have issues looking ahead because they spend so much time thinking about what is behind them.

Finally, we have sameness and difference. Sameness people have a love for familiarity: they spend their time around things they already know. Things they don't know will make them fearful, so these people avoid them at all costs. On the other hand, different people are always craving new experiences to have new people meet, fresh foods to eat, etc. If there is something they haven't experience yet, different people want to share it.

These are the five significant dichotomies in metaprograms. Whoever the co-worker is who you want to use our dark psychology tricks on will want to sort them into these metaprograms. Now, when you use the Aristotelian technique of envisioning the future, you have a more objective stand-in for the person you will interact with.

When we imagine someone in our heads, it isn't always accurate to how they are. NLP's metaprograms are useful because they make us think carefully about our subject's kind of person.

Metaprograms are particularly useful for the work environment because they force us to think about the people we work with more objectively. When you do Step 1 and prepare to get into the co-worker's mind with Step 2, you can use these metaprograms to paint a fuller picture of who you will use dark psychology on.

Since these are often just people we interact with exclusively in work environments, we can be surprised by how little we might know about them from a metaprogram standpoint. If you are honest with yourself as you sort them into these dichotomies, you might realize you don't know very much about them at all. When this turns out to be the case, don't just go along with the dark psychology technique anyway. There is no point in doing this when it won't always work—you can't adapt to the social cues of a person you don't even know yet.

That's why from here, you will have to do more intel-gathering on them first before you can even move on to Step 1. Step 1 can't successfully happen until you know the person and how they fit into all the metaprograms. Until you do that, you won't be able to properly imagine your interactions with them for Steps 2 and 3.

With that said, after you get to know the co-workers' metaprograms, let your senses do all the work in perceptual sharpness, use our exercises to prepare your state control, and imagine the interaction in your imagination, you are ready for Step 2.

For Steps 2 and 3, things go about the same when you are dealing with someone from your workplace. However, some techniques seem tailor-made for use in the work setting. We will go over these before moving onto our big lesson on neurolinguistics programming in psychology.

We will cover three big dark psychology techniques for the workplace before diving into the world of NLP. Social framing is a technique in which we paint a picture for the subject where adopting a particular behavior or idea will help them with social climbing.

Our social lives are one of the most important things to us as humans. That's why framing the truth about the subject's social environment is such a powerful tool for manipulating and mind-controlling people. As long as we make them believe they get a social reward for doing what we say, they will jump at the opportunity.

Executing this technique is simple. Assuming you have already mentally sorted these techniques into the proper metaprograms, controlled your state, and paid close attention to your senses.

Chapter 56. Dark Personalities

Dark psychology is not a single, universally applicable medical diagnosis that can be applied across all cases of deviant personalities. In fact, there are a wide variety of ways that dark psychology may manifest itself in someone's psychological and behavioral makeup. There is no absolute division of one deviant personality type from another. Many bizarre personalities with prominent dark psychology features may display more than one manifestation of dark psychology.

We will explore three types of dark psychology personalities. It is important to remember that although the internet has spawned a massive growth in problems resulting from dark psychology, these traits have been part of human culture since ancient times. One of the dark psychology profiles we will explore here, Machiavellianism, takes its name from a medieval politician. Another narcissism takes its name from an ancient mythological character. Together, the three dark psychology profiles talked about here—psychopathy, Machiavellianism, and narcissism—make up what is known as "the Dark Triad."

The Dark Triad Personalities

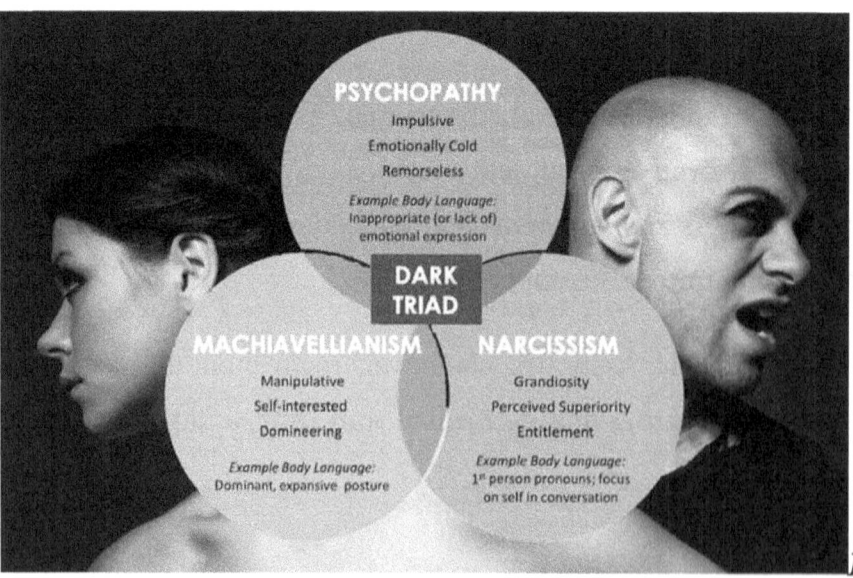

Narcissism

The term "narcissism" originates from an ancient Greek myth about Narcissus, a young man who saw his reflection in a pool of water and fell in love with the image of himself. In clinical psychology, narcissism as an illness was introduced by Sigmund Freud and has continually been included in official diagnostic manuals as a description of a specific type of psychiatric personality disorder.

In psychology, narcissism is defined as a condition characterized by an exaggerated sense of importance, an excessive need for attention, a lack of empathy, and, as a result, dysfunctional relationships. Commonly, narcissists may outwardly display a too high level of confidence. Still, this façade usually hides a very fragile ego and a high degree of sensitivity to criticism. There is often an enormous gulf between a narcissist's highly favorable view of himself or herself, the resulting expectation that others should extend to him or her favors and special treatment, and the disappointment when the results are quite negative or otherwise different. These problems can affect all areas of the narcissist's life, including personal relationships, professional relationships, and financial matters.

As part of the Dark Triad, those who exhibit traits resulting from Narcissistic Personality Disorder (NPD) may engage in relationships characterized by a lack of empathy. For example, a narcissist may demand constant comments, attention, and admiration from his or her partner but will often appear unable or unwilling to reciprocate by displaying concern or responding to their partner's circumstances, thoughts, and feelings.

Narcissists also display a sense of entitlement and expect excessive reward and recognition, but usually without ever having accomplished or achieved anything that would justify such feelings. There is also a tendency toward excessive criticism of those around him or her. Combined with heightened sensitivity when even the slightest amount of criticism is directed at him or her.

Thus, while narcissism in popular culture is often used as a pejorative term and an insult aimed at people like actors, models, and other celebrities who display high degrees of self-love and satisfaction. NPD is a psychological term that is quite distinct from merely having high self- esteem. The key to understanding this aspect of dark psychology is that the narcissist's image of himself or herself is often completely idealized, grandiose, and inflated and cannot be justified with any real, meaningful accomplishments or capacities make such claims believable. As a result of this discord between expectation and reality, the demanding, manipulative, inconsiderate, self-centered, and arrogant behavior of the narcissist can cause problems not only for themselves but also for all people his or her life.

Machiavellianism

Strictly defined, Machiavellianism is the political philosophy of Niccolò Machiavelli, who lived from 1469 until 1527 in Italy. In contemporary society, Machiavellianism is a term used to describe the popular understanding of people who are perceived as displaying very high political or professional ambitions. In psychology, however, the Machiavellianism scale is used to measure the degree to which people with deviant personalities say manipulative behavior.

Machiavelli wrote The Prince, a political treatise. He stated that sincerity, honesty, and other virtues were indeed admirable qualities. In politics, the capacity to engage in deceit, betrayal, and other forms of criminal behavior was acceptable if there were no other means of achieving political aims to protect one's interests.

Popular misconceptions reduce this entire philosophy to the view that "the end justifies the means." To be fair, Machiavelli himself insisted that the more critical part of this equation was ensuring the end itself must first be justified. Furthermore, it is better to achieve such ends using means devoid of treachery whenever possible because there is less risk to the actor's interests.

Thus, seeking the most effective means of achieving a political end may not necessarily lead to the most treacherous. Also, not all political fortunes that have been justified as worth pursuing must be pursued. In many cases, the mere threat that a particular course of action may be followed may be enough to achieve that end. In some cases, the betrayal may be as mild as making a credible threat to take action that is not intended.

In contemporary society, many people overlook the fact that Machiavellianism is part of the "Dark Triad" of dark psychology and tacitly approve of the deviant behavior of political and business leaders who can amass great power or wealth. However, as a psychological disorder, Ma- Machiavellianism is entirely different from a chosen path to political power.

The person displaying Machiavellian personality traits does not consider whether his or her actions are. The most effective means of achieving their goals, whether there are alternatives that do not involve deceit or treachery, or even whether the ultimate result of his or her actions is worth achieving. The Machiavellian personality is not evidence of a strategic or calculating mind attempting to reach a worthwhile objective in a contentious environment. Instead, it is always on, whether the situation calls for a cold, calculating, and manipulative approach or not.

For example, we had all called in sick to work when we just wanted a day off. But for most of us, such conduct is not how we usually behave. After such acts of dishonesty, many of us feel guilty. Those who display a high degree of Machiavellianism would not just lie when they want a day off; they see lying and dishonesty as the only way to conduct themselves in all situations, regardless of whether doing so results in any benefit.

What's more, because of the degree of social acceptance and tacit approval granted to Machiavellian personalities who successfully attain political power, their presence in society does not receive the kind of negative attention accorded to the other two members of the Dark Triad—psychopathy and narcissism.

Psychopathy

Psychopathy is defined as a mental disorder with several identifying characteristics: antisocial behavior, amorality, an inability to develop empathy, establish meaningful personal relationships, extreme egocentricity, and recidivism, with repeated violations resulting from an apparent failure to learn from the consequences of earlier transgressions. In turn, antisocial behavior is defined as behavior based upon a goal of violating formal and/or informal rules of social conduct through criminal activity or through acts of personal, private protest, or opposition, all of which are directed against other individuals' society in general.

Egocentricity is the behavior when the offending person sees himself or herself as the central focus of the world, or at least of all dominant social and political activity. Empathy is the ability to view and understand events, thoughts, emotions, and beliefs from others' perspectives. It is considered one of the most essential psychological components for establishing successful, ongoing relationships.

Amorality is entirely different from immorality. An immoral act is an act that violates established moral codes. An immoral person can be confronted with his or her actions with the expectation that they will recognize that their actions are offensive from a moral, if not a legal, standpoint. Amorality, on the other hand, represents psychology that does not realize that any moral codes exist, or if they do, that they have no value in determining whether or not to act in one way or another.

Thus, someone displaying psychopathy may commit horrendous acts that cause tremendous psychological and physical trauma and not ever understand that what he or she has done is wrong. Worse still, those who display signs of psychopathy usually worsen over time because they cannot connect the problems in their lives and the lives of those in the world around them and their own harmful and destructive actions.

The Dark Triad in Practice

The professional workplace has acknowledged the presence of people exhibiting Dark Triad characteristics.

The following diagram illustrates that they are tolerated for their efficiency and their ability to get things done but contrasts that ability with the adverse effects it has on their ability to form personal relationships:

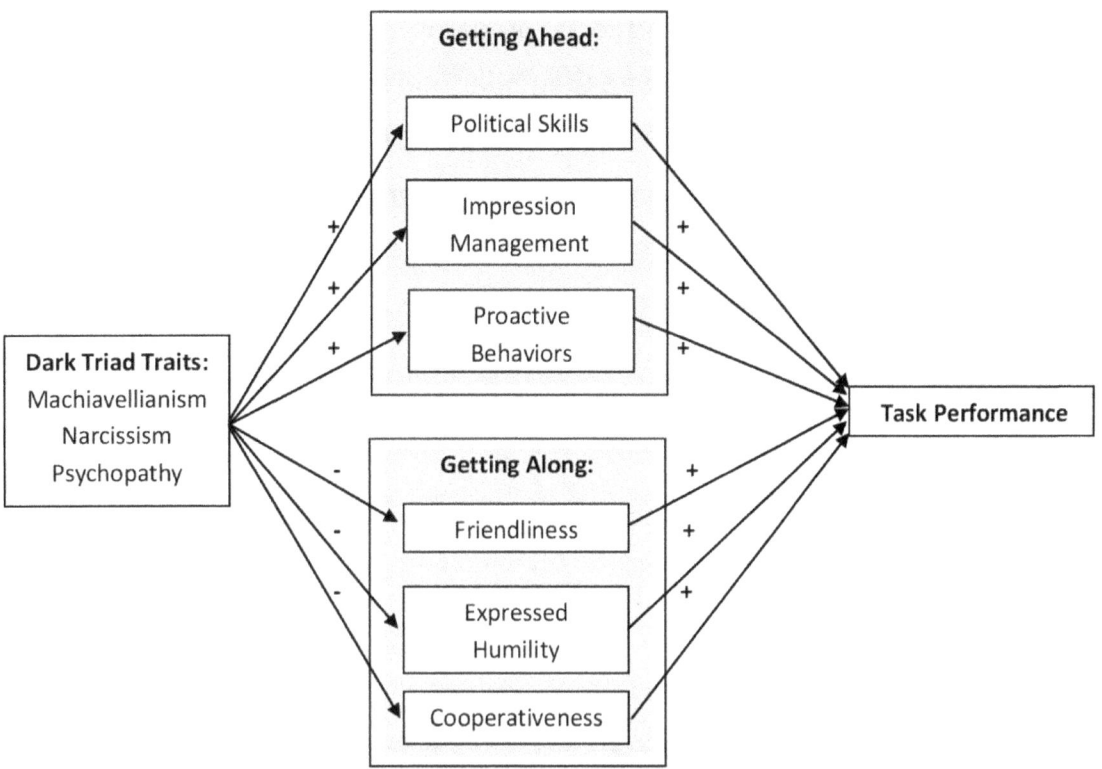

(Benjamin McLarty, Mississippi State University, 2015)

The remainder will discuss a wide variety of people and situations where you may find one, two, all three, or some combination of these Dark Triad personalities working in concert around you.

The clinical descriptions are easy enough to categorize. In isolation, it can be reasonably straightforward to separate one type of dark psychology from another. The real world is a lot messier. Many of us have grown accustomed to so-called "toxic relationships," whether they are relationships with our partners, co-workers, family members, bosses, or political and community leaders.

Also, dark psychology manifestations are often far more mundane than the dramatic examples we see in major television and film productions about serial killers and other criminals' romantic lives. The more we accept these relationships, as usual, the more difficult it will be to identify them as problematic.

Remember that psychological, emotional, and social predators do not think of themselves as sick. Their lack of morality and empathy, and their adaption from a very early age to live according to rules and methods you may find wrong, can make their presence intimidating. However, you should also remember that even when their amorality and lack of empathy may allow them to enjoy it. An unfair advantage in relationships, their mental capacities result from underdevelopment, not a higher evolutionary state.

Chapter 57. The Dark Triad

The dark triad is a psychology term that refers to a person's behavioral characteristics, which is, in most cases, defined as narcissism, Machiavellianism, and psychopathy. Some people rate it as a mental disorder and some as a disaster that just dawns on someone changing their behavior and how they relate to others. Dark triad generally affects a person's personality, making them take advantage of others. People with these traits tend to be manipulative, deceptive, and egoistic. They attempt to brainwash others to gain success and fame.

Politicians are, on most occasions, the worst group of people affected by this personality disorder. Their lives are full of lies, ego, and manipulation. To gain power, most of them only deceive other people to get public support and seem successful. Many people fall victim to the dark triad because they are not well exposed to the point of understanding what it is. They cannot easily tell when this is being used against them.

Persons with dark triad personalities have no empathy for others. They always attempt to have everything for themselves, ignoring other people's importance around them. Narcissists still want to be regarded as the most influential people in society. They want to be praised and admired all the time, a kind of behavior that only manipulates others for the benefit of their interests.

You may be tempted to think that these people are insane. From my perspective to some extent, they are. No one in his normal state of mind would want to have everything go their side at the expense of others. To these people who possess a Machiavellianism trait, they always want to win and be declared successful. They go as far as deceiving everyone around them to turn out the right person. They easily exploit the "less fortunate" in society to open their ways.

Apart from politicians, bloggers are another group of people that are overwhelmed by these traits. For example, in Kenya, we have Dr. Miguna, who is all over the social media busy manipulating people—the youth and young politicians being the most affected. He tries to make everyone his psychopath through his blogs, twits, books, and constant drama here and there.

Can we Say Dr. Miguna is insane? He is all over seeking fame and wants everyone to believe he is always right, and the rest are wrong. He manipulates everyone, and those who follow his steps end up being disappointed at the end. Once he gets what he is looking for, he turns against you and uses your negatives to manipulate others that are not in the same line as him. He comes up with dramas to attract attention and convince everyone to believe whatever he does.

While politicians everywhere are fighting him back, the youth become psychos by his blogs and believe that he is right because he is fighting politicians whom he claims to be narcissists. Not to be personal, I would like to say that if you research deeply into psychology, you will find most bloggers with the same interest showing narcissism, Machiavellianism, and psychopathy traits. They won't feel guilty or ashamed because they don't even notice that they are too much.

Anyone can be a victim of these traits. You may, at one point in your life, find yourself in a relationship with a narcissist. Before you notice it, you will be exploited and used by your partner. Your partner can be that antagonistic person that only feels superior to you and those around you. They will always want to be treated special and can exploit you to serve their interests. They often interact in a way that shows you are less important and not as good as them.

This kind of person usually wants to be listened to. They will prefer seeking attention than empathizing with you or even recognizing your needs. Everything they do is always for their benefit. They only concentrate on feeling better in the relationship and are never ready to give you a listening year. You have no say in their decisions because this makes them feel less important to you and don't respect their decisions.

To know that you are in a relationship with a narcissist, you will realize that your partner doesn't really care about how you feel. They only expect you to make them happy and superior without considering what you go through for them to be what they want. Failing to meet their interests makes them feel so low and unwanted in the relationship. They make you feel like you are of no good to them and that you don't deserve them.

They can also be antisocial and low self-esteemed. They will always think of their mistakes as the worst ever and that none can be compared. Whenever they fail in something, they will feel like they don't fit in society anymore and imperfect. They feel so drowned and depressed as a result of one mistake. This is always brought about by the fear of being a normal person.

On some occasions, narcissists attempt to praise themselves too much without realizing how majestic they can be. They never stop talking about their achievements and plans in life. They always talk about how intelligent and successful they are and even exaggerate what they are capable of. They always want people to believe that their success cannot be related to someone else's. Stopping them from doing this makes them feel stupid, and they can easily hate you for pinpointing their imperfections.

These persons' living standards are always set high by them, which is becoming realistic because they are in a way that has low standards. Their lives are usually filled with a fantasy about success, and they expect everyone around them to respect them because their destinies are thought to be successful. No one can ever change their perception in their minds without hurting them and making them feel useless.

At some point, these people are always depressed, and no one will ever understand the reason for their depression. Understanding them becomes difficult. If you are not a psychologist, you will always be brainwashed to serve their interests before noticing what you are getting yourself into. Other people can advise you, but you will not have the time to listen to what they have to say because you will have fallen victim to narcissism. The narcissist will, by that time, have full control of you.

You are always left torn between thoughts when it reaches a point that you no longer understand a friend or a partner who has a dark personality. Failing to listen to them makes them feel worse than other people while listening to you is useless to them, on the other hand. They never have time to listen to you but to seek the audience all the time.

Machiavellian leaders are the most dangerous leaders because they are always cunning and duplicitous. They always manipulate everyone from doing what they want, whether they like it or not, and never reveal any reason for their actions. They only do that when the favor is on their side. They always make people believe that they are the most intelligent and that no one's intelligence can be compared to theirs. Those who believe in this kind of leaders are never ready to listen to other people's advice unless they align with the Machiavellian heads.

Dark triad strikes too much due to several reasons and the following additional reasons.

1. The Understanding of Dark Triad Is Not Everybody's Cup of Tea

Not everyone has the psychology of understanding dark personality. This leads to many of us fall victim to dark triads without noticing it. We get manipulated easily and exploited to serve the interest of narcissists and Machiavellian leaders without a choice of thinking a second time or even the chance to take an alternative move.

2. The Fear of Standing Alone

Narcissists always manipulate the big number from being on their side and supporting their ideas. This has left many people stranded between thoughts because they fear being left alone for making an opposing decision. They fear of not getting back up from those around you led many people to fall, victims of the dark triad since they are forced to take steps they were not ready to take.

This usually happens with people who are often close to this kind of person or whose friends are involved with those with dark personalities.

3. I Don't Want to Lose a Friend

Many people tend to value friendship more than their own safety. They are too much into their friend's decisions and way of life that they even forget they are also important. Such people are the most common victims of the dark triad. They easily get exploited by their friends into doing what their friends want, what makes them happy.

In this case, when you're are friends with a narcissist, then you have no choice. You will always be a tool for happiness. You will be ready to listen to all sorts of boasting and exaggerated stories from your friends.

4. Investing Your Trust in the Wrong Person

On many occasions, we don't always know the right person to trust. Laying your trust in someone without considering their personality opens a gate for you to be used by narcissists. This normally occurs in relationships that are just beginning, and partners wish to travel miles away together.

Many fall into traps of their partners because they invest too much trust in them that they can never think of the negative side of them. This is what makes the narcissists overjoyed and leave them feeling so highly of themselves.

5. Believing Too Fast

These narcissists always have their stories told everywhere by them and by those who believe helplessly in them. They always catch the interests of those who believe in all stories they are told because they believe the people telling the story are always right, intelligent, and successful.

The narcissist always catches others' attention with their striking success that makes others believe in them desperately and follow their steps blindly without a third eye to see into the future and the consequences of following these people.

6. Most People Don't Care

The tendency of assuming everything said by those in authority is final is what makes us victims of manipulation and exploitation. Some of us don't even care about what is going on around them, and having no idea about it for them is even much better. Some say that something you don't know does not hurt.

People with dark personalities easily exploit such people because they know the favor will always be on their side no matter what. No one will stand against them because they don't even care in the first place.

7. Psychopathy

Being too possessed with someone is what leads you to become their psychopaths. You will always want to listen to what they say, and at the end of it, you will be convinced they are right, and anything said against them is wrong. You will feel pain when they are in pain are depressed when they are depressed because you have become their shadow. Whoever sees you see the person you have invested your personality in.

Conclusion

Now that you've learned some of the basic dark psychology disciplines, you have a great deal more power than you had before. At the very least, you will be better able to recognize controlling techniques and behaviors when other people try to use them against you. If someone is trying to manipulate or even persuade you, you can now see through their tricks and resist.

But you also have the unique opportunity to use dark psychology for your personal growth and improvement. Just because these tools and techniques are labeled 'dark' doesn't mean they're inherently destructive. Many techniques, including hypnosis and NLP, were first developed as self-improvement tools. Only when people learned how to turn these techniques against other people did they become relegated to the field of 'dark' psychology.

NLP, persuasion techniques, body language, and even hypnosis are all regularly taught in social spheres that we would not normally consider 'dark.' Athletes, business people, teachers and educators, actors, entertainers, and marketers all regularly use these techniques to improve their performance, increase their productivity, make themselves better negotiators, and yes, to convince others to do what they want. There's nothing inherently amoral about social influence, especially if the thing you're persuading the other person to do is good for them. Using NLP techniques to persuade your alcoholic partner to get help is hardly an act of evil or manipulation. Neither is learning to read your teenager's body language to improve your communication and defuse potential conflict.

With great power, however, does come great responsibility. Whenever you decide to employ any of these techniques against another person, always take a step back and ask yourself, "What are the consequences for the other person if I get my desired outcome? Will the other person be hurt? Will this put them in danger? Will this compromise their core values or beliefs in some way?" If the answer to any of these three questions is yes, you have to find another way to get what you want without manipulating tactics. All of the techniques that you've learned are extremely powerful. With patience and practice, they do work. Suppose you become skilled in any of these disciplines and decide to use them for the wrong reasons. In that case, you could cause some serious damage to another person's psychological well-being and risk losing your important relationships if someone else becomes aware of what you're doing.

I hope that, you re-enter your life as a more secure and empowered person. Psychological techniques are subtle and often context-based. It's normal to be clumsy when you first begin, and you should always be aware of how the other person is responding so that you can make necessary and appropriate adjustments to your techniques.

With these tactics at your disposal, you are no longer at the mercy of other people. If you find yourself constantly rubbing other people the wrong way, perhaps receiving labels like 'bossy' or 'pushy,' you now have a variety of subtler ways to get what you want. If you're someone that's constantly fighting and barreling over others, you know that sometimes being straightforward isn't the best option. Being too blunt can often backfire on you. Asking for what you need more subtly won't only get you more success in life—it may even make it easier for you to build healthy relationships with other people.

If you find yourself in the opposite position, these tactics can work for you, too. If you feel that you're just too timid to get what you want or find yourself easily pushed around by other people, you now have a way to succeed. Instead of running headlong into conflicts that scare you, you can try a different approach, one that may feel much more comfortable. As you start to achieve results, you'll probably feel a big improvement in your confidence. And the more confident you feel, the more comfortable you will be with straightforward communication, making you a much better communicator all the way around.

Most importantly of all, now that you are aware of dark psychology, those who would wish to do you harm have significantly less power over you. Suppose someone does try to manipulate, persuade, or use NLP against you in the future. In that case, you will be better able to recognize their tactics before something bad happens. And suppose you are currently in a relationship with a manipulative person. In that case, you now have a better idea of their tactics and therefore take steps to free yourself from their influence.

www.ingramcontent.com/pod-product-compliance
Lightning Source LLC
Chambersburg PA
CBHW081344080526
44588CB00016B/2375